Yale Historical Publications, 136

Kenyan Communities in the Age of Imperialism

in the

Age of Imperialism

The Central Region in the Late Nineteenth Century

CHARLES H. AMBLER

Yale University Press
New Haven and London

Published under the direction of the Department of History
of Yale University with assistance from the income
of the Frederick John Kingsbury Memorial Fund.

Designed by Jill G. Breitbarth
and set in Sabon type, by Eastern Graphics.
Printed in the United States of America by
BookCrafters, Inc., Chelsea, Michigan.

Library of Congress Cataloging-in-Publication Data

Ambler, Charles H.
  Kenyan communities in the age of imperialism.

  (Yale historical publications.   Miscellany; 136)
  Bibliography: p.
  Includes index.
    1. Kenya—History—To 1895.   2. Kenya—Economic
conditions—To 1963.   I. Title.   II. Series.
DT433.57.A43   1988   967.6′2   87-14801
ISBN 0-300-03957-3 (alk. paper)

The paper in this book meets the guidelines for permanence
and durability of the Committee on Production Guidelines
for Book Longevity of the Council on Library Resources.

10 9 8 7 6 5 4 3 2 1

Contents

Maps

Acknowledgments

In the course of researching and writing I have accumulated a great many debts, but the greatest is to my family. My wife, Gloria Miglietta Ambler, our parents, and our children, Peter and Catherine, gave the encouragement—and offered the diversions—that kept this project on track. As readers will become aware, I also owe special gratitude to the women and men who offered me their time and trust in the interviews that to a very great extent form the basis of this study.

This book began as a dissertation at Yale University, and the exchanges that I had there with faculty and fellow students continue to shape my approach to history. Sally Moore, Kennell Jackson, and Jack Glazier provided important suggestions during the initial phase of research; Bill Worger and Jerry Carpenter gave support along the way. Generous financial assistance came from the Fulbright-Hays Dissertation Research Abroad program, from the Yale Concilium on International and Area Studies, and from the Whiting Foundation.

I am grateful to the Kenya government for permission to conduct research, and to many Kenyan officials for their assistance and forbearance. The history department of the University of Nairobi provided me a research associateship. I owe thanks to the then chairman, Godfrey Muriuki, and to my fellow researchers David Brokensha, David Miller, and H. S. K. Mwaniki for sharing their thoughts and experience. The Kabaa and Kyeni Missions and the Embu County Council kindly gave me access to sources in their possession. The staffs of the Kenya National Archives and the Nairobi University library made me welcome, as did those at the Public Record Office, Rhodes House Library, the Church Missionary Society archives, and Syracuse

University library. Moore Crossey at the Yale library obtained several important documents on my behalf.

For practical help in Kenya thanks are due to Richard and Mary Oates, to the Roman Catholic mission fathers at Mwingi, Kyuso, and Siakago, and to the principals of Nyangwa Secondary School and Gi-kuuri Primary School. My fifteen months of research would have been much less pleasant had it not been for their generosity, and that of Richard Kakoi, John Kuyu, and all of our friends at Thatha, the community Gloria and I were fortunate enough to call home.

The history department at the University of Texas at El Paso provided not only the release from teaching duties that allowed me to complete the manuscript, but a stimulating and collegial atmosphere in which to work. Final revisions were undertaken while I was Andrew W. Mellon Faculty Fellow in the Humanities at Harvard University. The manuscript was prepared by Florence Dick and the maps by Cynthia Renteria, both at the University of Texas at El Paso.

Gloria Ambler painstakingly read and criticized each draft. For comments on all or part of various versions, I am grateful also to David Robinson, Sherry Smith, Thomas Spear, the reader for the press, and especially to Robert Harms. I owe final and particular thanks to Leonard Thompson. From the inception of this project I have benefited repeatedly from his ideas, assistance, and example.

Abbreviations Used in the Footnotes

PRO: Great Britain, Public Record Office
F.O.:   Foreign Office
C.O.:   Colonial Office
KNA: Kenya National Archives
IBEAC: Imperial British East Africa Company
s/o: son of
w/o: wife of

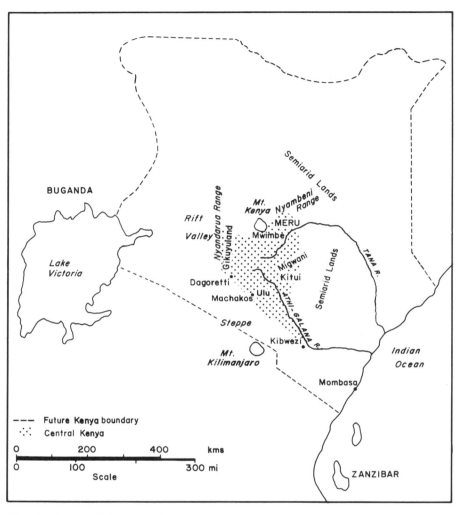

BUGANDA

Lake
Victoria

Rift
Valley

Nyandarua Range

Gīkuyuland

Semiarid Lands

Mt.
Kenya

Nyambeni Range

MERU

Mwimbe

Migwani

Dagoretti

Ulu

Kitui

Machakos

ATHI-GALANA R.

Semiarid Lands

TANA R.

Steppe

Mt.
Kilimanjaro

Kibwezi

Indian
Ocean

Mombasa

ZANZIBAR

— — — Future Kenya boundary
∴∵∴ Central Kenya

| 0 | 200 | 400 | kms |
| 0 | 100 | | 300 mi |

Scale

Map 1. Nineteenth-Century Kenya

Introduction

Beginning in 1897 a famine spread across central Kenya, the agricultural region stretching south and east from the highlands of the Nyandarua Range and Mount Kenya. Inadequate rainfall plagued much of East and Central Africa during the last years of the nineteenth century, and many areas suffered repeated food shortages; but in central Kenya this drought provoked a crisis that endured with terrible consequences for more than three years.[1] For the people of Migwani, a farming society on the northernmost margins of the Kitui Hills, this was a time of intense privation. Here, as in many other areas of central Kenya, a convergence of gradually accumulating ecological, political, and economic pressures had left local farmers unusually vulnerable to drought. As stunted crops withered in the fields, households rapidly exhausted their small stores of food. A season of drought turned into an almost unrelenting succession of failed harvests, and hunger became pervasive. Community after community was reduced to the point of disintegration.

As hunger intensified, its effects radiated outward. For many, the only real hope for survival lay in the highlands that formed the region's northern perimeter, from the Nyandaruas in the west, across Mount Kenya to the Nyambeni Range in the northeast. There, food remained available. In growing numbers, Migwani residents took their livestock and other property north some eighty miles to trade for food supplies in the Mount Kenya highlands. But by late in 1898, only wealthy men had possessions left to sell; for many others, the very survival of their families and community seemed in doubt. The frantic struggle for exis-

1. See maps 1 and 3.

1

tence interrupted the established relationships of authority and obligation, stretching the bonds of social order to breaking. In Migwani, in an atmosphere increasingly marked by insecurity and violence, a local leader, Nzambu wa Ndove, took action.[2] Trading on his wealth and prominence in the northern section of Migwani, Nzambu managed to gather a large group of destitute families and lead them to refuge in Mwimbe on the eastern edge of the Mount Kenya foothills.

The refugees, with their small herds of livestock, headed directly north across the Tana River. Skirting settled areas, they made their way toward Mwimbe on the eastern slopes of Mount Kenya. From his experience as hunter and trader, Nzambu had become familiar with this route; but many of his followers lacked his confidence, having had little experience with travel beyond their home areas. They had real cause for concern: weak from persistent hunger, they faced not only a physically arduous journey across rough country, but the threat of attack from raiders and bandits as well. After several days of difficult travel, and apparently without incident, Nzambu's exhausted and hungry party reached its destination. In this area of the highlands surplus food remained available, and with the agreement of local lineage leaders, the migrants built makeshift villages on the fringes of the settled areas of Mwimbe.

The worst effects of drought did not touch the people of Mwimbe and their highland neighbors, but their relative agricultural security could not isolate them from the general crisis which gradually enveloped the entire central Kenya region. The refugees who traveled from Migwani to Mwimbe made up only one small group in a much larger movement of people from the drought-plagued areas into the highlands. First traders and then refugees by the thousands pushed into sections where stocks of food were still available. In time this flow of refugees placed a severe economic and social burden on the highland societies. Worse yet, the travelers who swarmed over the paths of central Kenya carried with them the threat of disease. By 1899 a major outbreak of smallpox had engulfed the entire region. Together, hunger and epidemic killed thousands, depopulated entire settlements, and left community life in many areas thoroughly disrupted. Central Kenya ap-

---

2. The details of Migwani's experience in the famine are drawn largely from oral evidence, notably interviews with Wamui w/o Munyasia and Paul Ngutu s/o Ngutha, Migwani. Informants are cited by name and place of residence. Further explanation of the oral material is found in the List of People Interviewed. The impact of the famine across the region is examined in chap. 6.

proached the edge of chaos. In one man's words, this was "the famine that swept away all the people."[3]

The drought that began in 1897 pressed hard on farming communities already threatened externally and from within by an accumulation of traumatic changes: a deterioration of agricultural resources, the sudden decline of surrounding pastoralist populations, the advance of European economic and political power. In central Kenya during the last decades of the nineteenth century men and women and their families, in their small, often isolated communities, struggled to adjust and maintain autonomous societies, economies, and cultures in the face of these challenges. With time, however, the traditions of this period have gradually compressed the diverse elements of change into a single crisis of transition. An elder recalled, "People did not know what to do; they consulted healers and promised them as many pots as they wanted, but they had no success."[4] To people pressed from every side by famine and epidemic, it seemed as if forces beyond their control and comprehension had conspired to challenge and ultimately destroy established society.

During their stay in Mwimbe, the refugees from Migwani managed a precarious existence. Despite threats of violence and disease, Nzambu wa Ndove held his following together. But when the Migwani people finally could return home, their vision of a reconstructed community proved a chimera. There was no room for small, independent societies like Migwani in the new world of colonial Kenya. Not surprisingly, people saw a connection between the disaster of drought, famine, and disease on the one hand, and the advance of European economic and political power on the other. In the collective memory of central Kenya societies the two became increasingly closely entwined. The traditions of communities like Migwani portray the famine not as a natural disaster, but as the most immediate and punishing element of a larger social and cosmological crisis. The famine is seen not as a critical event in the modern history of the region, but as a terrible symbol of the advent of colonialism.

In a similar process, scholars have characterized the late nineteenth century as a period of transition to colonial rule, focusing their attention almost exclusively on the developing relationships between Kenyan and European societies. This tendency has been marked in

3. Interview: Mbele s/o Nguli, Migwani.
4. Interview: Wamui w/o Munyasia, Migwani.

Kenyan history not only because of the country's particular experience as a settler colony and as a supposed outpost of neocolonialism, but also because the nineteenth-century Kenyan interior lacked the indigenous states that in many parts of Africa have provided an alternative subject of study. The people of Migwani, like all the people of central Kenya, lived out their lives in small, independent communities—beyond the power of any indigenous state.[5] In general, historians have given little attention to the experiences of the vast numbers of people in precolonial Africa who lived in such societies, or even to those who lived relatively autonomous lives within the perimeters of great states.[6] This is regrettable but hardly surprising. By their size and structure, states not only dominated the landscape but generated bodies of evidence—written, oral, and material—from which historians could conveniently work.

The larger history of central Kenya must be pieced together from the accumulation of the separate histories of communities like Migwani and men and women like Nzambu wa Ndove. For circumstances such as these, where the effective reach of social and political institutions scarcely extended beyond a neighborhood, it is difficult to define an appropriate historical context. During the nineteenth century an intense localism colored the outlook of every society in central Kenya, yet the fortunes of all were bound up together. A circle of formidable physical features set the region off from areas beyond: on the north and west, the mountains and the Rift Valley; on the south and west, arid steppe and semidesert. Within this circle lived some one million

5. I use *community* to mean the area—generally quite small—whose residents were sufficiently bound together by local social and political institutions (e.g., elder councils) to permit unified action on a regular basis. *Small society* refers to a collection of communities that together possessed a substantial sense of common identity and experience. Given the diversity and fluidity of central Kenya societies, the boundary between the two categories is by no means clear-cut. This issue is pursued below, chap. 1.

6. Note the similar laments in Robin Horton, "Stateless Societies in West Africa," in *History of West Africa*, ed. J. F. A. Ajayi and Michael Crowder (London, 1972), vol. 1, pp. 78–119; and more than a decade later in Jan Vansina, "The Peoples of the Forest," in *History of Central Africa*, ed. D. Birmingham and P. Martin (London, 1983), pp. 75–117. Caroline Neale has related the lack of interest in stateless societies to nationalist tendencies in African historiography. "The Idea of Progress in the Revision of African History, 1960–1970," in *African Historiographies: What History for Which Africa?* ed. B. Jewsiewicki and David Newbury (Beverly Hills, 1986), pp. 116–17. Among the most successful histories of small-scale African societies are D. W. Cohen, *Womunafu's Bunafu: A Study of Authority in a Nineteenth-Century African Community* (Princeton, 1977); R. Harms, *River of Wealth, River of Sorrow: The Central Zaire Basin in the Era of the Slave and Ivory Trade, 1500–1891* (New Haven, 1981); and David Northrup, *Trade Without Rulers: Pre-Colonial Economic Development in Southern-Eastern Nigeria* (Oxford, 1978).

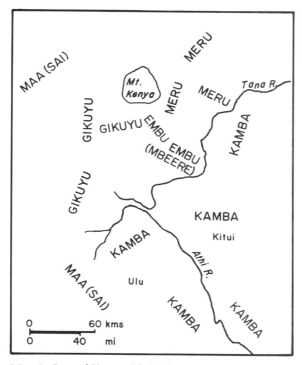

Map 2. Central Kenya: Major Languages

people, most of whom shared fundamental cultural assumptions and spoke one of several closely related languages.[7] Kamba-speakers lived in the southern section of the region, Gikuyu-speakers in the western highlands, those who spoke Embu on the southern side of Mount Kenya, and Meru-speakers on the eastern slopes.

The experience of famine put into relief the complex mass of connections that linked people throughout this area. Nzambu led Kamba-speaking refugee families from Migwani to Meru-speaking Mwimbe because of the history of trade between the two areas and because there he could invoke the widely held—if contrived—notion that Migwani and Mwimbe people shared a common ancestry. Contacts like those between the people from Migwani and Mwimbe reveal complicated layers of competing identities and interdependencies, from the most lo-

7. This represents a conservative estimate. The first Kenya census, conducted in 1948, revealed a central Kenya population of more than two million. See Charles H. Ambler, "Central Kenya in the Late Nineteenth Century: Small Communities in a Regional System" (Ph.D. dissertation, Yale University, 1983), p. 10, *n*11.

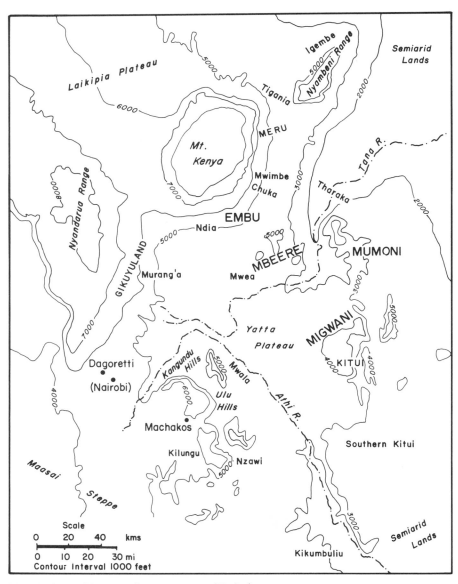

Map 3. Central Kenya: Place-Names and Relief

cal to the largest scale. But whatever elements defined the relationship that existed between communities in the two areas, it is clear that this was not essentially a meeting of representatives of two tribes or ethnic groups. No settled and exclusive ethnic order defined social and economic relationships in nineteenth-century central Kenya. Indeed, the histories of small communities reveal nothing more clearly than the themes of dynamism, movement, and newness. This was a social order in the making.[8]

In my reconstruction of the central Kenyan past, I have sought as much as possible to develop an approach that responds to these circumstances. This is people's history—a story that is rooted in the experience of individuals and families and shaped by the institutions that dominated people's lives: the neighborhood, the community, the region.[9] The scope is broad, but woven through this study are the histories of several small societies, located in the area from northern Kitui to the Mount Kenya highlands: the hill communities of Kamba-speaking Migwani; to the northeast, the drier and more open country of Mumoni, whose residents spoke a dialect of the same language; several communities located in Mbeere, north and west across the Tana River from Migwani and Mumoni; and finally the highland society of Embu, whose residents were culturally and linguistically closely tied to their neighbors in Mbeere.[10] While the experiences of these communities are not necessarily representative, they do encompass an impressive diversity of situation. Their histories, pieced together largely from oral evidence, reveal societies that in the late nineteenth century were independent and insular, but by no means isolated from one another or from larger forces of change.

The structures of environment, economy, and culture imposed a degree of order on the evolution of central Kenya's myriad small and autonomous societies. As Migwani's experience in famine suggests, the patterns of the availability or want of resources could have a profound

8. John Lonsdale emphasizes the newness of Kenyan societies in "When Did the Gusii (or any other group) Become a 'Tribe'?—A Review Essay," *Kenya Historical Review* 5, no. 1 (1977): 123–33.

9. Raphael Samuel, "People's History," in *People's History and Socialist Theory,* ed. Raphael Samuel (London, 1981), p. xviii. An important discussion of this problem for African history is found in D. W. Cohen, "Doing Social History from Pim's Doorway," in *Reliving the Past: The Worlds of Social History,* ed. Olivier Zunz (Chapel Hill, N.C., 1985), pp. 191–235. In my attempt to conceptualize the central Kenya past in indigenous terms, I am developing approaches pioneered by B. A. Ogot, *A History of the Southern Luo* (Nairobi, 1967); and Godfrey Muriuki, *A History of the Kikuyu, 1500–1900* (Nairobi and London, 1974).

10. The histories of these small societies are examined in detail in chaps. 1–3.

impact on the development of local societies and the development of their relationships with others. But at the same time the environment certainly did not determine the processes of social evolution. The people of communities such as Migwani drew on and continually reproduced a body of critical social and cultural traditions as they struggled to cope with new circumstances, such as those presented by the severe drought of 1897–1900. The relationship between Migwani and Mwimbe also points to the way that the existence of a gradually evolving complex of interdependent relationships among individual communities within central Kenya—a regional system—ordered events within small localities.[11] Finally, over the course of a century or more central Kenya had been drawn gradually within the larger structures of the international economy. After 1880 this process accelerated rapidly. During the last two decades of the century the shape of Migwani society would be altered significantly by the emergence of new patterns of long-distance trade. By the late 1890s the residents of Migwani were well aware of the establishment of a permanent imperial foothold in Machakos, some fifty miles to the west. When the famine struck, a sizeable number of men from Migwani sought work or relief not in the highlands but in the railway camps and administrative stations of the new colonial order.

We can see in retrospect that the most dynamic late nineteenth-century processes of change originated in the expansion into the Kenya interior of forces associated with the international economy. Yet the crisis of central Kenya societies during this period was by no means monolithic. As the advance of external forces steadily constricted local autonomy, people in their small communities struggled to cope with a variety of sometimes contradictory pressures. Moreover, the strategies that they devised in response were by no means insignificant. In late nineteenth-century Migwani the combination of a growth in long-distance trade and a decline in the local resource base encouraged a decided concentration of individual wealth and power. This development, and parallel developments across the region, far from being irrelevant, would have a substantial influence on the character of the colonial society that emerged after 1900.

11. See Allen M. Howard, "The Relevance of Spatial Analysis for African Economic History," *Journal of African History* 17 (1976): 365–88; and Carol Smith, "Analyzing Regional Social Systems," in *Regional Analysis*, vol. 2, ed. Carol Smith (New York, 1976), pp. 3–20. In *Political Systems of Highland Burma: A Study of the Kachin Social Structure* (Cambridge, Mass., 1954), E. R. Leach demonstrated the usefulness of a regional approach for the study of fluid social and economic systems.

1

The Formation
of New Societies

The nineteenth-century history of central Kenya is dominated by
a single process: the spread of agricultural settlement across
the region and the concomitant rise of the closely related
Kamba, Gikuyu, and Meru cultural-linguistic traditions. The extension
of farming economies occurred gradually over many centuries, but
after 1800 agriculturalists gained an undisputed dominance. The out-
lines of the last phase of this expansion are clear; it is unlikely,
however, that we will ever have a full understanding of the history of
central Kenya before the nineteenth century. Archeological evidence
shows that farmers have occupied areas of central Kenya since at least
1000 A.D., approximately the same time that the divisions were occurring which led to the gradual development of the several closely related
Bantu languages that were spoken in the region by the late 1800s.[1] But
little is known of the people concerned or of their links to successor
populations. Less yet is known of other peoples, hunters and pastoralists, who also inhabited central Kenya.

The popular histories of present ethnic groupings open only a narrow view of the past.[2] Ethnic traditions portray the distant past as the

---

1. Thomas Spear provides a stimulating introduction to the early history of the Kenya
interior in *Kenya's Past: An Introduction to Historical Method in Africa* (London, 1981),
chaps. 1–3. See also Derek Nurse and Thomas Spear, *The Swahili: Reconstructing the History and Language of an African Society, 800–1500* (Philadelphia, 1985), pp. 43, 53–54;
D. W. Phillipson, "The Early Iron Age in Eastern and Southern Africa: A Critical Reappraisal," *Azania* 11 (1976): 20; Robert Soper, "Iron Age Archaeology and Traditional History in Embu, Mbeere and Chuka Areas of Central Kenya," *Azania* 14 (1979): 44, 54; and
Muriuki, *History of Kikuyu*, pp. 52–54. Archeological investigations may yet yield important new information on pre-nineteenth-century central Kenya.

2. By *popular histories* I mean the vision of the past generally held today in central
Kenya. These views have been received mainly in the form of ethnic traditions—now some-

story of the movement of groups of outsiders into central Kenya and the subsequent and inexorable expansion of their descendants, the now dominant Gikuyu, Kamba, and Meru ethnic populations, throughout the region. These traditions of migration are typically self-contained; they obscure the contribution of earlier inhabitants, exclude the evidence of interaction, and generally avoid inconsistencies. In short, the popular histories reduce complicated processes of movement and social formation to a few clean lines on a map.

According to these accounts, the ancestors of Kamba-speaking people migrated from the Mount Kilimanjaro area northward into Ulu, then spread throughout the Ulu Hills and eastward into Kitui. Ethnic traditions trace the forebears of the Gikuyu to the east slopes of Mount Kenya, from where they are said to have moved westward through Mbeere some 150 miles into Gikuyuland and then north and south along the foothills of the Nyandarua Range. Finally, popular accounts of Meru history tell of a migration from the Kenya coast that followed the Tana River into the interior and the subsequent diffusion of Meru-speaking people across the country east of Mount Kenya.[3]

These ethnic traditions—now disseminated in published form—describe widely separated and distinct origins for peoples that have had extensive and intimate interconnection and whose languages and cultures clearly possess some common origins.[4] This does not mean, however, that one version is necessarily correct, while others are inaccu-

---

times published—which are comprised of relatively fixed texts recounting the origins, elsewhere, and subsequent migration to and settlement in the territories of present-day ethnic populations. Robert Harms relates the development of similar traditions among the Bobangi people along the Zaire River to a growth in social scale and the concomitant redefinition of what it meant to be Bobangi. "Bobangi Oral Traditions: Indicators of Changing Perceptions," in *The African Past Speaks: Essays in Oral Tradition and History*, ed. Joseph Miller (Folkestone, England and Hamden, Conn., 1980), pp. 178–200. On the historicity of migration traditions, see Joseph Miller, "Listening for the African Past," in Miller, *African Past Speaks*, pp. 31–34.

3. Kennell A. Jackson, "The Dimensions of Kamba Pre-Colonial History," in *Kenya Before 1900*, ed. B. A. Ogot (Nairobi, 1976), pp. 181–203; Jeffrey Fadiman, "The Meru Peoples," in Ogot, *Kenya Before 1900*, pp. 139–56; and Muriuki, *History of Kikuyu*, chaps. 2–3.

4. J. Forbes Munro looked at these contradictory traditions of origin in "Migrations of the Bantu-speaking Peoples of the Eastern Kenya Highlands: A Reappraisal," *Journal of African History* 8 (1967): 25–28. For evidence of the remarkable similarities among central Kenya societies, see John Middleton and G. Kershaw, *The Central Tribes of the North-Eastern Bantu: The Kikuyu, including Embu, Meru, Mbere, Chuka, Mwimbi, Tharaka, and the Kamba of Kenya*, Ethnographical Survey of Africa (London, 1965). On the irreconcilability of origins traditions, see J. Lamphear, *The Jie: Traditional History of the Jie of Uganda* (Oxford, 1976), p. 61.

rate. Rather, the inconsistencies speak of the attempts of people in their traditions to come to grips with diverse roots and a complex past.[5] Over centuries, as central Kenya societies were established and matured, they continually drew in new people from various other parts of the region and from beyond. Such migration rarely involved large numbers of people, but consisted of the gradual filtering of individuals, families, or small groups of kinsmen and associates into new areas.[6] Over generations, the accumulation of short movements left patterns roughly corresponding to the traditions of migration—a series of communities linked by bonds of language and culture. The migrants who settled a particular area did not see themselves as part of a greater historical process; they were simply people looking to build more secure and prosperous lives. What appear in retrospect to have been way stations along the routes of migration were often stable communities to the people who inhabited them.[7]

Although traditions usually trace the origins of central Kenya communities to the arrival of a single group of pioneer farmers, this was rarely the case. In Gikuyuland, for example, at a certain point migrating farmers—or more precisely their language, culture, and economy —must have overwhelmed the previous agricultural society, in the process expunging those predecessors from collective memory. New societies incorporated men and women of various backgrounds, in-

5. Thomas Spear pointed out some of the dangers of the literal reading of Meru oral traditions in his review of J. Fadiman, *Mountain Warriors*, in *International Journal of African Historical Studies* 11 (1978): 131–34. Possible lines of interpretation are suggested in Jurg Mahner, "The Outsider and Insider in Tigania, Meru," *Africa* 45 (1975): 400–09; and for other areas of Africa in Robert Harms, "Oral Tradition and Ethnicity," *Journal of Interdisciplinary History* 10 (1979): 61–85; and D. W. Cohen, "Reconstructing a Conflict in Bunafu: Seeking Evidence Outside the Narrative Tradition," in Miller, *African Past Speaks*, pp. 201–20.

6. This discussion of movement is based on Muriuki, *History of Kikuyu*, chaps. 2–3, and my own analysis of oral evidence of nineteenth-century migration. Those oral records largely consist of semiformalized lineage traditions and genealogies; relatively fixed stories of particular events or famous individuals; and highly individual personal or family testimonies or recollections. I made no systematic effort to collect the texts of ethnic traditions. For recent discussions of the methodological issues arising from the use of oral materials, see J. Miller, "Listening for the African Past," pp. 1–59; and Jan Vansina, *Oral Tradition as History* (Madison, Wisc., 1985), notably, pp. 189–99.

7. Muriuki, *History of Kikuyu*, pp. 37–61; H. S. K. Mwaniki, "A Political History of the Embu, c. A.D. 1500–1906" (M.A. thesis, University of Nairobi, 1973), p. 140; and H. E. Lambert, *Kikuyu Social and Political Institutions* (London, 1956). An important overview of migration is found in Richard Waller, "Ecology, Migration and Expansion in East Africa," *African Affairs* 23 (1985): 347–70. Joseph C. Miller relates migration to climate cycles in "The Significance of Drought, Disease and Famine in the Agriculturally Marginal Zones of West-Central Africa," *Journal of African History* 23 (1982): 22.

cluding people from hunting or herding communities. Numerous accounts attest to the biological and cultural intermixture evident in societies in nineteenth-century central Kenya, notably on the frontiers of Gikuyuland and Meru.[8] Migrants sometimes settled down in country that was largely uninhabited; but more commonly, they encountered existing populations, however sparse, that had previously made use of the land. Written and oral sources abound with references to indigenous non-Bantu-speaking hunters and gatherers—known as Okiek—whom farmers encountered as they spread across central Kenya.[9] The nature of the confrontation between farmers and hunters is difficult to reconstruct, since by the last part of the nineteenth century the remaining, small and scattered groups of hunter-gatherers had been confined almost entirely to the region's outer margins. Some of the relatively fixed texts of lineage or ethnic traditions describe clashes that culminated in expulsion or annihilation for hunting groups. But it is more likely that evolving farming societies incorporated many of those original residents who supposedly disappeared. This was certainly what occurred during the nineteenth century as Gikuyu-speaking farmers expanded southward.[10] Once established, of course, societies continued to draw in new people: wives, adoptees, captives, slaves, clients, and independent settlers.

As the agriculturalists expanded, they had also to contend with groups of pastoralists who occupied the neighboring grasslands. By the nineteenth century the threat to the northern and eastern frontiers from Oromo herders had apparently subsided, but on the northwest, west, and south farmers confronted the still-rising power of Maasai and related peoples.[11] The rapid advance of the Maasai south along the Rift Valley coincided roughly with the emergence of the new agricultural societies of central Kenya. By 1800, Maasai groups had occupied lands on the northern and southern fringes of farming areas and

8. See in particular the testimony of African witnesses to the Kenya Land Commission. Great Britain, Kenya Land Commission, *Evidence and Memoranda* (London, 1934), for example, 1:267.

9. For example, William A. Chanler, *Through Jungle and Desert: Travels in Eastern Africa* (New York, 1896), pp. 373–74. See R. H. Blackburn, "Okiek History," in Ogot, *Kenya Before 1900*, pp. 53–83.

10. G. St. J. Orde-Browne, *The Vanishing Tribes of Kenya* (Westport, Conn., 1970 [1925]), pp. 20–21; Mwaniki, "History of Embu," pp. 129–39; Muriuki, *History of Kikuyu*, pp. 77–78, 100–02; and G. Kershaw, "The Land is the People: A Study of Kikuyu Social Organization in Historical Perspective" (Ph.D. diss., University of Chicago, 1972), pp. 256–59.

11. Spear, *Kenya's Past*, pp. 105–09. Also, Fadiman, "Meru Peoples," pp. 156–58.

were ranging into the heart of central Kenya itself. As they extended their sway over the vast territory surrounding the Rift Valley, the pastoralists raided ever more widely, reaching as far west as Lake Victoria and to the east almost to the coast.[12] But Maasai power was neither monolithic nor invincible; and after the mid-1800s internecine conflicts increasingly sapped the strength of the small subdivisions that made up Maasai society.[13] Still, the presence of pastoralist raiders certainly restricted the extension of agricultural settlement on the frontiers of Gikuyuland and Ulu.

The characterizations of the late nineteenth-century region drawn from oral accounts generally emphasize the violent elements of contacts between farmers and pastoralists. But local histories assembled largely from oral evidence also suggest that in most areas raids occurred infrequently.[14] In those many areas that possessed few cattle, the likelihood of pastoralist raids was rather remote. Even where farmers owned substantial herds, contacts were by no means uniformly hostile. In Meru and in northern and southern Gikuyuland, trade, intermarriage, and adoption commonly took place across the boundaries of language, economy, and culture that divided cultivators from herders. Often, Maasai men or women who had abandoned—or been forced to abandon—their pastoral ways of life settled with farming families or became clients to agricultural communities. In a reverse process, Gikuyu-speaking farmers sometimes sought to build their wealth in livestock by attaching themselves to Maasai patrons.[15] In fact, societies in the outlying sections of the region often were culturally fluid and diverse, as emerges in this description of northern Meru in the early 1890s:

12. John L. Berntsen, "Pastoralism, Raiding and Prophets: Maasailand in the Nineteenth Century" (Ph.D. diss., University of Wisconsin, 1979), pp. 23–40, 140, 223–67.

13. Ibid., p. 294; F. J. Jackson, "Journey to Uganda via Masailand," *Proceedings of the Royal Geographical Society* 13 (1891): 193–208; Charles Dundas, "History of Kitui," *Journal of the Royal Anthropological Institute* 43 (1913): 485; J. R. L. MacDonald, *Soldiering and Surveying in British East Africa, 1891–1894* (London, 1973 [1897]), p. 41; J. Forbes Munro, *Colonial Rule and the Kamba: Social Change in the Kenya Highlands, 1880–1939* (Oxford, 1975), pp. 26–27; Richard Waller, "The Maasai and the British, 1895–1905: The Origins of an Alliance," *Journal of African History* 17 (1976): 536.

14. Also, John Berntsen, "The Maasai and their Neighbors: Variables of Interaction," *African Economic History* 2 (1976): 1–11; Muriuki, *History of Kikuyu*, p. 97.

15. Muriuki, *History of Kikuyu*, pp. 67–71, 83–101; Fadiman, "The Meru Peoples," pp. 156–68; Peter Marris and Anthony Somerset, *African Businessmen: A Study of Entrepreneurship and Development in Kenya* (Nairobi, 1971), pp. 32–47; Berntsen, "Maasailand," pp. 279, 284–87; Margaret Gillman, "Concepts of 'Inter-tribal Relations' Applied to the Kamba-Masai Border," *Kenya Historical Review* 1 (1973): 33–44; F. Jackson, *Early Days in East Africa* (London, 1969 [1930]), p. 174; Chanler, *Jungle and Desert*, pp. 350–53.

the land is cultivated by natives, who are numerous here, the tribes being those of Mnyithu and Katheri. All these people are akin to those of Kikuyu. But there is also a clan of Wakwafi (a branch of the Masai), living alongside of Katheri, and a community of Ndorobos [hunters], too; thus three distinct races with different customs live side by side.[16]

THE ESTABLISHMENT OF SMALL SOCIETIES

By the late nineteenth century, farmers had occupied most of the areas of central Kenya that could support settled farming. In the Ulu Hills, in central Gikuyuland, and on the slopes of Mount Kenya the existence of highly cohesive communities reflected several centuries of relatively dense agricultural settlement. Despite the challenge posed by pastoralist raiders, pioneer farmers gradually expanded the boundaries of these major centers of population. During the course of the nineteenth century, settlers cut down the dense forests of Gikuyuland and Mount Kenya; they advanced onto the margins of the highlands and the Ulu Hills. Most migrants probably moved only a short distance, but some advanced well beyond the limits of established communities and founded or joined new communities on the frontier, especially in the more arid eastern sections of the region. Most were escaping what they saw as the insufficient or declining resources of their home communities. Land hunger drove many to migrate, the trauma of food shortages, others. Every new community also drew in free spirits or scoundrels attracted by adventure or fleeing from debts or scandal. Although many of the migrants were poor, migration was by no means the preserve of the impoverished. Prosperous men often moved as well, seeking greater opportunities in long-distance trade or livestock herding.[17] The communities these migrants founded differed sharply from those they had left behind. In the late 1800s, newly established societies in Mumoni and eastern Kitui and on the southern edges of Gikuyuland were still very much in the process of formation.

Beginning during the mid-1700s, some groups of Kamba-speaking

16. A. H. Neumann, *Elephant Hunting in East Equatorial Africa* (London, 1898), p. 128.

17. H. E. Lambert, "The Social and Political Institutions of the Tribes of the Kikuyu Land Unit of Kenya," manuscript, 1945, University of Nairobi Library (microfilm, Yale University Library), p. 107; Mwaniki, "History of Embu," p. 160; Muriuki, *History of Kikuyu*, p. 55; Kennell A. Jackson, "An Ethnohistorical Study of the Oral Traditions of the Akamba of Kenya" (Ph.D. diss., University of California, 1972), pp. 117–23. Interviews: Maritha w/o Nthereru, Muruachuri Nyaga, and Muruaringo s/o Muyakagio, Embu; Paul Ngutu s/o Ngutha and Muito s/o Muthama, Migwani; Ruguca Nthimbu and Gatema Muyovi, Mbeere.

farmers abandoned Ulu and migrated some fifty miles eastward to the
drier country of Kitui. As these pioneer farmers established new communities, they increased their stake in livestock raising. Farmers everywhere in the region kept some domestic animals, but as a rule settlers
on the frontier tended to be more oriented toward pastoralism. In Kitui, as in most of the new areas of settlement, the emphasis on herding
sustained a continual push for new grazing land. A period of drought
around 1830 also encouraged movement, forcing some families into
immediate migration and putting into relief for all the limitations and
fragility of local resources.[18] Thus, as elders died and village settlements broke up, many of the younger men left their home areas and
moved out onto the frontier. By the early 1800s pioneer farmers had
already established themselves in Migwani, on the northern extremes
of the Kitui Hills, while descendants of these and later settlers rapidly
spread beyond the hills into the lower and drier lands to the south, to
the east, and especially to the northeast into Mumoni, into areas where
cultivation was only barely practicable. Some of the migrants left central Kenya altogether, establishing Kamba-speaking colonies hundreds
of miles distant, near the Indian Ocean coast, in the area of Mount
Kilimanjaro, and in northern Tanganyika.[19] In these newly forming
societies, where social relationships were in flux, men could advance
rapidly. To the Kitui migrants, life on the moving frontier of settlement offered not only apparently limitless grazing lands, but a wider
scope for individual initiative and the acquisition of property and
influence.[20]

The farmers who moved into Migwani built their homesteads
along a twenty-mile range of hills, rising above four thousand feet. Although erratic, rainfall there normally supported extensive fields of
grains, pulses, and a few root crops. To the north and west these higher
lands faced out on an open, unoccupied plain that stretched twenty-
five miles to the Tana and Athi rivers; to the northeast, dry and simi-

18. Jackson, "Kamba History," p. 215.

19. Interviews: Mutia s/o Mboo, Mukusu s/o Mututhu, and Muito s/o Muthama,
Migwani.

20. Jackson, "Kamba History," pp. 191–93, 203; John Lamphear, "The Kamba and
the Northern Mrima Coast," in *Precolonial African Trade*, ed. R. Gray and D. Birmingham
(London, 1970), pp. 82–86. Dating of Migwani and Mumoni settlements is based largely on
the analysis of genealogies. Also see J. L. Krapf, Journal Description of a Journey made to
Ukambani [Kitui] in November and December 1849 (received, C.M.S., Aug. 1850), entry for
29 Nov. 1849, Krapf Papers, Church Missionary Society Archives, London, CA5/0 16/174.
Dundas incorrectly claims a much later date for Mumoni settlement, "History of Kitui," pp.
480–81.

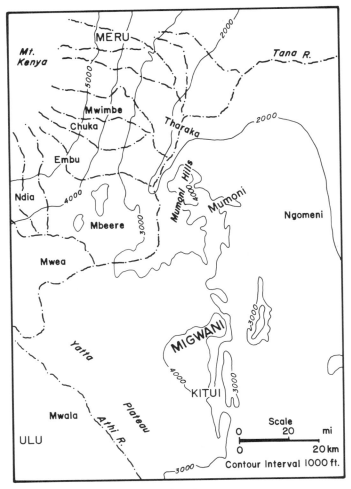

Map 4. Migwani and Surrounding Areas

larly unpopulated brush country reached toward Mumoni; to the east and south, a series of narrow valleys and rugged hills separated the newly settled areas from other areas of population concentration in Kitui. This geographical isolation meant that Migwani settlers were forced to give up close contact with their areas of origin quickly and decisively. Consequently, an autonomous local society and economy rapidly developed, encouraging the emergence—within the Kamba linguistic and cultural tradition—of a clearly separate sense of identity.[21]

21. Interviews: Salim Ndongo, Kitui Town; Mbulwa s/o Ndoo, Migwani. By the late 1960s the area had a population of about seventy-five thousand. Government of Kenya, *Cen-*

A Kitui riddle collected around 1900 poses this statement: "I went to Yatta [the vast open plain between Migwani and the Tana River] just now, and I returned." The solution, "My eyes," refers to the enormous distances that people living on the outlying Ulu or Kitui hills could travel by sight.²² For Migwani residents, for example, the hills of Mbeere and Mumoni and the highlands of Gikuyuland and Mount Kenya were not imagined distant territories but everyday facts of life. In spirit, communities in Migwani and other fringe areas faced outward, very much attuned to the opportunities and threats posed by external contact. In a pattern repeated across the region, Migwani attracted migrants not only from the neighboring farming areas of Mbeere, but from pastoralist groups as well. Outsiders were rapidly assimilated, but because population was scattered and the local society hardly formed these newcomers—with their diverse backgrounds— had the opportunity to play a significant if subtle role in the evolution of Migwani society.²³

Across central Kenya, pioneer farmers established themselves in the small, lineage-based settlements that were the fundamental units of agricultural societies throughout the region. The extended families of a small group of men, closely related by patrilineal descent, generally made up the core of residents, but on the frontier in particular these small villages often also included more distant lineage-mates as well as people from other lineages. The members of families within these settlements cooperated closely in the allocation of land and labor, in the conduct of community affairs, and in the organization of relations with the outside and outsiders.²⁴ The adjacent settlements of a number of lineages merged loosely into communities or neighborhoods, whose

sus (Nairobi, 1969), pp. 27–28. For a wide-ranging discussion of the formation of new societies in precolonial Africa, see Igor Kopytoff, "The Internal African Frontier: The Making of African Political Culture," in *The African Frontier: The Reproduction of Traditional African Societies*, ed. I. Kopytoff (Bloomington, Ind., 1987), pp. 3–84.

22. Gerhard Lindblom, *Kamba Folklore, vol. 3: Proverbs and Songs*, Archives D'Etudes Orientales, vol. 20 (Uppsala, 1934), p. 10.

23. PRO: John Ainsworth to J. Pigott, 28 Feb. 1895 in IBEAC to F.O., 3 May 1895, FO 2/97. K. Jackson, "Traditions of the Akamba," pp. 123–27. Interviews: Kilungi s/o Kithita, Rose Makaa w/o Mutia, and Ngatu s/o Mauna, Migwani.

24. This statement is based essentially on my own field research. The substantial, if uneven, ethnographic literature covering the peoples of central Kenya is ably summarized in Middleton and Kershaw, *North-Eastern Bantu*. See also, K. Ndeti, *Elements of Akamba Life* (Nairobi, 1972); Satish Saberwal, *The Traditional Political System of the Embu of Central Kenya* (Kampala, 1970); and Jack Glazier, "Conflict and Conciliation among the Mbeere of Kenya" (Ph.D. diss., University of California, 1972), pp. 48–83. K. Jackson emphasizes the diversity of local communities in "Kamba History," pp. 206–08. Jane Guyer has pointed out many of the problems in defining communities in "Household and Community in African Studies," *African Studies Review* 24 (1981): 87–137.

cohesiveness increased as local residence patterns stabilized. Except in emergencies, the scope of communal action rarely extended beyond this narrow sphere. According to an early colonial administrator's description of Kitui society, "The members of a *thome* [neighborhood] hang very close together and form almost a little state by themselves, perhaps the only form of state known to the Mkamba."[25]

In Migwani, as elsewhere across the region, communities were not defined in neat territorial terms, but as aggregates of relationships. The movement of people continually recast the patterns of these relationships, particularly in the fluid frontier zones. But even in established communities, the arrival or departure of families or groups of families shifted the local political balance by changing the composition of settlements and disrupting the bonds that linked residential groups in neighborhoods. Thus, the extent of territorial units continually fluctuated, drawing in or excluding groups of residents according to the particular circumstances.

The processes of territorial relations emerged essentially from the circulation of property and labor that resulted from the exchange between lineages of women for bridewealth.[26] No definitive rules governed where husbands or wives should be found, aside from prohibitions against incest and marriages within the clan (and hence within the lineage). But if local custom did not demand absolute reciprocity in marriage relations, in practice, husbands and wives usually did come from the same small community. Because bridewealth was often paid in installments spread over many years, the lineages within a locality became locked in a complicated web of marriage contracts.[27] Most elders could draw on an array of relationships with other lineages to which they were connected through mothers, stepmothers, sisters, wives, sisters-in-law, daughters, and daughters-in-law. Over genera-

25. Dundas, "History of Kitui," p. 493.
26. C. Meillassoux, "The Social Organization of the Peasantry: The Economic Basis of Kinship," *Journal of Peasant Studies* 1 (1973): 84. Most of the ethnographic studies place excessive emphasis on corporate descent groups. An interesting exception is Jomo Kenyatta, *Facing Mount Kenya* (New York, n.d. [1938]), pp. 19–20. Also see W. E. H. Stanner, "The Kitui Kamba: A Study of British Colonial Administration in East Africa," manuscript, 1939, pp. B.43–48, KNA; and Colin Maher, "Soil Erosion and Land Utilization in the Ukamba (Kitui) Reserve," Nairobi, Government of Kenya, Soil Conservation Service, 1937, p. 4.
27. Kenyatta, *Facing Mount Kenya*, pp. 19–20; Dundas, "History of Kitui," pp. 517–20; L. S. B. Leakey, *The Southern Kikuyu before 1903* (London and New York, 1977), 1:508. The reconstruction from interviews of late nineteenth-century marriage patterns in the Kagaari section of Embu revealed that almost all marriages involved spouses from the same immediate area. Regina Oboler found a similar situation in Nandi, western Kenya. *Women, Power and Economic Change: The Nandi of Kenya* (Stanford, 1985), p. 41.

tions, marriage connections created dense networks of personal relationships within a community; gaps in the concentration of such links corresponded to the boundaries among neighborhoods. In the heavily populated districts of Gikuyuland, Ulu, and on Mount Kenya, however, such boundary areas would have been difficult to discern.

The life of the Migwani community centered on the numerous hillside neighborhoods, each comprising a collection of lineage homesteads. Within each of these neighborhoods, families dispersed their plots to take advantage of local variations in soil types, vegetation, and climate. In the process, farmers spread their risks and found the best possible conditions for raising different crops. The resulting complicated patterns of land use ensured that in every locality a number of different lineages would own or utilize land. This fragmentation and interpenetration of lineage residence and land holdings effectively blurred the boundaries among lineages.[28] After 1850, Migwani society entered a period of consolidation and stability. By the 1880s several thousand people lived in the area, concentrated in hillside settlements. As Migwani society lost its frontier character, residents increasingly identified with the larger community rather than with individual lineage settlements. Still, no political superstructure institutionalized this identification.

Adjacent communities did sometimes cooperate in military actions, but such common enterprises were rarely institutionalized. Rather, the scope of military mobilization continuously shifted, focusing at times on a single lineage settlement, a collection of neighboring settlements, or at times much larger areas. In Kitui, for example, groups of several hundred men assembled rapidly in response to aggression, while in Embu as many as a thousand warriors could be called into the field. Raiding parties in the region sometimes included more than one hundred warriors.[29] In fact, forces numbering at least

28. Interviews: Kilungi s/o Kithita, Vungo s/o Ngonzi, Sali w/o Mulewa, Wamui w/o Munyasia, Kaliungi s/o Ikenga, Nelson Kangu s/o Imeli, and Muito s/o Muthama, Migwani. Testimonies correspond with the earliest travelers' impressions. See J. W. R. Pigott, "Diary of my Journey up the Tana River and Back Through Ukambani and along the Tabaki River, 1889," entries for 24–25 May 1889, typescript of original, University of Nairobi Library; and C. W. Hobley, Original Safari Diaries, Rhodes House Library, Oxford, Mss. Afr. R. 148, entries for 21–25 Nov. 1891. Also Maher, "Erosion in the Kitui Reserve," pp. 19, 70; and Dundas, "History of Kitui," p. 499.

29. PRO: Lt. R. Meinertzhagen, Intelligence Report, in Capt. Dickinson to Adjutant, 3rd. K.A.R., 17 March 1904 in Eliot to F.O., 4 May 1904, FO 2/836. Alfred Arkell-Hardwick, *An Ivory Trader in North Kenia* (London, 1903), p. 71; Chanler, *Jungle and Desert*, pp. 489–90; John Boyes, *John Boyes: King of the Wa-Kikuyu*, ed. C. W. L. Bulpett (London, 1968 [1911]), pp. 94–95; Hobley, Safari Diary, 24–25 Sept. 1891.

one thousand men were said to have launched attacks from Ulu against
Maasai settlements and herds during the 1890s.[30] But most such expeditions were much smaller, in many cases hardly more than raider
bands. Even larger "armies" were the product of a temporary amalga-
mation of independent local units.[31]

THE EVOLUTION OF ESTABLISHED SOCIETIES

The qualities of newness and fluidity that still marked Migwani society
during the late nineteenth century were less evident in the long-estab-
lished communities located in the highlands and in the hill country of
Mbeere and central Ulu. The larger economic and political developments that disturbed communities in many sections of the region after
1850 touched Embu country only slightly.[32] In Embu a slow expansion had entrenched basic patterns of authority that had been laid
down by the late 1700s. In contrast to the motion that characterized
Migwani society, Embu lineages had—over several generations—become closely identified with particular localities. In the absence of large
herds of livestock, the problem of excessive pressure on limited grazing
lands did not arise as it did repeatedly in Kitui and Mumoni. Soils were
rich and with care could be kept in almost continuous use. Widespread
banana cultivation also tended to stabilize residence patterns because
once seedlings were established, these plants produced fruit over many
years with little attention.[33]

30. Letter from Francis Hall to Edward Hall, Kikuyu [near present-day Nairobi], 4
July 1893, typescript of original, Francis George Hall Papers, 1895–1901, Rhodes House Li-
brary, Oxford (copies at Syracuse University Library). Unless otherwise noted, all Francis
Hall's letters cited below were written at Kikuyu, to his father, Edward Hall.
31. Gerhard Lindblom, *The Akamba in British East Africa* (Uppsala, 1920), pp. 186–
201; and H. S. K. Mwaniki, *Embu Historical Texts* (Nairobi, 1974), pp. 69, 264. Interviews:
Ngatu s/o Mauna, Munuve s/o Lingwa, Komba w/o Nzoka, Nguuti s/o Ndana, Kaliungi s/o
Ikenga, Muli s/o Ndulwa, Mbulwa s/o Ndoo, Migwani; Kiliungi s/o Muuru, Mwinzi s/o
Kathinzi, Paul Makuu s/o Kiwa, Mumoni; Wagatu w/o Mucirwa, Gatema Muyovi, Abedinego Kagundu Njangaruko, Mbeere. Information regarding raiding can also be found in
Jeffrey Fadiman, *An Oral History of Tribal Warfare: The Meru of Mt. Kenya* (Athens, Ohio,
1982).
32. Mwaniki, "History of Embu," pp. 168–72; and Orde-Browne, *Vanishing Tribes*,
p. 38. Embu oral records contain relatively little information on trade and traders.
33. KNA: Embu District, Political Record Book, Part II [entry written ca. 1927], DC.
Ebu/3/2. A. R. Barlow testimony in East African Protectorate, Native Labour Commission,
1912–13, *Evidence and Report* (Nairobi, 1913), p. 205; Philip Curtin et al., *African History*
(Boston, 1978), p. 171; Lambert, "Institutions of the Kikuyu," p. 124. Interviews: Kanjama
s/o Njanguthi and Muruwanyamu Kathambara, Embu.

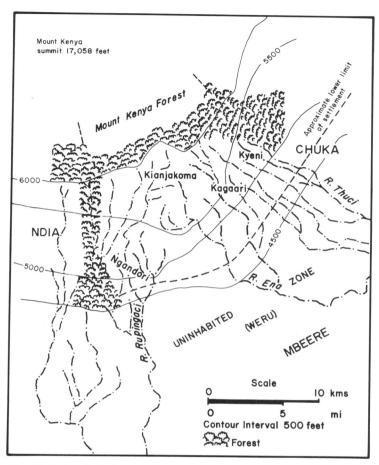

Map 5. Embu: Relief

Embu occupied a small, well-defined wedge of land—no more than twenty miles wide—on the lower southern slopes of Mount Kenya, bordered on the west by the Ndia section of Gikuyuland and on the east by Chuka. Mountain forest gave way to cultivated land at an altitude around six thousand feet; settlements stretched from there about ten miles—and fifteen hundred feet in elevation—down the mountain to the beginning of the open plain that separated Embu from the Mbeere hills. In contrast to its highland neighbors, Embu had substantial amounts of good farmland located higher up on the mountain, where rainfall was greater and more reliable.[34]

34. PRO: Hayes Sadler to C.O., 31 Aug. 1906, CO 533/16. KNA: Central Province, Embu District Political Record Book, PC.CP 1/5/1. Arkell-Hardwick, *Ivory Trader*, p. 75; R.

Ample rainfall and rich volcanic soils enabled many Embu farmers to produce a regular surplus of foodstuffs. Serious drought rarely if ever struck the country during the 1800s, although poorer people sometimes experienced hunger in the periods before harvest.[35] Around 1900 a visitor noted that "M'bu [Embu] seemed to be prodigiously rich in food. We saw thousands of acres planted with Muhindi [probably sorghum] stretching as far as the eye could reach."[36] Various beans, millets, peas, finger millet, greens, maize, and pumpkins were among the foods grown. Farmers also planted cassava, yams, sweet potatoes, castor, tobacco, and as many as thirteen types of bananas. The wide range of crops gave people a relatively varied diet as well as protection against occasional plant diseases or insect damage.[37] Every Embu family also kept some livestock, usually sheep and goats, although the local climate and vegetation did not favor herding.

Families generally were able to satisfy essential needs within their neighborhoods, but sectional economic variation did result in considerable trade, notably involving communities at the ecological extremes. A farmer who had surplus tobacco might, for example, arrange through a relative to exchange it for sugar cane to use in brewing beer. Transactions occurred informally in homesteads; markets served only as conduits for trade with the outside.[38]

In Embu, as across much of the central Kenya highlands, numerous streams descended rapidly from the forest, cutting the rugged landscape into a series of parallel, isolated ridges. The shape of local societies closely reflected the terrain. The small settlements found on a ridge formed a tight-knit, autonomous neighborhood, within which three concentrations of power and authority competed and overlapped: the

Meinertzhagen, *Kenya Diary, 1902–1906* (London, 1957), p. 147 (9 March 1904); and E. May Crawford, *By the Equator's Snowy Peaks* (London, 1913), p. 156. Interviews: Muruwanyamu Kathambara, Simeon Njage, Jason Njigoru, Njorano Ndarwa, and Kabogo w/o Gacigua, Embu.

35. Colin Maher, "Soil Erosion and Land Utilization in the Embu Reserve," Nairobi, Kenya Government, Soil Conservation Service, 1938, pp. 36–37.

36. Arkell-Hardwick, *Ivory Trader*, p. 70.

37. KNA: Central Province, Embu District Political Record Book [documents from ca. 1913 and ca. 1916], PC.CP 1/5/1. Hobley, Safari Diary, 4 Oct. 1891; and Orde-Browne, *Vanishing Tribes*, p. 97.

38. Mwaniki, "History of Embu," pp. 70–73. Rainfall levels varied widely between upper and lower Embu. Jon Moris, "The Mwea Environment," in *Mwea: An Irrigated Rice Scheme in Kenya*, ed. J. Moris and Robert Chambers (Munich, 1973), p. 29. Interviews: Muruakori s/o Gacewa and Paulo Njega, Embu. Discussion of the role of markets in central Kenya is found below, chap. 4.

residential lineage, the age set, and the generation.[39] The lineage settlements—fragments of highly dispersed clans—usually included a
small number of extended families closely related by descent. While the
boundaries among these settlements were clearly defined, this exclusivity was mediated by the attachment of members to the locality or
neighborhood where they and their ancestors had long resided. In societies in Gikuyuland and around Mount Kenya, the bonds of community were further reinforced by a system of genealogically defined generation sets.[40] At twenty-five- to thirty-year intervals a new generation
(made up of men of all ages) would be invested with the responsibility
for the moral direction of the society. Within any locality, elders of the
designated generation administered the local sacred groves and thus
regulated the ritual life of their community.[41]

While there is a good deal of confusion about the nature of generational affiliation in those areas where it existed, there is no question as
to the role and importance of the bonds of age. Everywhere in the region, the ceremonies of male and female initiation created attachments
among people of the same age that cut across other loyalties and reinforced localized concentrations of kinship relations. In Mbeere and
Embu, and in Meru and Gikuyu-speaking areas, corporate age sets
provided an alternative to lineage affiliation, balancing the power of elders in community politics. Even in Ulu and Kitui, where formal age

39. The description of Embu society is drawn largely from my own field work, which
was concentrated in the Kagaari section of central Embu. See also Saberwal, *Political System
of Embu*, pp. 4–16.

40. For a somewhat different view, see Saberwal, *Political System of Embu*, pp. 4–16.
A similar identification of lineage and locality existed in Mbeere. KNA: Asst. District Com-
missioner, 1917, Embu District, Political Record Book, Division III, Emberre, DC/EBU.3/1.
David Brokensha and Jack Glazier, "Land Reform among the Mbeere of Central Kenya,"
Africa 43 (1973): 183–98. As Jack Glazier has recently shown, the experience of land reform
in Mbeere during the 1970s generated a considerable body of exaggerated and fictitious
"evidence" of land occupation and ownership. *Land and the Uses of Tradition among the
Mbeere of Kenya* (Lanham, Maryland, 1985), esp. p. 27.

41. Lambert, *Kikuyu Institutions*, pp. 40–52. Kershaw has pointed out the many contradictions in the various accounts of generations. "Land is the People," p. 149. Generational
organization was complicated in Embu and Mbeere by the existence of two parallel sets of
generations. Jack Glazier, "Generation Classes among the Mbeere of Central Kenya," *Africa*
46 (1976): 313–26; Saberwal, *Political System of Embu*, pp. 61–68. Interviews: Waweru
Kamwea and Kanjama s/o Njanguthi, Embu; Kanguru s/o Kirindi, Mbeere. The reshaping of
generational institutions in the context of colonial society has made reconstruction of the
nineteenth-century system difficult. See C. Ambler, "The Remodeling of Custom in Colonial
Kenya: The 1932 Generation Succession Ceremonies in Embu," paper delivered at the African Studies Association, Annual Meeting, Madison, Wisconsin, November 1986.

sets did not exist, loosely defined associations of age-mates played a similar role in local politics. The rituals of initiation themselves, together with various rites tied to the agricultural cycle, not only brought the residents of a neighborhood or group of neighborhoods together, but also gave spiritual basis to the community, however flexibly defined.[42] The organization of trading and hunting expeditions and of work parties helped sustain these communal ties, but it was community dances especially that provided the opportunity for the periodic reaffirmation of local solidarity. The peace that elders imposed on the dance ground provided a context within which men from sometimes antagonistic lineage settlements and neighborhoods could rehearse cooperation. The dance ground was itself sometimes the site for the planning and preparation of raids or defense. Not surprisingly, the elders and senior warriors who controlled community dances also organized and often led military actions.[43]

Male elders within each neighborhood controlled the political direction of communities and the processes of reproduction and accumulation, although women and youths could wield substantial influence in family, lineage, and community affairs. Local elder councils constituted the visible apparatus of government throughout central Kenya. The role of these councils, however, was not really to rule but to mediate disputes and identify common concerns among various groups or individuals, different lineages or villages, competing leaders, age groups, and particular economic interests.[44] In Embu, councils were formed and operated within a broader and more precisely defined hi-

42. KNA: Kitui District, Quarterly Report, Dec. 1909, DC/MKS.1/3/1. Kenyatta, *Facing Mount Kenya*, pp. 246–50; H. E. Lambert, "Land Tenure among the Akamba," *African Studies* 6 (1947): 139; and Charles Dundas, "The Organization and Laws of some Bantu Tribes in East Africa," *Journal of the Royal Anthropological Institute* 45 (1915): 245–47. Interviews: Elizabeth Kitumba w/o Kisenga, Sali w/o Mulewa, and Kinyenye s/o Mbuvi, Migwani.

43. I. M. Hildebrandt, "Ethnographic Notes of Wakamba," KNA: Machakos District, Political Record Book, vol. I, part II, DC/MKS.4/3. KNA: Kitui District, Annual Report, 1928, DC/KTI/1/1/3. C. W. Hobley, *Ethnology of A-Kamba and other East African Tribes* (London, 1971 [1910]), p. 70; and Carolyn Clark, "Land and Food, Women and Power in Nineteenth Century Kikuyu," *Africa* 50 (1980): 364–65. Interviews: Kaungo s/o Mutia, Munyoki s/o Mutui, Kaungo s/o Mutia, and Ikiriki s/o Masila, all Mumoni; Paulo Njega, Embu. Robert Cummings links the rise of local trade in Ulu and Kitui to the mobilization of community work groups in "The Early Development of Akamba Local Trade History, c. 1780–1820," *Kenya Historical Review* 4 (1976): 91–92.

44. Lindblom, *Akamba*, pp. 159–60; Lambert, "Institutions of the Kikuyu," p. 139; and Clark, "Women and Power in Kikuyu," pp. 358–59. For an analysis of the extent and limits of women's influence in a male-dominated society, see Oboler, *Women, Power and Economic Change*, esp. p. 241.

erarchy than equivalent bodies found in societies elsewhere around Mount Kenya, let alone the ad hoc groupings that characterized the Migwani and Mumoni societies.[45]

WEALTH AND POWER IN SMALL SOCIETIES

A few elders had far greater influence than their peers. In each generation there were a number of men (and very rarely a woman) whose talents or success made them genuine community leaders.[46] Wealth and influence were inextricably intertwined in the societies of central Kenya. Since land was freely available, prosperity and security depended essentially on access to and control over labor—a fact that was illustrated in the popular aphorism *andu ni indo*, "people are wealth." The richest men were therefore those who could command the resources of labor necessary to open new fields for cultivation, watch over large herds, protect their settlements, and engage in trading, hunting, and raids. The importance of labor resources to the definition of wealth comes across in a song that Kitui women sang while grinding flour:

> At Kitili's there are 'boys' (servants) males
>   and females,
> there are goats and young sheep and cattle.
> Do I not call you I poor person!
> I have not our family and I have not my mother,
> and I have not relatives to call.[47]

Men built up their bases of wealth first by expanding their families, generally by marrying additional wives and sometimes through the adoption of dependents. They gained control over more labor through

---

45. Saberwal, *Political System of Embu*, pp. 67–70, 81; Mwaniki, "History of Embu," pp. 191, 225. Interviews: Alan Kageta, Gatere Kamunyori, and Gideon s/o Mwea wa Methumu, Embu.

46. The best known of female leaders was Ciarume from Mavuria in Mbeere, who apparently gained a reputation in combat and who may have served briefly as a colonial chief. Orde-Browne, *Vanishing Tribes*, p. 54; and Glazier, "Conflict and Conciliation among the Mbeere," p. 59. Interviews: Abedinego Kagundu Njangaruko and Anna Njira w/o Munyi, Mbeere. There may have been a female chief during the first years of colonial rule in Kitui. KNA: Kitui District, Quarterly Report, June 1910, DC/MKS.1/3/2. Of course, in every community women recognized their own leaders. Clark, "Women and Power in Kikuyu," p. 360.

47. Lindblom, *Kamba Folklore*, 3:50. The song was collected around 1908. The use of the English word "boy" for servant at this time must have suggested a direct comparison between Kitili and the European officials, missionaries, and settlers, who routinely employed servants. Kitili was a well-known, wealthy man in eastern Kitui.

hire, through the development of patron-client relationships, and through the manipulation of social obligations.[48] Those who found themselves on the opposite side of such arrangements were relatively poor, but the poorest people in any society were those who lacked even the protection and opportunities that a patron could offer. It was not, for instance, the refugees whom Nzambu wa Ndove led from Migwani to Mwimbe who suffered most severely in the famine of 1897–1901, but those unfortunate individuals who were left alone to scrape together an existence without family or patron for support. To repeat the women's work song from Kitui: "I poor person! . . . I have not relatives to call." While poverty was certainly to be avoided, wealth did not carry entirely positive values. In Embu it is recalled that men who became too rich were sometimes poisoned or cursed or accused of witchcraft.[49] Likewise, Migwani traditions include a cautionary story of the dangers of excessive wealth: As a young man, a local resident named Mwilile managed in rapid succession to acquire substantial herds and marry several wives. He moved away from the hillside settlements and isolated himself somewhat from the community. The contempt that he apparently felt for his poorer neighbors is conveyed in the memory that he permitted his livestock to trample their fields. But in his preoccupation with acquiring property, Mwilile neglected to provide adequate protection for his livestock. When raiders struck and he sent out the alarm, his neighbors are said to have responded, "You are a strong man, go and take your cattle back."[50]

Wealth was self-perpetuating. Access to labor gave a man the resources to enhance his stature and develop a following. Because his household could produce more food and livestock, a relatively rich man was in the position to reward workers and offer them the hospitality of beer parties and feasts that was an essential part of building a position of leadership.[51] Ownership of large numbers of livestock allowed wealthy individuals to obtain yet more wives, clients, and other dependents. Again, in the Kitui work song, the wealth of Kitili's homestead is illustrated in parallel mentions of servants and livestock. In-

---

48. At midcentury J. L. Krapf described the qualities that made leaders in Kitui. *Travels, Researches and Missionary Labours during an Eighteen Year Residence in Eastern Africa* (London, 1860), p. 355. Also, Lindblom, *Akamba*, p. 80; K. Jackson, "Kamba History," pp. 226–27; and Spear, *Kenya's Past*, pp. 125–27.

49. Interview: Kanjama s/o Njanguthi, Embu.

50. Interviews: Nguuti s/o Ndana and Ngavi s/o Mwanzi, Migwani.

51. Clark, "Women and Power in Kikuyu," p. 366. See also Margery Perham, ed., *The Diaries of Lord Lugard* (Evanston, Ill., 1959), 1:161 (entry for 27 March 1890).

deed, *andu ni indo* could be translated to mean not only "people are wealth" but "people are livestock." The scale of livestock accumulation was the surest indicator of wealth in nineteenth-century central Kenya.[52]

During the last decades of the nineteenth century, the push to accumulate cattle drove a steady expansion of agricultural settlement out of hillside communities in Meru, Gikuyuland, Kitui, and Ulu onto adjacent plains. In response to increased competition for grazing lands, larger-scale livestock owners moved beyond the bounds of established homesteads into areas where ample pasturelands were available. The potential for profit apparently offset the agricultural and military vulnerability of these new settlements.

This expansion occurred gradually. In Migwani, settlers first established cattle camps out on the plain and only later made these outposts their permanent homes.[53] While the majority of people in Migwani continued to live in the hillside neighborhoods, the leadership of the society as a whole and the impetus for change increasingly belonged to men who had chosen to move away from the hills. Few men would ever acquire herds of the size owned by the leaders, but poorer men nonetheless found the idea of settlement in the plains attractive. The patronage of wealthy cattle-owners and traders provided security, access to marriage capital, and a situation that promised rapid natural increase for smaller herds. Moving onto the plain usually involved traveling no more than a few miles, but the shift nevertheless involved a major reorientation. The newly established villages were located at the edge of the foothills, at altitudes some five hundred to one thousand feet lower than neighborhoods in the hills. Different soil, climate, and vegetation conditions required new modes of farming, which in turn opened the way to new political and social relationships. In the recently settled areas, families gathered their homesteads in hamlets or villages rather than in the smaller, dispersed homestead groupings that characterized hillside neighborhoods.[54]

The concentration in small villages was linked to the development

52. Stanner, "Kitui Kamba," p. B.148; and A. R. Barlow and T. G. Benson, *English-Kikuyu Dictionary* (Oxford, 1975).

53. This discussion is based on oral evidence collected in Migwani. See also, G. C. M. Mutiso, "Kitui Ecosystem, Integration and Change," in *Ecology and History in East Africa* (*Hadith 7*), ed. B. A. Ogot (Nairobi, 1979), p. 135; and Lambert, "Land Tenure among the Akamba," p. 143.

54. Pigott, Diary, 24–25 May 1889; and Hobley, Safari Diary, 22 Nov. 1891. Interviews: Ngavi s/o Mwanzi, Mbulwa s/o Ndoo, and Nguli s/o Kinuva, Migwani.

of an economy more oriented toward pastoralism and trade, and a society marked by increasing inequalities in the distribution of wealth. Village residence permitted greater efficiency in the mobilization of labor and encouraged the labor discipline that was necessary for activities such as herding or trade that sometimes took men away from home for extended periods.[55] Village concentration also reflected defense considerations. Each of the settlements was fortified with a palisade to provide a measure of protection against both raiders and wild animals. The residents of the settlements on the fringe of Migwani feared attacks not only from Maasai warriors, but from pastoralist-oriented communities like their own in Kitui or eastern Ulu. While military concerns helped shape residence patterns and encouraged the emergence of individual leaders, Migwani society was not preoccupied with defense. Had the external threat been constant and oppressive, it is unlikely that men would have moved their families away from the security of the hills.[56]

A fragment or fragments of a single lineage formed the core of each village. As a rule, other residents were drawn in through their close marriage ties to families in the core group, and it would have been unusual to find people living in a village who could not claim some kinship connection to the central lineage. Whatever the actual relationships among the people within a village, the residents tended to act as a unit and were identified both by themselves and by others with the dominant lineage and its leader. In fact, for many if not most, considerations other than marriage or descent underlay their village loyalties. As circumstances demanded, people made use of a rich and flexible idiom of kinship to convey the quality of an array of individual relationships. Often, when conditions changed, different loyalties asserted or reasserted their primacy.[57] Thus, the ties that supposedly bound many Migwani people to Nzambu wa Ndove during the 1890s faded into relative insignificance when he was later eclipsed by other leaders.

55. Hildebrandt, "Ethnographic Notes," KNA: Machakos District Political Record Book, vol. 1, part II, DC/MKS.4/3. Interviews: Mulango s/o Ngusia, Rose Makaa w/o Mutia, and Elizabeth Kitumba w/o Kisenga, Migwani.

56. PRO: J. Ainsworth, "Report on Kitwyi," 6 Feb. 1895, and Ainsworth to Pigott, 20 Feb. 1895, in IBEAC to F.O., 10 April 1895, FO 2/97. Pigott, Diary, 24–25 May 1889. Interviews: Thitu s/o Nzili, Ngatu s/o Mauna, Vungo s/o Ngonzi, Mukusu s/o Mututhu, Nguuti s/o Ndana, Kikwae w/o Thambu, Ngavi s/o Mwanzi, Komba w/o Nzoka, and Mbasia s/o Muliungi, Migwani.

57. Dundas, "History of Kitui," p. 493; and Stanner, "Kitui Kamba," pp. B.39–40. For a similar argument, see Ivan Karp, *Fields of Change among the Iteso of Kenya* (London, 1978), pp. 76–77.

Little is known about the careers or personal motivations of even the most prominent of Migwani's new leaders—Sila wa Ivuli, Ngulu wa Siviri, and Nzambu wa Ndove. But because the rise of such leaders was so widespread a phenomenon in Kenya during this period, it is possible to piece together the elements of their success. Each built his position on a base of support from lineage associates. Through involvement in trade and by various other means, local notables gradually expanded their herds, using these livestock holdings in turn to build the personal relationships that would permit an expansion of support and ultimately the accumulation of still greater wealth.[58] Migwani people did not see men like Ngulu, Sila, and Nzambu, however, only as wealthy traders and cattle owners, but also as leaders in political and military matters. None of these men, however, systematically involved himself in raiding in order to build up support, as did a number of their contemporaries in other parts of the region.

In some of the established communities in the highlands, the personal accumulation of wealth and power was much less pronounced than in areas like Migwani. In the context of such tight, elder-dominated societies, it was difficult for individuals, no matter how ambitious, to accumulate wealth. In areas like Embu, climate and vegetation conditions tended to keep herds small and hence restrict the scope for accumulation. At the same time, strictly enforced social and ceremonial obligations effectively redistributed property through the lineage and community. Although polygyny was certainly accepted, men rarely had the resources to marry more than one or at most two women. In short, during the late 1800s, there were few rich men in Embu society and thus few of those aggressive individuals whose quest for greater wealth and power shaped events in many other parts of the region.[59] Embu traditions, unlike those of Migwani or Mumoni, tend to be concerned with the experience of the mass of the people and make only sporadic reference to prominent individuals. Few of those who are recalled had reputations that extended across all of Embu, and most owed their prominence not to their wealth but to skills in combat,

---

58. A stimulating discussion of the rise of local leaders in Mijikenda society is found in Thomas Spear, *The Kaya Complex: A History of the Mijikenda Peoples of the Kenya Coast to 1900* (Nairobi, 1978), pp. 115–28. For the careers of the Migwani leaders, see the following Migwani interviews: Ngatu s/o Mauna, Paul Ngutu s/o Ngutha, Sali w/o Mulewa, Ngavi s/o Mwanzi, Wamui w/o Munyasia, and Komba w/o Nzoka.

59. Mwaniki, *Living History of Embu*, pp. 50–61; and Saberwal, *Political System of Embu*, pp. 10, 69–70. The reconstruction of late nineteenth-century marriages in Kagaari, Embu that I attempted uncovered no man who had had more than two wives.

healing, or conciliation.[60] The influence of local leaders did not often extend beyond the bounds of the individual's home community or particular area of talent. Military leaders, for example, could not necessarily claim leadership roles in other spheres of life. Partly as a consequence, these societies escaped much of the local violence that disrupted communities in Migwani and the rest of Kitui.[61]

This pattern held across much of the highlands, but outlying communities did produce a number of "big men." In Macang'a, on Mbeere's southwest margins, one such leader—a man named Munyiri —managed to accumulate considerable wealth and power during the late 1800s.[62] Macang'a was, like Migwani, situated on the edge of the populated hills, overlooking the plain that ran down to the Tana River. Local farms produced adequate if unreliable harvests, and the residents of Macang'a, like their counterparts in Migwani, had the advantage of easy access to good grazing country, well supplied with water and relatively remote from intruders. However, the expansion of raiding into central Kenya during the late nineteenth century left Macang'a less secure, since the area lacked good natural defenses.[63] Nevertheless, the growing need for military preparedness provided an opportunity for men like Munyiri to gain a reputation, some wealth, and a core of followers.

60. Mwaniki, *Living History of Embu*, pp. 154–66; and many of the testimonies in Mwaniki, *Embu Texts*. Interviews: Erasto s/o Runyenge and Girishom Mukono, Embu.

61. Interviews: Ngonju Ngunyaka, Kanguru s/o Kirindi, Nderi Ndigica, Anna Njira w/o Munyi, Ngira s/o Katere, and Mwageri Njuguara, Mbeere.

62. See Map 9. KNA: Central Province, Embu District Political Record Book, PC/CP.1/5/1. Interviews: Gachone Rukeni, Gatema Muyovi, and Ngonju Ngunyika, Mbeere. The localism of Mbeere society is reflected in the absence of information regarding Munyiri in testimonies collected outside his section.

63. Ndegerie wa Ngenu in Kenya Land Commission, *Evidence*, 1:251.

2

Community and Identity

The narrowly circumscribed sphere of the small society shaped the outlook of the vast majority of people living in central Kenya during the nineteenth century. In communities throughout the region, ideals of self-reliance and self-sufficiency engendered an intense localism; men and women looked at the world beyond a few contiguous neighborhoods with suspicion and fear and often with ignorance. People organized their lives and acted to protect and promote their interests through local institutions. As prominent and successful a leader as Nzambu wa Ndove in Migwani still drew followers only from one area, and his name scarcely appears in the oral records of other sections. In contrast, most alien observers organized their impressions of the Kenyan societies within a rigidly defined framework of tribal exclusivity. Worse, the subsequent appropriations of this framework have left a historical legacy of order where little existed, an assumption of coherent tribal outlook and interest that the record does not support.[1]

DEFINING IDENTITY

That the earliest European visitors to the region were able to record tribal names and approximate boundaries with apparent ease argues

---

1. For examples of the perceptions of early European observers, see H. R. Tate, "Further Notes on the Kikuyu Tribe of British East Africa," *Journal of the Anthropological Institute* 34 (1904): 256; and G. St. J. Orde-Browne, "Mount Kenya and its People: Some Notes on the Chuka Tribe," *Journal of the African Society* 15 (1915–16): 227. The "tribalization" of Kenya's history is discussed below in chap. 7.

strongly that ethnic divisions were widely acknowledged.[2] But the fact that a century ago people recognized the existence of populations corresponding roughly to the present-day Gikuyu, Kamba, Embu, Mbeere, and Meru ethnic groups is not evidence that during the 1800s Kamba-speaking people, for example, possessed a clear notion of ethnic identity, let alone any sense of common experience or destiny. In their fervor to draw tribal boundaries, nineteenth-century commentators generally failed to comprehend that ethnic populations encompassed substantial diversity and that ethnic affiliations were not infrequently competing or contradictory.[3] Residents of Kamba-speaking communities, like men and women throughout the region, moved in a complex world of overlapping, layered, and shifting associations. The strongest and most persistent of these centered on family, lineage, and locality.

The processes of population movement and local social formation that were such prominent features of nineteenth-century central Kenya had resulted by the late 1800s in the emergence of a myriad distinctive, small societies.[4] Within the sprawling Gikuyu, Kamba, and Meru-speaking populations, people identified themselves as residents of these local societies, not as members of any monolithic tribe or ethnic group. In fact, armed conflict among communities within an ethnic population was commonplace. In the 1800s, Kamba-speaking people apparently used the word *Akamba*, which today refers to all Kamba-speakers, most often in conjunction with a place name, as in *Akamba a Migwani*, meaning effectively, "people of Migwani."[5] In an area such as Migwani, local identity expressed itself on the surface in distinctive traits: styles of dress and decoration, hairstyles, popular songs and dances, and nuance of language. In other cases, particular patterns of body scarification, styles of teeth carving, or techniques of male cir-

2. For example, see J. L. Krapf's records of his two visits to Kitui, in particular, Journal, 21 Nov. 1849; and M. Guillain, *Documents sur L'Histoire, La Geographie et le Commerce de L'Afrique Orientale*, vol. 2 (Paris, 1856), pp. 289–97.

3. C. S. Lancaster explores similar circumstances in "Ethnic Identity, History and 'Tribe' in the Middle Zambezi Valley," *American Ethnologist* 1 (1974): esp. pp. 709–10. See also Morton Fried, *The Notion of Tribe* (Menlo Park, Cal., 1975); and the often cited essays in Fredrik Barth, *Ethnic Groups and Boundaries: The Social Organization of Cultural Differences* (Boston, 1969), especially the editor's Introduction, pp. 9–38.

4. Charles H. Ambler, "Population Movement, Social Formation and Exchange: Central Kenya in the Nineteenth Century," *International Journal of African Historical Studies* 18 (1985): 201–22.

5. Interview: Muito w/o Muthama, Migwani; Mutia s/o Mboo, Migwani. D. R. Lambert, memorandum based on the testimony of three Kamba-speaking witnesses, Kenya Land Commission, *Evidence*, 2:1291; and C. R. W. Lane, memorandum, in ibid., 1:399–400.

cumcision set people apart. The existence of localized subcultures is hardly surprising, but in central Kenya differences ran much deeper than variations in accent or particular styles of dress or ornamentation.[6] A common language often masked substantial differences among small societies. Kamba-speaking people in Ulu, for example, used the term *utui* to denote their basic social institution, the neighborhood; but in Migwani and especially in Mumoni, where neighborhoods were more fluid, *utui* had a much broader and less specific application.

Despite this intense parochialism, people did feel a connection to communities beyond their home areas, particularly but not exclusively to those within the same ethnic and linguistic tradition. Such broader loyalties, however weakly defined, provided men and women with a crucial sense of where they fit into a larger, and substantially foreign, world. Individuals and lineages established their links to others within the same ethnic population through membership in widely dispersed clans, which traced their histories, genealogically, to a place and time of common genesis. Widely repeated stories of origin and migration further reinforced identification with a particular ethnic tradition. The settlers of Migwani, although remote in space and experience from many other Kamba-speakers, nevertheless continued to pass on the Kamba legends of their beginnings in the Mount Kilimanjaro area and migration to Ulu.[7]

Not every community fit neatly into a grand ethnic tradition, however. People living in settlements in Tharaka, located along both sides of the Tana River to the east of Mount Kenya, spoke a Meru-related

6. KNA: Machakos Political Record Book, vol. 1, pt. 2, DC MKS 4/3. Krapf, Journal, 3 Dec. 1849. Lindblom, *Akamba*, pp. 392–97; Orde-Browne, *Vanishing Tribes*, pp. 28, 139–40, 168–69, 173–76; Hobley, *Ethnology of Akamba*, p. 17; W. Scoresby Routledge and Katherine Routledge, *With a Prehistoric People: The Akikuyu of British East Africa* (London, 1968 [1910]), pp. 30–35; and H. S. K. Mwaniki, *The Living History of Embu and Mbeere to 1906* (Nairobi, 1973), p. 129. Evidence of the mutability of styles is found in H. R. Tate, "Notes on the Kikuyu and Kamba Tribes of British East Africa," *Journal of the Anthropological Institute* 34 (1904): 255; Perham, *Lugard Diaries*, 1:320 (12 Oct. 1890); and Dundas, "History of Kitui," p. 498. For an early and sophisticated exploration of the question of local subcultures, see S. F. Nadel, *A Black Byzantium* (London, 1942), pp. 12–23.

7. Lindblom, *Akamba*, pp. 113–25, 136–38; Muriuki, *History of Kikuyu*, pp. 113–15; Glazier, "Conflict and Conciliation," pp. 40–46; Mwaniki, "History of Embu," pp. 118–76. The Gikuyu creation myth incorporates the formation of clans. Kenyatta, *Facing Mount Kenya*, pp. 5–10. Interviews: Mavuli s/o Makola and Paul Ngutu s/o Ngutha, Migwani. Krapf heard the traditions of Kamba origins and migration in Kitui at midcentury. Journal, 3 Dec. 1849. For evidence of ethnic categorization, see Krapf, Journal, 6 Dec. 1849; Lindblom, *Akamba*, pp. 21–22; and Hobley, *Ethnology of Akamba*, p. 3.

language, but their traditions as well as their speech and material culture showed clear signs of extensive contact with their neighbors in Mbeere and Mumoni. This circumstance would prove troubling to later colonial administrators, who in their preoccupation with monolithic tribal units would find it difficult to tolerate a society that not only defied official taxonomy, but occupied land on both sides of the "natural" district boundary formed by the Tana.[8]

For people living in central Kenya communities, ethnic tags such as Gikuyu, Kamba, and Embu also served as a convenient—if highly imprecise—means of categorizing outsiders. If for the most part such broader identities had little effective meaning, the perception of ethnic categories did sometimes influence the contacts between strangers. During his visit to Kitui in 1851, the missionary J. Krapf accompanied the Kitui-based merchant, Kivui wa Mwendwa on a journey north across the Tana River toward Mount Kenya. Along the route, on the fringes of Mbeere, the party was attacked and Kivui among others was killed. Krapf managed to make his way back to Kivui's village in Kitui; and there, in an apparent act of retribution, he saw some of Kivui's associates kill a small contingent of petty traders from Mbeere who had the misfortune to be visiting Kivui's settlement at the same time. According to Krapf, the Mbeere traders had no direct connection with Kivui's attackers, yet the fact of their origin was reason enough to determine their fates.[9]

As a rule, however, people saw ethnic groupings as only one layer of the larger social and cultural system into which they were joined. Most families, lineages, and communities possessed a range of links with counterparts in other sections of the region. The clan affiliations that tied local lineages into ethnic traditions also cut across language boundaries, creating connections, for example, between particular clans in Gikuyuland and in Kamba-speaking areas. Although such links generally had little practical significance (and perhaps little basis in fact), they did provide individuals with networks of putative clan-mates in other parts of the region. Similarly, a system of sectional part-

8. Arthur Champion, "The Atharaka," *Journal of the Royal Anthropological Institute* 42 (1912): 68–90; Hobley, *Ethnology of Akamba*, p. 2; and Muriuki, *History of Kikuyu*, pp. 46–61. Also, KNA: D. R. Crampton, "Early History of Chuka and Mwimbe," Embu Political Record Book, DC EBU/45 A1. For the issue of administering Tharaka, see KNA: D.C., Meru to D.C., Kitui, 9 Oct. 1933, D.C., Embu to D.C., Kitui, 9 Oct. 1934, and D.C., Meru to P.C., Nyeri, 30 Nov. 1934, in DC/KTI/7/3.

9. J. L. Krapf, "Journey to Ukamba and a two Months Residence in that Country, Journal from 11 July to 30 Sept. 1851," entries for 3–4 Sept. 1851, Krapf Papers, Church Missionary Society Archives, London, CA5/016/176.

nerships, expressed in a kinship vocabulary but essentially rooted in economic complementarity, established connections between communities across the region.[10] Thus, when the refugees fleeing famine in Migwani arrived in Mwimbe they were able to invoke a mutually accepted claim of common ancestry to manage their contacts with people who spoke a different language and had a quite distinct history. These entrenched associations (and parallel animosities among competing societies) overlapped in complex profusion, apparently without regard for ethnic boundaries.

Within central Kenya, farmers saw themselves—collectively—as distinct from pastoralists or hunters. To the agriculturalists, the close economic, cultural, and linguistic affinities among all the Bantu-speaking communities of central Kenya were signs of shared destiny. Mumoni residents, for example, described farming people from other parts of the region in positive terms, as "people who speak with 'light' tongues." A Migwani man explained the animosity between farmers and pastoralists like this: "We and the Maasai did not understand one another's language."[11] Even so, some popular tales asserted common origins for the Bantu-speakers and neighboring Nilotic-speaking Maasai people. Such traditions clearly violated linguistic and cultural logic just as they accurately reflected a history of interchange.[12]

As agricultural settlement steadily expanded, the patterns of identity were continually recast by the evolving relations among communities within central Kenya and between people from inside the region and those from beyond. Migrating farmers created a series of new communities, each an offshoot of an established society, yet each increasingly distinctive and autonomous. In the early decades of the century, migrants had to contend especially with neighboring groups of hunters and herders; by the end of the century, intruders from the Indian Ocean coast and beyond were increasingly influential in the equations of social formation and social definition. The history of Migwani shows how Kamba-speaking settlers gradually defined a local society that differed in important if often subtle ways from similarly Kamba-

10. K. R. Dundas, "Notes on the Origin and History of the Kikuyu and Dorobo Tribes," *Man* 8 (1908): 137; Lindblom, *Akamba*, p. 18; and Lambert, "Institutions of the Kikuyu," pp. 107–08. Carole Buchanan has described how, in Uganda, traditions of clan migration provided the "cognitive maps" that facilitated the movement of people across ethnic lines. "Perceptions of Ethnic Interaction in the East African Interior: The Kitara Complex," *International Journal of African Historical Studies* 11 (1978): 415–16.

11. Interview: Manderi s/o Munzungi, Mumoni.

12. Lambert, "Institutions of the Kikuyu," p. 416; and Lindblom, *Akamba*, pp. 153–54.

speaking communities elsewhere in Kitui and in Ulu. These processes of differentiation were repeated continually across the region, but they were particularly pronounced during the last decades of the century in the frontier areas on the margins of Meru country, on the northeastern fringes of Gikuyuland, and especially in Mumoni.

THE EMERGENCE OF MUMONI SOCIETY

Whereas Migwani developed as a direct extension of societies in central Kitui, the emergence of Mumoni society involved the establishment of autonomous communities in conditions that were ecologically, culturally, and strategically different from those which existed in Migwani or central Kitui. The mere distance involved and the rough country separating Mumoni from Kitui made communications difficult. The resulting isolation of Mumoni from the main concentrations of Kamba-speaking people encouraged the development and persistence of local dialects and a distinctive material culture and speeded the rise of a separate society.[13] In the journal of his visit to Kitui in 1849, J. Krapf referred to the Kamba-speaking areas to the east and north as "occupied by the tribes Mumoni, Udeitsu, Kauma, and others."[14] Some fifty years later, an early colonial official reported the existence of "practically two sets of customs" for Kitui and Mumoni.[15]

Unlike the pioneers who settled Migwani, the Kamba-speaking settlers who moved into Mumoni encountered a substantial preexisting population of hunters, herders, and settled farmers. Few records remain of the ensuing processes of interaction. Communities in this area probably adopted an identification with Kamba traditions and culture only gradually; at the very least, a great deal of intermixture occurred, accounting in part for the distinctive qualities of Mumoni society. Traditions agree that the newcomers to Mumoni met scattered small groups of people identified as Atwa, a term that probably refers both to Oromo (Galla) pastoralists and the hunter-herders (often called Ndorobo) who still frequented the upper Tana country in the 1880s and 1890s.[16]

13. Lindblom, *Akamba*, pp. 17, 392, 436, 582; Lambert, "Land Tenure among Akamba," p. 133. Interviews: Musyoka s/o Ndeto and Muthuvi s/o Mui, Mumoni.

14. Krapf, Journal, 29 Nov. 1849.

15. KNA: Kitui District, Annual report, 1911, DC/KTI/1/1/1.

16. Interviews: Mwangangi s/o Mathenge, Musyoka s/o Ndeto, and Munyasia s/o Mutilu, Mumoni.

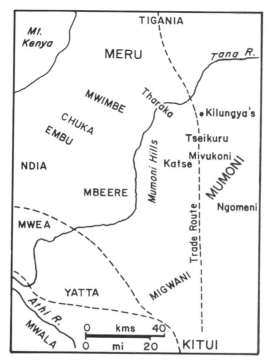

Map 6. Mumoni and Surrounding Areas

The migrants from Kitui also found in the Mumoni Hills area small settlements of Bantu-speaking farmers who were linked culturally and linguistically with Mount Kenya peoples. These communities were presumably incorporated into a new Mumoni society or retreated to Tharaka, the society that since the mid-nineteenth century, if not well before, has occupied both banks of the Tana River, just to the north of the Mumoni Hills. Toward the end of the century, as Kambaspeakers pushed increasingly northward in Mumoni, cattle-owners increasingly encroached on Tharaka grazing lands. Unsurprisingly, traditions emphasize the conflict that became increasingly more serious and frequent during this period. But there is every reason to believe that the Kamba-speaking residents of the longer established settlements near the Mumoni Hills had had regular contact—including substantial intermarriage—with their neighbors in Tharaka.[17] These contacts as

17. C. Dundas, "History of Kitui," p. 542; Muriuki, *History of Kikuyu*, p. 50. Interviews: Nason Muindi s/o Ngumbau, Munithya s/o Nganza, and Mutisya s/o Muthaaka, Mumoni; Muthura s/o Nthiga, Tharaka.

well as the incorporation of earlier Bantu-speaking settlers would account for the presence of the *r* sound—characteristic of Meru and Gikuyu speech—in Mumoni dialects. Such connections might also explain why in the early 1900s some Mumoni residents still recounted a story of origin that corresponded more closely to the Meru traditions of migration from the Indian Ocean coast than to those commonly repeated in other Kamba-speaking areas.[18]

The Mumoni environment was harsh. Most of the area lay between two thousand and three thousand feet above sea level, significantly lower, drier, and hotter than Migwani. Only the presence of scattered, prominent rock outcroppings broke the monotony of a forbidding landscape of flat brushland and stands of low scrub trees. On its eastern margins, Mumoni faded into bleak semidesert; but in the west, near the Tana River, a stark line of heavily forested hills rising above five thousand feet interrupted the open expanse. The Mumoni Hills not only formed a landmark visible from many miles in every direction, but included on the lower slopes and near the base the only reliably arable lands in Mumoni. Elsewhere, poor soils and lack of rainfall limited agricultural possibilities, although pockets of land along the few seasonal rivers supported small plots of crops such as sugar cane and bananas that ordinarily would not grow in Mumoni.[19]

The first Kamba-speaking pioneers in Mumoni established homesteads in the Mumoni Hills area, but by the mid-1800s the flow had changed course. Settlers moved into the open country on the east, apparently attracted by the availability of pastures and the opportunities for trade. Some of these migrants came from Migwani, but most traveled north from the central valley of Kitui. The settlers advanced rapidly; by the 1890s some had reached the boundary of Tharaka and the banks of the Tana.[20] The late nineteenth-century history of Mumoni

18. Hobley, *Ethnology of Akamba*, p. 2; Lindblom, *Akamba*, p. 17. Interviews: Muasya s/o Munene, Kitevu s/o Ndaku, and Kiteng'o s/o Mutui, Mumoni.

19. PRO: C. W. Hobley, Report of a Journey to Mumoni, 18 March 1908, CO 355/42. Pigott, Diary, 20 May 1889; Hobley, Safari Diary, 21–22 Nov. 1891; Maher, "Soil Erosion in Kitui," pp. 13, 49, 57, 192; Neumann, *Elephant Hunting*, p. 133; Karl Peters, *New Light on Dark Africa* (London, 1891), trans. H. W. Duicken, p. 191. Interview: Musyoka s/o Ndeto, Mumoni.

20. Linguists have identified two separate dialects spoken in Mumoni. Wilhelm Mohlig, "Bantu Languages," in *Language and Dialect Atlas of Kenya*, vol. 1: *Geographical and Historical Introduction*, ed. Bernd Heine and W. Mohlig (Berlin, 1980), pp. 24–25. The patterns of movement have been reconstructed from collected genealogies. Note especially interviews with the following Mumoni informants: Muthuvi s/o Mui, Ngumu s/o Munithya, and Muthuka s/o Nzuvi.

was dominated to a large extent by these later pioneers, in particular by a number of men whose involvement in long-distance trade enabled them to amass large herds of cattle and assemble substantial followings. The most important of these men, Kilungya wa Mutia, established a settlement on Mumoni's northeastern frontier, where he could command access to a key Tana River ford and graze his livestock over an enormous territory.[21]

In eastern Mumoni, near the major north–south trade route, other men founded similar fortified villages, known as *mbenge*, the largest of which included as many as five hundred people—substantially more than equivalent settlements in Migwani. Security considerations as well as the paucity of suitable settlement sites encouraged migrants to congregate in these villages. At the same time, the success of the village enterprise and of its leader depended on a sizeable population and a ready pool of labor.[22] The term *mbenge* derived from the word for the substantial pole fences, reinforced with brush, that enclosed the settlements. The strength of this palisade spoke of the need for protection, against pastoralist raiders, competing villages, and wild animals. Most *mbenge* villages were located at the bases of the great rock outcroppings that punctuated the Mumoni landscape. The rock face generally formed one side of the village, the heights serving as a lookout point and as a hiding place for women, children, and livestock in case of attack. The runoff from the rocks also provided water for irrigation and domestic use.[23]

The growth of fortified villages in Mumoni was an aspect of the emergence of a highly personalized social structure. The talent of individual charismatic leaders and the web of connections that each built up gave villages coherence and solidarity. Men like Kilungya wa Mutia, Muyanga wa Kathenge, Mutui wa Ndai, and the hunter Vere wa

21. Chanler, *Jungle and Desert*, pp. 56, 59; and Neumann, *Elephant Hunting*, p. 133.
22. Pigott, Diary, 20 May 1889; Hobley, Safari Diary, 21–23 Nov. 1891; Dundas, "History of Kitui," p. 492; and C. W. Hobley, *Kenya: From Chartered Company to Crown Colony* (London, 1929), p. 53. Interviews: Kiliungi s/o Muuru, Mwinzi s/o Kathinzi, Muthuvi s/o Mui, Mulatya s/o Mutia, Kele s/o Kanandu, Muthungu s/o Musango, Ngumu s/o Munithya, Nzilu s/o Siongongo, and Muli s/o Sumbi, Mumoni. Michael O'Leary describes similar processes in eastern Kitui in "Aspects of the Environment, Economy and Social Structure of the Kitui Akamba—Before the Influences of the Colonial Era Took Root," Dept. of Sociology, University of Nairobi, Staff Seminar Paper, no. 23, March 1977. Carolyn Clark mentions large, fortified settlements established on the frontiers of southern Gikuyuland. "Women and Power in Kikuyu," p. 362.
23. Pigott, Diary, 24 May 1889; Hobley, Safari Diary, 18, 21–22 Nov. 1891; Dundas, "History of Kitui," p. 492; and Lindblom, *Akamba*, p. 434. Interviews: Munithya s/o Mati, Kavindu s/o Ikunga, Kimwele s/o Kyota, and Muthungu s/o Musango, Mumoni.

Nzui attracted followers and accumulated wealth on a scale that altogether overshadowed the achievements of their contemporaries in Migwani.[24] These leaders did not rise to prominence by relying, as others in Migwani did, on a base of lineage support; lineages in Mumoni were simply too small and weak. An *mbenge* was usually identified popularly with the name of its leader's lineage, but members of that particular lineage did not necessarily dominate the settlement; some *mbenge* villages contained fragments of as many as ten lineages, although the members of two or three generally constituted the bulk of residents.[25] Those people who were not members of the main lineage were often designated as *athoni*, "in-laws," but the numerous fragments of lineages found within an *mbenge* usually were drawn together out of common interests rather than kinship bonds. Once the *mbenge* had been established, marriages within the village further solidified links among various families. The major leaders used multiple marriages as a means to strengthen and extend their bases of support and some of the wealthiest had ten or more wives.[26] The most successful leaders exercised considerable authority within their villages and gained influence that extended over surrounding, smaller hamlets. These outlying settlements often had close ties to a nearby *mbenge*, looking to the large village for leadership, contributing labor for various enterprises, and cooperating in defense.[27]

Even though household agricultural production provided basic sustenance, *mbenge* village economies were oriented fundamentally toward trade, herding, and, to a lesser degree, hunting. In fact, the concentration of people in *mbenge* villages was partly an extension of the cohesive and relatively disciplined labor organization required to engage in such activities on a substantial scale. Given the uncertainty of harvests on the dry Mumoni frontier, pioneers could have had no illu-

24. John Ainsworth, Diaries, 1895–1902, 1917, entries for March and April 1898, Rhodes House Library, Oxford, Mss. Afr. S 377-378 (on microfilm). Chanler, *Jungle and Desert*, p. 482; Lindblom, *Akamba*, pp. 149–50; and Lambert, "Land Tenure among the Kamba," p. 138. Interviews: Muli s/o Kakuru, Kaungo w/o Mutia, Muthuvi s/o Mui, and Muasya s/o Munene, Mumoni.
25. Notably from interviews with the following Mumoni informants: Kiliungi s/o Muuru, Nzilu s/o Siongongo, Mwinzi s/o Kathinzi, Muli s/o Sumbi, and Munithya s/o Mati.
26. Lindblom, *Akamba*, pp. 80–82, 87. Interviews: Munithya s/o Mati and Kimwele s/o Kyota, both Mumoni. Evidence collected in Kitui District during the period between the World Wars, while not necessarily accurate nor applicable to the late 1800s, showed that of some thirty thousand male taxpayers about two hundred had five or more wives, while only six men had eight or more. Maher, "Soil Erosion in Kitui," appendix 5.
27. Pigott, Diary, 15 May 1889. Interviews: Kavindu s/o Ikunga and Muthungu s/o Musango, Mumoni.

sions of self-sufficiency. Rather, they saw in Mumoni's ample grazing lands and strategic position the opportunity to make sufficient profit in commerce and livestock-rearing to more than compensate for inadequate harvests. Indeed, Mumoni communities regularly turned to outside sources to supplement their own production.[28] Although *mbenge* leaders dominated local involvement in major trade and fielded the most formidable military forces in the area, the *mbenge* villages were far from stable. Each village was dependent for unity on the personality of a leader and the cooperation of disparate collections of men who held their personal careers and the interests of their families paramount.

The villages constantly underwent changes, as families left and others were drawn in. Fluctuations in trade, the decline of water supplies, the deterioration of pasturelands, or intense personality conflicts sometimes led to a breakup of a village. Most of the *mbenge* villages disintegrated in the wake of a leader's death, since the solidarity of the village was largely based on the personal relationships he had built in his lifetime. With no clearly established succession and with polygynous marriage dividing descendants, the possibility of sustaining that unity in the leader's absence was small. Moreover, once young men had acquired sufficient property and connections, they were often anxious to break away and join with others like themselves to establish new villages and build their own careers.[29]

Councils of elders theoretically regulated contact among the various settlements, but they functioned only in exceptional circumstances. Instead, patronage ruled relationships between *mbenge* villages and nearby hamlets, and contacts among the various larger villages and their leaders were conducted like those among autonomous polities. Indeed, these contacts were often acrimonious and sometimes violent.[30] The community dance and the community dance ground provided the main opportunity for regular interaction among the villages. The bonds among members of local dance groups created solidarity

28. Hobley, Safari Diary, 23 Nov. 1891. Interviews: Munithya s/o Mati, Kavindu s/o Ikunga, Kimwele s/o Kyota, Muthungu s/o Musango, and Kele s/o Kanandu, Mumoni. Mumoni's involvement in trade is discussed further in chaps. 3, 5.

29. Dundas, "History of Kitui," pp. 487–88, 506. Interview: Muasya s/o Munene, Mumoni. For a description of the qualities of individual leadership in midcentury Kitui, see Krapf, Journal, 3 Dec. 1849.

30. Dundas, "History of Kitui," pp. 484–85, 493; and Lambert, "Land Tenure among the Akamba," p. 135. Interviews: Mwangangi s/o Mathenge, Kimwele s/o Kyota, and Muthuvi s/o Mui, Mumoni.

within the *mbenge*, and the dances themselves provided the rare chance for establishing connections among widely separated villages.[31]

Despite the dominant role played by the *mbenge* villages in commerce, during the late 1800s the majority of people probably lived in the communities that dotted the countryside nearer the Mumoni Hills. The settlements in this area effectively constituted a distinct society. In contrast to the rapid movement of Kamba-speakers into the eastern section of Mumoni, localities in the west had developed through a long process of interaction and intermixture with neighboring peoples. Again, unlike the dynamic and fluid *mbenge* villages, neighborhoods near the Mumoni Hills were relatively entrenched and stable. Many residential lineages traced their settlement of the area back several generations. Moreover, the trend toward individual accumulation of wealth that so marked *mbenge* society was much less evident in the communities near the hills. Although agriculture was more reliable in this area, settlements there were not well situated for involvement in long-distance commerce, and local conditions generally precluded extensive cattle herding. This absence of cattle restricted accumulation, and at the same time reduced the likelihood of raids. Given their relative security, people in this area did not congregate in larger villages or associate their fortunes with powerful and wealthy men.[32] Ties of trade and kinship between the two sections were relatively rare; what contact did occur was frequently not amicable.[33]

During the last decades of the century the rise of Mumoni as a commercial center helped create some sense of common destiny among these disparate communities.[34] By the 1880s and 1890s the commercial opportunities offered by association with *mbenge* villages had begun to draw in ambitious men from the western sections of Mumoni. By the 1890s, settlements in the middle area were turning increasingly to the larger villages for leadership. Still, this small measure of integration was never expressed in concrete political or economic terms. No

31. Lindblom, *Akamba*, p. 148; Dundas, "History of Kitui," p. 508; and Lambert, "Land Tenure among the Akamba," p. 138. Interviews: Mwangangi s/o Mathenge, Kimwele s/o Kyota, and Ngungu s/o Mwaniki, Mumoni.

32. PRO: C. W. Hobley, Report of a Journey to Mumoni, 18 March 1908, CO 533/42. Maher, "Soil Erosion in Kitui," Part 3. Interviews: Muvali s/o Kilanga, Kavindu s/o Ikunga, Ngumu s/o Munithya, Kauwima s/o Mutia, Munithya s/o Nganza, and Musyoka s/o Ndeto, Mumoni.

33. Interviews: Kisalu s/o Kilatya, Kitevu s/o Ndaku, Kiteng'o s/o Mutui, Kisilu s/o Katumo, Muvali s/o Kilanga, Kauwima s/o Mutia, and Munithya s/o Nganza, Mumoni.

34. Chanler, *Jungle and Desert*, p. 486; and C. W. Hobley, "Nairobi to Fort Hall: A Survey of Ukamba Province," in *East Africa: Its History, People, Commerce and Resources*, comp. S. Playne (London, 1908–09), p. 262.

joint enterprise ever mobilized people across the entire society; in fact, instances of even temporary alliances including more than several villages were exceedingly rare.[35]

The processes of fragmentation and cultural differentiation that characterized the evolution of Mumoni society were hardly particular to that area. The same themes recur in the histories of many of the newly forming societies of the central Kenya frontier during this period, notably in eastern Kitui, in parts of northern Meru, and especially on the northeastern fringes of Gikuyuland. There, in eastern Nyeri, between the Nyandarua foothills of Gikuyuland and Mount Kenya, a number of aggressive Gikuyu-speaking leaders drew farmers, herders, and hunters into dynamic commercial and raiding-oriented communities.[36] The pace of social change may have been less rapid and dramatic in densely populated sections, but gradual cultural differentiation was nevertheless evident in a number of areas. During the nineteenth century, for example, the isolated Kilungu section of southern Ulu became increasingly separated from its neighbors despite their common language.[37] These developments were not, however, intermediate stages in a neat process of segmentation in which outpost communities gradually separated from parent societies and asserted their own exclusive identities. The boundaries were never so clear-cut. Rather, layers of identity accumulated and intermingled as the balance among loyalties continually shifted. Whereas intense localism marked the experiences of Mumoni, Nyeri, and Kilungu, in other societies broader bonds increasingly superceded local identities. Nowhere in the region was this tendency more evident than on Mount Kenya, in Embu.

SOCIAL COHESION AND ISOLATIONISM IN EMBU

The unity and stability of late nineteenth-century Embu society contrasted sharply with the dynamic and unsettled conditions that existed in much of central Kenya. To the people of Embu their fertile highland

35. PRO: John Ainsworth to J. Pigott, 20 Feb. 1895, in IBEAC to F.O., 10 April 1895, FO 2/97. Interviews: Kalundu s/o Ndai, Mwangangi s/o Mathenge, Muli s/o Kakuru, and Kaungo s/o Mutia, Mumoni.

36. Peter Rogers, "The British and the Kikuyu, 1890–1905: A Reassessment," *Journal of African History* 20 (1979): 267; Ambler, "Population Movement," pp. 213–14; and Muriuki, *History of Kikuyu*, pp. 87–88.

37. J. W. Gregory, *The Great Rift Valley* (London, 1968 [1896]), p. 84; and Ludwig von Höhnel, *Discovery of Lakes Rudolf and Stefanie: A Narrative of Count Samuel Teleki's Exploring and Hunting Expedition in Eastern Equatorial Africa in 1887 and 1888*, trans. Nancy Bell (London 1968 [1894]), 2:312.

country was a land of plenty. Embu traditions are remarkably silent on the subject of famine; in contrast, vivid descriptions of hunger fill the oral records of Mumoni, Migwani, and Mbeere. As this oral evidence suggests, Embu communities most often felt the impact of famine indirectly, in the pressures created by refugees from hardship elsewhere. Oral accounts of nineteenth-century migration repeatedly equate the land of Embu with agricultural wealth and security.[38]

By the late 1800s several tens of thousands of people lived in Embu country.[39] The relative high density and even spacing of this population eased communications and encouraged the growth of a web of interrelationships among ridge communities. It would have been extremely difficult to delineate discrete sections of the larger society, since one area tended to flow into another. In fact, a wider sense of identity largely superceded the incipient loyalties to smaller communities that marked the emergence of small societies in Kitui, Ulu, or Gikuyuland. In contrast to other areas of the region, Embu society nurtured an ethos that emphasized commitment to common purpose and proscribed violence as a means of settling internal disputes.[40] An elder put it simply: "Embu was one thing."[41]

Occasional migrants were rapidly integrated in lineages and communities. Women and especially girls were most easily and thoroughly incorporated, since they became the daughters or wives—and therefore the permanent dependents—of established men in their new societies.[42] Male migrants experienced more difficulty and sometimes even hostility. In particular, those men who had already been initiated and circumcised before they arrived were by definition "different"—a

38. Saberwal, *Political System of Embu*, p. 96; and Mwaniki, "History of Embu," p. 160. Interviews: Muruaringo s/o Muyakagio, Muruachuri Nyaga, Lukah Nyaga s/o Kamuigu, and Kabogo s/o Gacigua, all Embu. Roy G. Willis makes a similar argument in *A State in the Making: Myth, History, and Social Transformation in Precolonial Ufipa* (Bloomington, Ind., 1981).

39. By the mid-1960s Embu had a population of more than 101,000. *Kenya Census*, p. 23. The first serious census was conducted in 1930 and revealed a population of about 38,000, very likely an undercount. KNA: Embu District, Annual Report, 1930, DC/EBU/1/2.

40. PRO: J. Hayes Sadler to C.O., 22 Aug. 1906, CO533/16. Arkell-Hardwick, *Ivory Trader*, p. 70; and Saberwal, *Political System of Embu*, p. 16. Interviews: Muruaringo s/o Muyakagio and Alan Kageta, Embu.

41. Interview: Njorano Ndarwa, Embu.

42. KNA: J. G. Hopkins, "Embu Land Tenure System," [1928], Embu District, Political Record Book, Part II, DC.EBU/3/2; Orde-Browne, *Vanishing Tribes*, p. 118; and Hobley, Safari Diaries, 4 Oct. 1891. Interviews: Mbutei s/o Mwangai, Tirisa Kanyi w/o Mbarire, and Njorano Ndarwa, Embu. Oral records reveal no evidence of land shortages in Embu. Also, Rudia Mairu w/o Mbiti, Mbeere; and Mwalimu Charley, Kitui Town. The last of these informants was a refugee in Embu from Kitui as a young man.

quality rarely valued in relatively homogenous societies like Embu. Moreover, male migrants would likely make claims on the wealth of the lineage, while theoretical rights to land in their areas of origin gave them an unwelcome measure of independence from lineage control.[43] Still, the process of the incorporation was relatively simple. One young boy from Mumoni who found shelter in an Embu household during the famine of the late 1890s was later adopted and promised land and bridewealth by his surrogate father. Without apparent difficulty, he "became Embu." In 1900, when hordes of raiders from Mumoni and Migwani attacked Mbeere and Embu communities, neither this boy nor his neighbors questioned his loyalty to his new family and community.[44]

Despite its small size and considerable unity, Embu society was not entirely homogenous. Localized dialectal and cultural idiosyncrasies continued in a number of areas, in some cases probably the result of immigrant influence.[45] The most striking discontinuity in Embu culture involved the persistence of two types of male circumcision. Most of Embu practiced the simple custom of cutting away the entire foreskin; a few communities in the western section of Embu followed a procedure—common in Meru-speaking areas to the east—that involved retaining a portion of the foreskin.[46] It speaks to the diversity and intense localism of central Kenya society that even in Embu, where the prevailing ideology emphasized harmony and homogeneity, differences could endure in a custom as central as circumcision. In contrast, the few immigrants from Meru who settled in Migwani apparently had to be recircumcised before they could be accepted.[47]

Broad-based political and social institutions bound Embu localities into the larger society. Sectional councils of representative elders from numerous ridges periodically met, deliberated, and determined actions and policies, while a more informal system of consultations among sectional councils provided a still wider unity. The ceremonies that sym-

43. Interview: Muvali s/o Kilanga, Mumoni. See Elizabeth Colson, "The Assimilation of Aliens among the Zambian Tonga," in *From Tribe to Nation in Africa: Studies in Incorporation Processes,* ed. Ronald Cohen and John Middleton (Scranton, Penn., 1970), pp. 35–54.

44. Interview: Muvali s/o Kilanga, Mumoni. In addition, see Mwaniki , *Embu Texts,* p. 167. Interviews: Nzunya w/o Mbondo, Mumoni; Mwalimu Charley, Kitui Town; Kilungi s/o Kithita and Nguli s/o Kinuva, Migwani; Muruaringo s/o Muyakagio, Tirisa Kanyi w/o Mbarire, and Girishom Mukono, Embu.

45. Saberwal, *Political System of Embu,* p. 23*n*.

46. Ibid. Interview: Kabogo s/o Gacigua and Muruachuri Nyaga, Embu. H. S. K. Mwaniki has confirmed this point in personal communication.

47. Interview: Mutia s/o Mboo, Migwani.

bolically accomplished the handing over of authority from one generation to another in each of the two generational cycles drew men from
all parts of Embu country, providing the opportunity for the celebration and dissemination of basic traditions and values. Elders may also
have used the occasion to set down or adjust community law, for example that having to do with marriage and bridewealth.[48] Certainly,
the capacity of Embu communities for collective action is well documented. Military operations frequently involved participants from a
wide area; for instance, raids to the east against Chuka communities
often drew contingents of warriors from many if not all sections of
Embu country. According to an account from 1900,

> The Wa'm'bu [Embu people], being a numerous and *united* people, are,
> therefore, very dangerous to tackle in their mountain fastnesses. The weak
> spot in most of the other tribes of that region is the fact that they are ruled
> by numerous petty chiefs, and have no cohesion and consequently no real
> strength.[49]

As this report suggests, invaders could expect a large-scale, unified,
and tenacious resistance from Embu warriors. In 1906, Embu became
the single central Kenya society to mount a collective armed opposition to the assertion of colonial authority.[50]

The Embu confrontation with the British came as the culmination
of several decades of accumulating antagonism toward outsiders and
outside contact. At midcentury, a number of Embu men had been actively involved in long-distance trade; by the late 1800s Embu communities had only the most peripheral involvement in the increasingly dynamic and expansive commerce that linked central Kenya to world
markets. At the same time that most of the societies of central Kenya
were moving toward greater external contact, Embu increasingly isolated itself. During the last decades of the century, Kuthathura, from
the western section of Embu, gained prominence first as a hunter and
later as a middleman and host to the merchants who occasionally vis-

48. Saberwal, *Political System of Embu*, pp. 61–68; and Lambert, "Institutions of the
Kikuyu," pp. 191-92. Interviews: Waweru Kamwea and Kanjama s/o Njanguthi, Embu. Several conversations with H. S. K. Mwaniki helped to clarify the intricacies of the generation
system.

49. Arkell-Hardwick, *Ivory Trader*, p. 72. Emphasis in original.

50. PRO: Sub-Commissioner Hinde to Eliot, 5 April 1905 in Eliot to F.O., 4 May
1904, FO 2/836; and Hayes-Sadler to C.O., 31 Aug. 1906, CO 533/16. Arkell-Hardwick,
Ivory Trader, pp. 57, 63; Meinertzhagen, *Kenya Diary*, pp. 146–51; Saberwal, *Political System of Embu*, pp. 34–36, 40; and Mwaniki, "History of Embu," pp. 255, 266, 282–87. Interviews: Kabogo s/o Gacigua, Muruachuri Nyaga, Kamwochere s/o Nthiga, and Arthur
Mairani, Embu.

ited Embu to purchase ivory.[51] He was very much the exception, however; a few other Embu men exchanged local products such as animal skins, tobacco, and occasional ivory for goods from the outside in this period, but generally the world beyond Embu had little to offer in return. Embu people apparently found unappealing the imported cloth and other items that were increasingly popular in other parts of the region.[52]

Embu's declining involvement in long-distance trading occurred in part because of a decline in elephant herds—and hence in supplies of ivory—in the area. Yet it is also clear that the Embu leadership deliberately discouraged outside contacts. Whereas trade expeditions entering Migwani, Mumoni, or Mbeere could always find local hosts and agents, in Embu such cooperation was by no means assured. By enforcing customary taxes on the movement and sale of ivory, elders made it difficult for alien merchants or their local agents to operate in Embu.[53] These policies reflected a broader ambivalence about external contact. Embu oral traditions and testimonies certainly have a martial orientation largely absent from similar records in Mumoni, Kitui, and Mbeere. Unlike most central Kenya societies, Embu communities displayed considerable hostility toward strangers, attitudes that were reinforced by initiation rituals that promoted assaults on outsiders. When parties led by coast men or Europeans tried to enter or traverse Embu country, they were generally met with undisguised hostility; and even petty traders and famine refugees who ventured near Embu were regularly raided.[54] A final testament to Embu's exclusivity is the fact that most of the destitute families who left Mumoni and Migwani dur-

51. Krapf, Journal, 6 Aug. 1851; Orde-Browne, *Vanishing Tribes*, p. 38; Mwaniki, "History of Embu," pp. 333, 344–46; S. Saberwal, "Social Control and Cultural Flexibility among the Embu of Kenya (ca. 1900)" (Ph.D. diss., Cornell Univ., 1966), p. 26. Interviews: Mbutei s/o Mwangai, Girishom Mukono, Kabogo s/o Gacigua, and Kamwochere s/o Nthiga, Embu; Mulango s/o Ngusia, Migwani. The first colonial chief in eastern Embu was Kuthathura's son. KNA: Central Province, Embu District Political Record Book, PC.CP 1/5/1.

52. Krapf, Journal, 6 Aug. 1851; Boyes, *King of Kikuyu*, p. 157; Orde-Browne, *Vanishing Tribes*, p. 38; Mwaniki, "History of Embu," pp. 317–45; and Mwaniki, *Embu Texts*, pp. 304–05. Interviews: Murwanthama s/o Gicandu, Jason Njigoru, Kabogo s/o Gacigua, and Alan Kageta, Embu; Muvali s/o Kilanga, Mumoni.

53. Mwaniki, "History of Embu," pp. 347–50. Interviews: Murwanthama s/o Gicandu, Tirisa Kanyi w/o Mbarire, Kabogo s/o Gacigua, and Muruachuri Nyaga, Embu.

54. PRO: Lord Elgin, 9 April 1906, CO 533/16. H. S. K. Mwaniki, "The Chuka: Struggle for Survival in the Traditional Days to 1908," *Mila* 3 (1972): 13–21; Mwaniki, *Embu Texts*, pp. 27–28, 69. Interviews: Paulo Njega and Alan Kageta, Embu; Ruguca Nthimbu, Mbeere. For attitudes of surrounding communities toward Embu, see Arkell-Hardwick, *Ivory Trader*, pp. 62–73.

ing the great famine of 1898–1901 chose destinations elsewhere on Mount Kenya, although Embu was not more distant and certainly possessed ample food to offer those stricken by famine.

For the leaders of Embu society, isolationism seems to have represented a means of resisting the processes of differentiation and disunity that they associated with external commerce and which they believed would inexorably undermine their own positions. Foreigners who traveled through Embu and through other areas of central Kenya often flaunted local authority in the areas they visited, indirectly challenging the legitimacy of the communal councils charged with the task of maintaining order.[55] Potentially even more dangerous were the activities of the local brokers of international trade. Embu elders were undoubtedly aware that leading brokers in other sections of the region had accumulated considerable personal wealth and power. Just to the west of Embu in Ndia, Gutu wa Kibetu had used his position in trade to amass sufficient wealth and warrior power to make himself the local strongman.[56] By containing external contact, Embu leaders apparently hoped to block similar developments at home. In that sense, isolationist policies were meant to protect and enhance not only the authority of the elders, but also the relative economic and social equality on which that domination was based.[57]

However insular, the societies of central Kenya were not fundamentally xenophobic. Feelings toward outsiders and outside contact encompassed a range of attitudes from outright hostility to enthusiasm, varying in space and time, from locality to locality or even neighborhood to neighborhood, and from season to season. More dynamic societies such as Mumoni tended to be more receptive to strangers, whereas the more stable and tight-knit communities on Mount Kenya sometimes inclined toward animosity. But no society—not even Embu—had a uniform attitude toward outsiders. The character of external relations reflected the evolving patterns of internal discontinuities and tensions: among various localities, between rich and poor, between

55. Arkell-Hardwick, *Ivory Trader*, p. 65; and Meinertzhagen, *Kenya Diary*, pp. 120–21. Interviews: Kabogo s/o Gacigua and Muruachuri Nyaga, Embu.

56. KNA: District Commissioner [ca. 1911], Central Province, Embu District Political Record Book, PC.CP 1/5/1. Interviews: Mbutei s/o Mwangi, Paulo Njega, and Kanjama s/o Njanguthi, Embu.

57. Interview: Kanjama s/o Njanguthi, Embu. See also John Lonsdale, "How the People of Kenya Spoke for Themselves, 1895–1923," African Studies Association, Annual Meeting, Boston, Nov. 1976.

men and women, and notably between the elders and the warrior class. The particular origins of outsiders also entered the equation of contact. Residents of central Kenya communities distinguished degrees of foreignness, viewing people who came from within the region in a different category from more exotic visitors from the Indian Ocean coast or from Europe.[58]

Even within the sphere of closely related cultures, people encountered unfamiliar customs, behavior, and styles of dress and decoration which they regarded as perplexing or even objectionable. People who spoke closely related languages or even dialects of the same language were nevertheless regarded as strangers—as people who lived beyond the area within which circumstances could be anticipated, influenced, and comprehended.[59] Travelers could rarely enter a community without having their intentions scrutinized and their presence widely reported. Some people carefully denied outsiders access to milk products, fearing that even indirect contact with strangers could endanger the family herds and perhaps even threaten the human relationships that herds symbolized. Men and women who ventured beyond their home places saw themselves moving into a social and political vacuum, a world of physical and psychological uncertainty and insecurity. Thus, those who went outside their home areas generally protected themselves with medicines and charms and ritually purified the routes before venturing over them.[60] Nevertheless, central Kenya communities were not entirely isolated, nor were they self-sufficient. Through a series of critical exchange relationships each of the region's small, autonomous communities was bound in a complex web of economic interdependency.

58. Note especially, Arkell-Hardwick, *Ivory Trader*, pp. 70–71; Chanler, *Jungle and Desert*, pp. 160, 246; and Muriuki, *History of Kikuyu*, pp. 138–41.

59. Dundas, "Laws of Bantu Tribes," p. 45. Interviews: Kasina s/o Ndoo, Migwani; Runji s/o Jigoya, Mbeere. The classic statement is Georg Simmel, "The Stranger," in *The Sociology of Georg Simmel*, ed. and trans. Kurt Wolff (New York, 1950), pp. 402–08. See also Donald N. Levine, "Simmel at a Distance: On the History and Systematics of the Sociology of the Stranger," in *Strangers in African Societies*, ed. William A. Shack and Elliot Skinner (Berkeley and Los Angeles, 1979), pp. 21–36.

60. J. M. Hildebrandt, "Travels in East Africa," *Proceedings of the Royal Geographical Society* 22 (1877–78): 452; and Krapf, Journal, 19–20 Nov. 1849. Interviews: Kimwele s/o Kyota and Mwangangi s/o Mathenge, Mumoni; Paul Ngutu s/o Ngutha, Nguli s/o Kinuva, and Kilungi s/o Kithita, Migwani; and Tirisa Kanyi w/o Mbarire, Embu. Philip Curtin relates the development of stranger trade diasporas to the absence of overarching political structures in *Cross Cultural Trade in World History* (Cambridge, 1984).

3

The Regional Economy

As farmers expanded across central Kenya, the residents of each community shaped and reshaped economic strategies that they hoped would provide immediate and long-term material security and perhaps the opportunity to attain wealth. The result, by the nineteenth century, was an intricate regional mosaic of distinctive local ecologies and economies. In each locality the household was the basic economic unit, and production depended primarily—although certainly not exclusively—on family labor. To meet basic needs, people looked largely to their own plots and herds; however, no family was entirely self-sufficient. Even within a small community, subtle gradations in elevation, topography, vegetation, and soils meant that certain areas would be better suited than others to the production of particular crops or to raising livestock. Variations in the timing of harvests for different crops, fluctuations in the size of harvests from farm to farm, and the presence of more and less successful farmers created further discontinuities in production.[1] The existence of such inequities meant that in any season a large proportion of households regularly bought and sold ordinary foodstuffs and other consumer goods. In a broader context, similar patterns of economic complementarity encouraged the development of trade beyond individual localities, ultimately drawing small communities into a larger system of exchange.

1. Stanner, "The Kitui Kamba," p. B-14; and Maher, "Soil Erosion in Embu," p. 71. Interviews: Musyoka s/o Ndeto and Ngumu s/o Munithya, Mumoni; and Mavuli s/o Makola, Migwani.

THE REGIONAL ENVIRONMENT

Rainfall, coming in two annual seasons, was the central element in the complex of factors which determined the boundaries of cultivation in the region and the possibilities for agricultural activity in each of three broad ecological zones. Because the areas located at higher elevations —above forty-five hundred feet—generally received greater and more reliable rainfall, the most secure and productive farming communities in central Kenya were found in the highland zone of Gikuyuland, Mount Kenya, and the Nyambeni Range in Meru. Through most of this country, as in Embu, rich soils and a favorable climate permitted farmers to raise a wide range of crops, including various grains, pulses, root crops, and bananas, and to produce beyond their immediate needs.[2]

The extensive zone of hills on the fringes of Gikuyuland and Meru and in Mbeere, Ulu, and Kitui received less rainfall than the highlands, but the amount was generally adequate to support reasonably intensive cultivation, at least at the higher elevations. Farmers in the hills of central Ulu, for example, regularly produced surplus, as did farmers in central Kitui and Migwani.[3] As a rule, however, the climate in this zone was harsher and the soils poorer than in the highlands, and thus harvests were less plentiful and less secure. This contrast was even more evident in the lowest sections of the hill zone, where rainfall was unreliable and high temperatures compounded the problems of insufficient precipitation. Outside the highlands, soils often absorbed water inefficiently; and despite careful application of traditional techniques of soil and water conservation, much rain was lost as runoff.[4] These

2. Philip W. Porter, *Food and Development in the Semi-Arid Zone of East Africa* (Syracuse, 1979), pp. 7, 22–23; C. G. Trapnell and J. F. Griffiths, "The Rainfall-Altitude Relation and its Ecological Significance in Kenya," *The East African Agricultural Journal* 25 (April 1960): 207–12; Frank E. Bernard, *East of Mount Kenya: Meru Agriculture in Transition* (Munich, 1972), pp. 20–21, 146; Orde-Browne, *Vanishing Tribes*, pp. 97–102; Routledge, *The Agikuyu*, pp. 41–43; Tate, "Kikuyu and Kamba Tribes," p. 132. Areas of poor soils also existed in the highlands. Bernard, *Meru Agriculture*, p. 25.

3. Krapf, Journal, 29 Aug. 1851; Hobley, "Survey of Ukamba," p. 260; Porter, *Food and Development*, p. 7.

4. M. Dagg, "Water Requirements of Crops," in *East Africa: Its Peoples and Resources*, ed. W. T. W. Morgan (London, 1969), p. 120; and Porter, *Food and Development*, pp. 18–20; R. F. van de Weg and P. Mbuvi, eds., *Soils of the Kindaruma Area* (Nairobi, Kenya Soil Survey, 1975), pp. 21, 30, 61–67; and W. MacLellan Wilson, "Mombasa to Nairobi," in *East Africa (British): Its History, People, Commerce, Industries and Resources*, comp. Somerset Playne (London, 1908–09), pp. 134–47. For descriptions of traditional soil

circumstances allowed extensive cultivation of only a limited number
of crops in many areas—a few varieties of pulses and grains. Farmers always tried to produce some surplus for trade and as insurance
against later drought, but the vagaries of climate and pest infestation
made planning difficult.[5]

Beyond the hills, farms in the dry plains of Mumoni and eastern
and southern Kitui could support an even smaller range of crops. The
outside boundary of cultivation ran through this zone, through the
areas below three thousand feet in elevation that received on average
less than twenty-five inches of rain in a year.[6] It was not only rainfall,
however, that determined the extent of agricultural settlement. Farmers continued to avoid the Mwea grasslands, south of Mount Kenya,
despite the fact that Mwea received as much rain as neighboring sections of Mbeere and considerably more than Mumoni. Mwea was un-
attractive to settlers because it lacked good soils and good permanent
sources of water and because it was particularly vulnerable to attacks
from mobile pastoralist raiders.[7]

Farmers outside of the highlands faced a continual battle with
drought. Figures for central Kitui show that, despite a substantial annual average, rainfall was insufficient during one of the two seasons in
at least seventeen of the forty years surveyed.[8] In the lower country of
southeastern Kitui the situation was even worse. There, during a period of fifty-three years, rains failed in one of the two yearly seasons
twenty-eight times and in the other, thirty-seven times. On eighteen
occasions the rains failed in consecutive seasons, inevitably creating
severe stress since stores of surplus could not last more than a few
months.[9] In fact, across the drier sections of the region periods of two

conservation practices, see Hobley, *Ethnology of Akamba*, p. 20; Porter, *Food and Development*, pp. 34–40; and Moris, "Mwea," p. 24.
    5. Charles Lane, "Report on Kitui," 30 June 1898 in "Report by Sir Arthur Hardinge
on the British East Africa Protectorate for the Year 1897–1898," Appendix A, p. 29, Great
Britain, Parliamentary Papers, London, 1899, C 9125; Hobley, "Survey of Ukamba," p. 262;
and Porter, *Food and Development*, pp. 22–28.
    6. Bernard, *Meru Agriculture*, pp. 20–21; and Mutiso, "Kitui Ecosystem," p. 22.
    7. PRO: Capt. B. Dickson, "Report on the Country between Nairobi, Mbirri and
Kitui," 12 Nov. 1901 in Eliot to F.O., 8 Dec. 1901, FO 2/451. Krapf, Journal, entries for
Aug. 1851; and Moris, "Mwea," pp. 17–22.
    8. Michael F. O'Leary, *The Kitui Akamba: Economic and Social Change in Semi-
Arid Kenya* (Nairobi, 1984), pp. 127–28. Rainfall in central Kenya is notoriously erratic. See
J. F. Griffiths, "Climate," in *East Africa: Its Peoples and Resources*, ed. W. T. W. Morgan
(London, 1969), p. 109.
    9. Philip Porter, "Climate and Agriculture in East Africa," in *Contemporary Africa:
Geography and Change*, ed. C. Gregory Knight and James L. Newman (Englewood Cliffs,
N.J., 1976), p. 120.

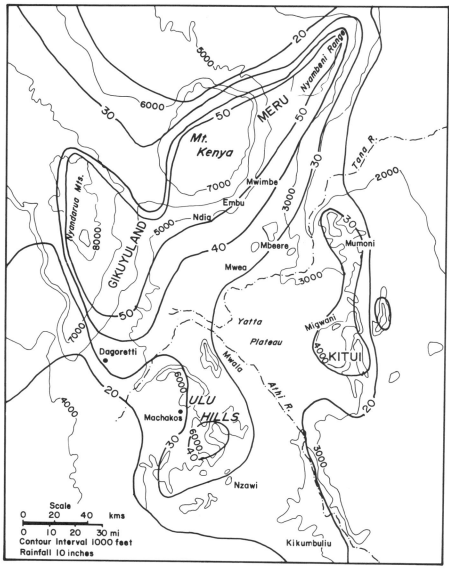

Map 7. Central Kenya: Relief and Rainfall

to three years rarely passed without a serious shortage of rainfall. Still, drought was often highly localized. The amount of rain could be dangerously low in one community in the Kitui Hills, while it was adequate in another only fifteen miles distant. Even where rainfall was uniformly low, variations of two or three inches between neighborhoods or communities could in a single season represent a critical difference in the amount and types of crops harvested. Thus, most years did not reveal sharp dichotomies between crop failure and abundance, but complicated patterns of production inequities within localities, sections of the region, and across the region as a whole.[10]

Despite the risks involved, during the late nineteenth century a growing number of families settled the parts of the region where rainfall levels ran perilously close to the minimum requirements for basic grain crops, eight to ten inches in a season.[11] In these areas farmers had to depend often on food obtained from the outside. Yet communities in these dry sections were certainly not impoverished. Unlike the highlands, plains country such as Mumoni usually offered excellent pasturelands and hence the chance to accumulate wealth.[12] The large-scale cattle owners were concentrated in dry, open country in Ulu, Kitui, Mumoni, and eastern Gikuyuland.[13] Elsewhere, farmers were more likely to own sheep and goats than cattle. Even in the plains, the presence of tsetse flies—and hence of trypanosomiasis—restricted the expansion of cattle-keeping into some areas, notably along the Tana River and in southern Kitui and Ulu.[14]

10. KNA: Kitui District, Political Record Book, 1868–1946 [entry written ca. 1919], DC.KTI 7/1. Krapf, Journal, 26 July 1851; Lane, "Report on Kitui," p. 28; Porter, *Food and Development*, p. 4; and P. Mbithi and P. Wisner, "Drought and Famines in Kenya," *Journal of East Africa Research and Development* 3 (1973): 115. Interview: Mutia s/o Mboo, Migwani.

11. Porter, *Food and Development*, p. 7.

12. B. E. Conn, "Ecology in Historical Perspective: An East African Example," Historical Association of Kenya, Annual Conference, 1972, p. 15. Interviews: Munithya s/o Nganza and Musyoka s/o Ndeto, Mumoni. Jack Glazier, personal communication. Helge Kjekshus draws attention to the complexities of the ecology of pastoralism in *Ecology Control and Economic Development in East African History: The Case of Tanganyika, 1850–1950* (Berkeley and Los Angeles, 1977), pp. 52–56.

13. Lionel Decle, *Three Years in Savage Africa* (London, 1900), p. 492; Hobley, Safari Diaries, 23 Nov. 1891 and 4 Oct. 1891; Boyes, *King of the Kikuyu*; Perham, *Lugard Diaries*, 3:387 (12 Aug. 1892); Dundas, "History of Kitui," p. 545; Maher, "Soil Erosion in Kitui," p. 76; and Maher, "Soil Erosion in Embu," p. 71. Interviews: Muvali s/o Kilanga and Ngumu s/o Munithya, both Mumoni; Muruakori s/o Gacewa and Johana Kavuru s/o Muruanjuya, Embu; and Mbiringi Kathande, Mbeere.

14. For a basic outline of tsetse fly distribution, see the map in Francis F. Ojany and Reuben B. Ogendo, *Kenya: A Study in Physical and Human Geography* (Nairobi, 1973), p.

SETTLEMENT AND ECOLOGICAL CHANGE

Although the contrasts among the ecological zones provided the essential basis for economic interchange, the regional patterns of production were by no means ecologically determined.[15] As established communities matured and new ones were founded, people consciously and unconsciously altered the natural world that they inhabited. Like small-scale farmers everywhere, the people of central Kenya were closely tuned to the nuances of local geology, vegetation, and climate; but there is no evidence that communities consciously sought any balance between human demands and natural resources. The environment was seen as open rather than enclosed; land was in unlimited supply.[16]

The expansion of cultivation occurred slowly and with great expense of labor, particularly in the highlands. Settlers clearing the forest had to make do with only the small, iron-bladed axe and a wide, double-edged, swordlike tool; it took two men using such implements a full day to fell a single large tree. Removing the trees and brush that covered the lower and drier country was less taxing, but turning the soil in preparation for planting was always arduous work. Moreover, it was accomplished without the aid of plows or metal hoes.[17] However slow and difficult, the extension of agricultural settlement brought dramatic changes in local environments. By cutting down trees, killing off game, clearing away ground cover, and turning over the soil, farmers changed the face of the land. These same farmers brought with them numerous herds of livestock which simultaneously increased pressure on the remaining grasslands.[18] Over a period of time, some-

---

97. This pattern is confirmed in a number of early accounts. See also Philip Porter, "Environmental Potential and Economic Opportunities: A Background for Cultural Adaptation," *American Anthropologist* 67 (1965): 410; and Kjekshus, *Ecology Control*, pp. 53–54.

15. See William Cronon, *Changes in the Land: Indians, Colonists, and the Ecology of New England* (New York, 1983), pp. 3–15, for an excellent discussion of this issue. Edward Soja has warned against conceptualizing the environment as a container within which history occurs. *The Geography of Modernization in Kenya* (Syracuse, 1968), p. 210. For a recent examination of the ecological impact of population movements in the forest zone, see Jan Vansina, "L'homme, Les Forêts et le Passé en Afrique," *Annales: Economie, Societés, Civilisations* 40 (1985): 1307–29.

16. Cronon, *Changes in the Land*, p. 165.

17. PRO: Agricultural Report by Mr. Linton on the Kenya District, 12 June 1903 in D. Steward to F.O., 1 Sept. 1904, FO 2/839. Hobley, *Ethnology of Akamba*, p. 20; Dundas, "History of Kitui," p. 496; Routledge, *Agikuyu*, p. 40; and Leakey, *Southern Kikuyu*, 1:169.

18. A. T. Grove, "Desertification in the African Environment," in *Drought in Africa*, vol. 2, ed. D. Dalby, R. J. Harrison Church, and F. Bezzaz (London, 1978), p. 60; and Marilyn Silberfein, "Differential Development in Machakos District, Kenya," in *Life before the Drought*, ed. E. Scott (Boston, 1984), pp. 101–02.

times not very great, the extension of agricultural settlement subtly reshaped local climates and substantially altered the ecological systems on which previous inhabitants—both animal and human—had depended. In the highlands the transformation could be particularly dramatic:

> The Kikuyu take a rugged wooded valley with a torrent flowing at the bottom. First they cut down all the trees and burn them. Then they bare the whole hillside till it is nothing but a mass of red earth. Then they plant it . . . leaving between the fields only enough room for their steep little paths running straight up and down the hill. At the top of the hill are built a few prim little huts, and a few bushes . . . are planted in a semicircle on their windward side. Next they tame the torrent, levelling the rocky places . . . till it flows quietly between two sloping banks of black earth planted with sugar cane. The transformation and beautification of the valley is now complete.[19]

The actions of the farmers made it more and more difficult for hunters and herders to hold on. Hunters faced the disappearance of the animals and plants that made up their diet; for herders, the growing population of farmers meant increased competition for water and a decline in pasturelands. Thus, pioneer farmers were able to win the struggle for preeminence as much with environmental weapons as through direct confrontation. By the late nineteenth century only scattered groups of herders and hunters still lived within the region, and most of those who remained had entered into highly dependent relationships with neighboring farmers.[20]

The environmental changes that undermined hunting and herding economies inexorably threatened the bases of the very pioneer communities whose establishment had initiated the changes in the first place. This insidious reverberation of ecological change was particularly rapid and pronounced in the drier frontier zones of settlement. In Mumoni, settlers often concentrated along the few seasonal streams, setting off a chain of events that ultimately forced a redistribution of population. Dry streambeds provided sources of water for domestic use the year round, and the rich, moist soils along the banks were particularly desirable for cultivation. As settlers gradually cleared the vegetation from the edge of the streams, the seasonal floods swept away the accu-

19. Chauncy H. Stigand, *The Land of the Zinj: Being an Account of British East Africa, Its Ancient History and its Present Inhabitants* (London, 1913), p. 236.

20. For example, see Neumann, *Elephant Hunting*, p. 128; and Muriuki, *History of Kikuyu*, p. 88. Also Corinne Kratz, "Are the Okiek Really Masai? or Kipsigis? or Kikuyu?," *Cahiers D'Etudes Africaines* 79 (1980): 355–68.

mulated rich topsoil at the edges, leaving a broad, sandy river bottom that retained less water for subsequent use. Meanwhile, a growing local population increased pressure on diminishing water, fuel, and soil resources as well as on surrounding pasturelands. In an area such as Mumoni, where ecologies were fragile, these interlocking developments might result—within particular localities—in long-term desiccation and thus in shifts in patterns of economic activity and residence. The rapid northward movement of settlers in Mumoni that occurred during the later part of the nineteenth century was almost certainly the product of this destructive cycle of settlement and land deterioration.[21]

REGIONAL EXCHANGE

The stark contrast between highlands economies and those in the drier hill and plains zones structured regional exchange, with active trades in food, livestock, and livestock products crossing and recrossing these ecological divides. Traders regularly moved back and forth along the paths between the fertile farmlands on Mount Kenya and the arid and somewhat forbidding country of Mumoni, only fifty miles to the east, but as much as three thousand feet lower. Men and women from Meru communities near Mount Kenya carried yams and bananas along the routes to Tharaka, where they could be traded for animal fats, hides, and various kinds of beans. Across the region, a series of similar exchange relationships joined settlements in the dry areas, such as Migwani or Mumoni, with communities in higher areas, in Gikuyuland, on Mount Kenya, in the Nyambeni Range, or even in the hill sections of Ulu.[22] Such trade connections spread out in every direction, creating an evolving complex of interlocking and overlapping networks of economic interdependence that by the second half of the nineteenth century constituted a coherent regional exchange system.[23]

The greater portion of trade in basic commodities moved through networks that linked neighboring areas rather than along the longer distance routes shown on the map. In both Meru and Gikuyuland, sub-

---

21. Maher, "Soil Erosion in Kitui," pp. 57, 192–94; and Mutiso, "Kitui Ecosystem," pp. 133–34. The point is amply demonstrated by the ecological impact of recent development programs, notably well-digging projects.

22. Chanler, *Jungle and Desert*, p. 218.

23. For the concept of the regional system, see Smith, "Analyzing Regional Social Systems," pp. 3–20.

stantial trade developed out of the complex interpenetration of areas that emphasized production of grains and those where farmers grew bananas and root crops. Nineteenth-century visitors to central Kenya often remarked on the variation in crops between adjacent areas.[24] Just within Mbeere, the variation in the types of beans produced in different localities stimulated an active trade.[25] The patterns of trade across the hill sections of the region were especially complex, since distinctions among small economies within this zone were often subtle. Depending upon the season or year and on personal circumstances, a Migwani farmer sold certain kinds of foodstuffs to people in Mumoni or in central Kitui; another Migwani farming family bought food in Kitui or in the highlands in exchange for various kinds of livestock, while others were trading elsewhere to expand their herds.[26] Of course, the level of trade along any given route varied substantially from year to year, becoming much more active when food shortages occurred; and, as conditions within the region changed, the flow of people and commodities shifted as well. But if the patterns of trade were not immutable, exchange relationships were nevertheless often deeply entrenched in practice and ideology. In the words of an elder in Migwani, "Since the beginning of time, we have gone to Gikuyu. It was a cold place where cattle could not be reared. . . . They would give us food; in return they would get livestock."[27]

The basis of the regional exchange economy was the demand for food and livestock products: to diversify diets, to alleviate regular inequities, to ease temporary shortfalls, to ensure adequate sustenance in areas facing chronic shortages, to meet social obligations, and to provide some degree of economic security. Thus, in central Kenya it was the production and circulation of ordinary consumer commodities— essentially food—and not the distribution of restricted commodities such as salt, iron, or imported goods that animated regional trade.[28]

    24. Von Höhnel, *Lakes Rudolf and Stefanie*, 1:328; and Chanler, *Jungle and Desert*, p. 218.

    25. Mwaniki, *Embu Texts*, p. 206.

    26. Migwani testimonies. See also, Chanler, *Jungle and Desert*, p. 218.

    27. Interview: Matha w/o Ngumbi, Migwani; Muthuku s/o Nzuvi, Mumoni.

    28. Studies of precolonial African trade have typically focused on the movement of high-value, restricted commodities. However, in a preliminary but highly stimulating investigation of the Lake Victoria region, D. W. Cohen has argued that "the domain of food production and consumption was neither enclosed nor local, and neither stable nor politically neutral." "Food Production and Food Exchange in the PreColonial Lakes Plateau Region," in *Imperialism, Colonialism and Hunger: East and Central Africa*, ed. Robert Rotberg (Lexington, Mass., 1983), pp. 1–18, quote p. 13. Other studies which emphasize the circulation of food commodities include D. Newbury, "Lake Kivu Trade in the Nineteenth Century,"

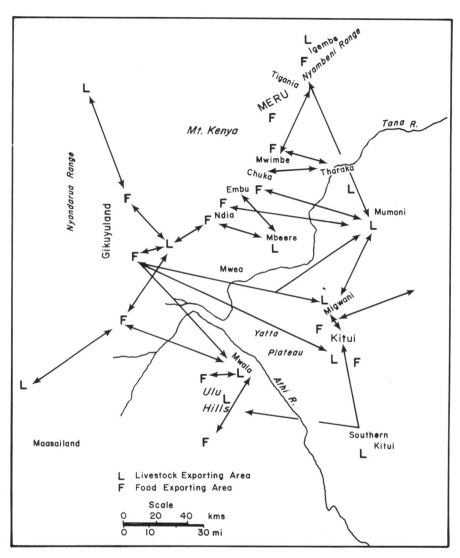

Map 8. The Patterns of Exchange in Basic Commodities

Unfortunately, the activities of the small groups of men and women carrying agricultural products from place to place rarely attracted the notice or interest of literate observers, or became the focus of formal oral traditions. Nevertheless, oral testimonies of individual and family experiences provide abundant evidence of the importance and pervasiveness of such trade. In fact, the very abundance of such detailed and highly personalized information on the trades in food and livestock makes the reconstruction of this commerce difficult.

Because the trade involved inexpensive and perishable commodities that most families produced or consumed, almost anyone could participate. Certainly, little of this exchange was in the hands of people who could be categorized as professional or specialist traders.[29] The sources permit no estimates of the volume of the nineteenth-century food trade, although the evidence makes plain that it was substantial, regular, and in many cases vital to the well-being of the societies involved. While the list of commodities carried is extensive, the bulk of trade was in the foodstuffs that were basic to local diets—millet, sorghum, yams, sweet potatoes, and various sorts of beans.

If it was food products that fueled regional exchange, it was livestock that oiled the machinery. For the farmers of central Kenya the intrinsic value of domestic animals was relatively small. Herds provided people with milk, fats, hides, and animals for sacrifice, but meat was not a significant part of local diets. Instead, the critical importance of domestic animals was their exchange value. Livestock served as a regional currency: an accepted medium of exchange in most transactions, a standard of value, and a means of accumulation and investment.[30] Livestock ownership provided a measure of security against the vagaries of harvests: if crops were inadequate, animals could be sold off. Thus, the heavy commitment to pastoralism in the dry sections of the region, such as Mumoni, made perfect sense. Moreover, livestock resources gave owners the opportunity to accumulate the

Journal des Africanists 50 (1980): 6–36; Bernard Lugan, "Echanges et Routes Commerciales au Rwanda, 1880–1914," *Africa-Tervuren* 22 (1976): 33–39; and Stephen Baier, *An Economic History of Niger* (Oxford, 1980).

29. The organization of these trades is discussed in chap. 4.

30. Kenyatta, *Facing Mount Kenya*, p. 62; Joseph Muthiani, *Akamba from Within: Egalitarianism in Social Relations* (New York, 1973), p. 62; Tate, "Kikuyu and Kamba Tribes," p. 136; Dundas, "History of Kitui," p. 501; and Lindblom, *Akamba*, pp. 108, 273, 313. Interviews: Ngatu s/o Mauna and Mbele s/o Nguli, Migwani; Malila s/o Nzoka, Mumoni. The definition of currency is drawn from Lars Sundstrom, *The Exchange Economy of Pre-Colonial Tropical Africa* (New York, 1974), pp. 84–85.

personal relationships—beginning with marriage—that were so critical to security and success in the social and economic life of central Kenyan societies. Understandably, families treasured their herds and guarded them closely.[31]

The transfer of various forms of casual labor was closely woven into the basic exchange of livestock for food. Typically, men or women worked briefly for farmers in their home areas or in nearby communities in return for measures of food. Women in Migwani regularly obtained supplementary foodstuffs from their neighbors by cultivating their fields; Mbeere residents often worked in nearby highland areas. Less commonly, men traveled into the stock-raising districts and contracted to work for goats or animal skins.[32] Such temporary laborers sometimes became the clients of their employers and settled down permanently in the societies where they had found work.[33]

While a substantial market for free labor existed during the late 1800s, much of the movement of workers from one area to another was to some degree coerced. Unfree or dependent labor took a variety of forms. Young boys sometimes became indentured servants or apprentices, working in households away from their home societies as farmhands, herd-boys, or, more rarely, traders' assistants.[34] But most unfree labor was female labor. Raiders sometimes seized young women or girls as hostages, and if not subsequently ransomed, the victims were forcibly integrated into their captors' communities.[35] The transfer of women was usually accomplished, however, through pawning agreements. Pawning was the basic customary instrument of the circulation

31. Stanner, "Kitui Kamba," p. B-156; Dundas, "History of Kitui," p. 501; R. M. A. Van Zwanenberg with Anne King, *An Economic History of Kenya and Uganda* (Nairobi, 1975), p. 86; and A. G. Hopkins, *An Economic History of West Africa* (New York, 1973), p. 42.

32. C. W. Hobley, *Ethnology of Akamba*, p. 84. Interviews: William Muriria, Embu; Elizabeth Kitumba w/o Kisenga, Nguuti s/o Ndana, and Ngatu s/o Mauna, Migwani; Munyasia s/o Mutilu, Malila s/o Nzoka, and Masila s/o Kivunza, Mumoni; Ngira s/o Katere, Maringa s/o Maunge, Wagatu w/o Mucirwa, and Nderi Ndigica, Mbeere. See also C. Ambler, "Labor Migration in Central Kenya, ca. 1880–1920: A Regional Interpretation," Social Science History Association, Annual Meeting, Washington, D.C., 29 Oct. 1983.

33. Ainsworth, Diary, 18 Nov. 1895.

34. Marris and Somerset, *African Businessmen*, p. 17. Interviews: Ngatu s/o Mauna, Muito s/o Muthama, and Nguli s/o Kinuva, Migwani.

35. Decle, *Three Years in Africa*, p. 489; and Neumann, *Elephant Hunting*, p. 132; and Mwaniki, *Embu Texts*, pp. 232–33. Interviews: Muruakori s/o Gacewa, Gatere Kamunyori, and Kabogo wa Gacigua, Embu; Malila s/o Nzoka, Mumoni; Mavuli s/o Makola, Migwani; Mwageri Njuguara, Mbeere.

of dependent labor within the region, and pawning arrangements were commonplace, particularly when food shortages occurred.[36] Typically, a young woman whose family was experiencing hard times was sent to live with people in a different community, in return for a negotiated payment or series of payments of foodstuffs or livestock. But ultimate control over the pawned woman continued to rest with the original parent, husband, or guardian; and most of the men who pawned their dependents apparently intended to redeem them when circumstances improved. Often such women never did go back to their homes, but the fact that their relatives could return and claim them provided a measure of protection from exploitation.[37]

REGIONAL EXCHANGE AND LOCAL ECONOMIES

The families who moved into frontier areas took into account not only the resources available locally, but the strategic positions of their new settlements, and in particular the possibilities for trade. Pioneer farmers maintained close ties with their previous homes—ties that often formed the basis for regular commerce—and also carried with them, and drew on, a legacy of established exchange relationships. In time, the existence of these new communities, with their particular resources and interests, reshaped the larger patterns of exchange. Many of the Kamba-speaking farmers who moved into new settlements on the northern fringes of Ulu were anxious to expand existing trade links with communities to the west in Gikuyuland. The establishment of these farming settlements in Ulu in turn drew a number of Gikuyu-speaking migrants, who further expanded exchange between the two areas. Likewise, Mumoni settlers depended heavily on their trade con-

36. The pawning or sale of people during famine was widespread in Africa. Miller, "Drought, Disease, Famine," pp. 28–29. Hopkins pointed to the need for further examination of pawnship in *Economic History of West Africa*, p. 27, but despite the rapid growth in slave studies the topic has received little attention. Paul Lovejoy, *Transformations in Slavery: A History of Slavery in Africa* (Cambridge, 1983), p. 13. The most useful discussion of the issue remains Mary Douglas, "Matriliny and Pawnship in Central Africa," *Africa* 34 (1964): 301–13.

37. Lane, "Report on Kitui," p. 29; Ainsworth, Diary, 25 April 1898; Dundas, "Laws of Bantu Tribes," p. 290; Berntsen, "Maasailand," p. 266; and Kennell A. Jackson, "The Family Entity and Famine among the Nineteenth-Century Akamba of Kenya: Social Responses to Environmental Stress," *Journal of Family History* 1 (1976): 205–06. Interviews: Ndithio s/o Mwangi and Musyoka s/o Ndeto, Mumoni; Mbatia w/o Mukumi, Mbeere. When a pawned woman married, her husband sometimes later paid a portion of bridewealth to her original guardian as well as to her new one.

tacts with central Kitui, while at the same time developing important new contacts in Meru and on Mount Kenya. The development of the *mbenge* villages of eastern Mumoni would scarcely have been possible if the settlers had not been able to depend upon external sources of food.[38]

Although frontier settlements often blatantly displayed their orientation toward trade, the commerce in food and livestock was sometimes even more closely interwoven into the social and economic fabric of established communities. The patterns of trade in basic commodities could be deeply embedded in the local political economy. Around the southern slopes of Mount Kenya, for example, the dense concentration of basic exchange relationships that linked Mbeere localities with communities in the Mount Kenya highlands clearly played an important role in the reproduction of the local social order.

By the 1880s, some ten to twenty thousand people lived in Mbeere, concentrated in a series of overlapping communities in the hill country that stretched east and south from the base of Mount Kenya toward the Tana River.[39] The dry, rocky country that sloped away from the hills supported little population, except in the few places where access to special resources, such as the iron deposits found in the Ivurori area, offset the otherwise harsh conditions. Few if any people lived permanently near the Tana River, in the arid expanse of land lying below twenty-five hundred feet, although this country was used for hunting and for honey collection. An open plain formed a boundary zone between the northern settlements of Mbeere and the foothills of Mount Kenya, lying some ten miles away.[40] But despite this distance, the mountain formed an awesome visual presence in every corner of

38. PRO: Ainsworth to Pigott, 28 Feb. 1895 in IBEAC to F.O., 3 May 1895, FO 2/97. Krapf, Journal, 25–29 Aug. 1851; Guillain, *Documents sur L'Afrique Orientale*, 2:294; Jackson, "Kamba History," p. 204; and Mbithi and Wisner, "Drought and Famines," p. 118. Interviews: Manderi s/o Munzungi and Nzilu s/o Siongongo, Mumoni. This point is discussed at greater length in Ambler, "Population Movement and Exchange," pp. 209–13.

39. KNA: Embu District, Political Record Book, Division III, Emberre [Mbeere], DC/EBU.3/1. Hobley, Safari Diary, entries for Oct. 1891; Maher, "Erosion in the Kitui Reserve," p. 129; and Brokensha and Glazier, "Land Reform among the Mbeere," pp. 182–83. Interviews: Gitavi s/o Kunyira and Kamdia Ndarabo, Mbeere.

40. KNA: Embu District, Political Record Book, Division III, Emberre, DC/EBU.3/1; and Central Province, Embu District Political Record Book [ca. 1916], PC.CP 1/5/1. Peters, *New Lights on Dark Africa*, pp. 200–05; Ernest Gedge, "A Recent Exploration Under Capt. F. G. Dundas, R.N., up the River Tana to Mt. Kenya," *Proceedings of the Royal Geographical Society*, 2d ser. 14 (1892): 525; and Brokensha and Glazier, "Land Reform among the Mbeere," pp. 182–83. Interviews: Ngari w/o Matha and Gitavi s/o Kunyira, Mbeere. Iron production and trade is discussed below, chap. 4.

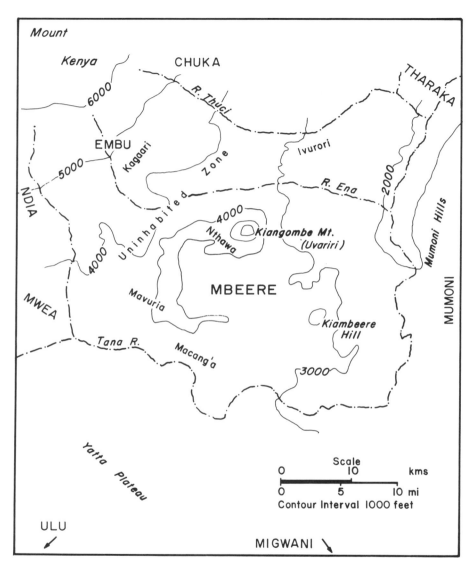

Map 9. Mbeere and Mount Kenya

Mbeere—symbolizing the close links that bound local communities to those nearby on the mountain's slopes, particularly in Embu. Indeed, though Mbeere society lacked the unity that distinguished Embu, communities in the two areas essentially shared a culture and language.

The Mbeere economy, however, contrasted strikingly to that of Embu. While highland communities regularly produced surpluses of a wide variety of foods, many Mbeere neighborhoods, at least during the late 1800s, were not self-sustaining in basic agricultural production.[41] The convenience of external sources of food apparently led farmers to plant crops that were preferred for their taste or labor requirements, but that were less well suited than others to the relatively dry conditions that prevailed in Mbeere.[42] Consequently, many Mbeere families looked, year after year, to the nearby communities on Mount Kenya to meet their food needs. Highland farmers offered not only regular supplies of basic grains, beans, and tubers, but also a number of crops, including sugar cane and bananas, that could not be grown successfully in most sections of Mbeere. Because these foods were readily available through trade, many Mbeere residents came to think of them as part of their regular diets. Thus even in years when basic supplies were adequate, trade in foodstuffs continued on a substantial scale.[43] This exchange between Mbeere and the mountain communities was not an encapsulated symbiosis between ecologically complementary neighbors, but part of broader commercial networks that linked localities all around Mount Kenya.[44] Farmers from Mbeere obtained food from several highland areas, while engaging in related trades in honey, iron, and livestock with neighbors to the east and south in Meru, Tharaka, Mumoni, and Migwani.[45] As a result, the economies of Mbeere communities were in fact more fundamentally oriented toward exchange than many of those in areas that were centers of long-distance trade.

Mbeere farmers ordinarily obtained food supplies in exchange for livestock, which were in considerable demand in the highlands. In

41. Hobley, Safari Diary, 8 Oct. 1891. Interviews: Mutinda s/o Ruanyaki and Ruguca Nthimbu, Mbeere. The relative superiority of particular crops in terms of yield, reliability, and nutritional value is difficult to determine because of the variability of local conditions. Marvin Miracle, *Maize in Tropical Africa* (Madison, 1966), p. 207.

42. Maher, "Soil Erosion in Embu," pp. 135, 170. Interviews: Ngira s/o Katere, Gachone w/o Mburati, and Njuguna Kivuli, Mbeere.

43. Interviews: Gachone w/o Rukeni, Ruguca Nthimbu, and Mutinda s/o Ruanyaki, Mbeere.

44. Van Zwanenberg and King describe local trade in northern Gikuyuland as symbiotic. *Economic History of Kenya and Uganda*, p. 149.

45. Ambler, "Central Kenya," pp. 179–82.

Embu, herding was clearly a secondary activity, but the ownership of livestock still represented the only practical means of accumulation. Moreover, the transfer or slaughter of animals occupied a central position in the basic relationships and ceremonies of Embu life, including the payment of bridewealth.[46] But with ample stocks of agricultural surplus to sell, Embu people could regularly obtain animals as well as iron and iron products from the outside.[47]

During the long dry season from June to September, when the ceremonies of initiation took place, men from Embu and the neighboring Mount Kenya society of Ndia often looked to Mbeere for the animals that they required to fulfill their various ritual obligations. Those Mbeere farmers who did not have adequate livestock to trade for food often sold their labor instead. Highlands farmers generally hired workers on a daily basis to clear plots or cultivate fields in return for a standard payment in foodstuffs. Men and women seldom worked for more than a few days at a time; they were limited by the size of the loads they could carry and were often anxious to get the food back to their families. For both parties, labor agreements had the potential to develop into more lasting relationships, which were in many cases formalized in blood partnerships.[48] The Embu farmer gained a contact who could provide assistance in the purchase of livestock, while the Mbeere family acquired a dependable source of food to cover shortages.

In the larger sense, this exchange of labor and livestock for food worked to the considerable advantage of Embu and the other highlands societies. Embu farmers used labor from Mbeere to expand production. The resulting surplus went to procure stock or to compensate additional workers, ultimately enabling the host employers to build up their herds and households. Embu farmers bought livestock and paid wages with a perishable commodity—food; men and women from Mbeere either gave up their savings—livestock—or sold labor that might have been expended on their own farms.

In Embu the availability of livestock and labor from the outside ac-

46. G. St. J. Orde-Browne in Kenya Land Commission, *Evidence*, 1:388; Maher, "Soil Erosion in Embu," p. 71; and Saberwal, *Political System of Embu*, p. 15. Interviews: Runji s/o Jigoya and Ngari s/o Matha, Mbeere; Muruakori s/o Gacewa, Paulo Njega, Rungai s/o Nthigai, and Tirisa Kanyi w/o Mbarire, Embu.

47. Interviews: Paulo Njega, Kanjama w/o Njanguthi, and Munduwathara Kunyaa, Embu.

48. Interviews: Mwige Kwigiriira, Nderi Ndigica, Muturi s/o Ruveni, and Kanake s/o Gikathi, Mbeere; William Muriria and Muruwanyamu Kathambara, Embu. For further discussion of blood partnership, see chap. 4.

tually discouraged the emergence of internal disparities in wealth. Because many Embu farmers had the capacity to produce surplus and thus could acquire the livestock and other goods that they required, large herds did not translate into the weapon of property that in many other societies allowed a few men to monopolize wealth and power. Even if an Embu man managed to command the labor of a substantial number of workers, pawns, or dependents, he would have little to gain from the resulting increased production. The surplus itself, of course, could not be stored for more than a few months, and the shortage of good pasturage meant that major investments in livestock were unlikely to yield satisfactory returns. In the absence of an easily convertible commodity, the profits of trade tended to go toward conspicuous consumption. Even here the scope was limited, since Embu farmers did not really possess the products that would have purchased typical imported luxuries such as cloth and jewelry in large quantities.[49] There is some evidence, however, that surplus production was used to buy leisure time, in particular for warriors. The availability of Mbeere workers to clear and prepare fields in Embu—work often done by young men—presumably freed Embu youths to concentrate their attentions on activities like dancing that built up the spirit and solidarity of warrior groups. This in turn may explain the distinctive martial spirit of the Embu warrior class, and Embu's wide reputation in central Kenya for unusually aggressive raiding. Embu warriors often directed their attacks against the very people who were underwriting these activities— the men and women from Mbeere who were crossing the plain to work for food in the highlands.[50]

THE REGION IN THE LARGER ECONOMY, CA. 1880

In 1880 only the slender thread of the caravan trade linked the central Kenya region to the Indian Ocean port of Mombasa and hence to the international economy. Commerce had moved along this route for a

49. Boyes, *King of Kikuyu*, p. 157; and Orde-Browne, *Vanishing Tribes*, p. 38. Interviews: Alan Kageta, Embu; Muvali s/o Kilanga, Mumoni.

50. Arkell-Hardwick, *Ivory Trader*, pp. 62–64. Interviews: Muturi s/o Ruveni and Manunga s/o Nguci, Mbeere; Muruachuri Nyaga and Muruakori s/o Gacewa, Embu. Unlike most other areas of central Kenya, Embu communities organized a unified armed resistance to British expansion. See Mwaniki, "History of Embu," pp. 388–96, 405–29. W. G. Clarence-Smith has described leisure time as a form of conspicuous consumption in "Slaves, Commoners and Landlords in Bulozi, c. 1875 to 1906," *Journal of African History* 20 (1979): 223.

century or more, but its impact on the eastern interior had been remarkably muted: a small number of communities had tied their fortunes to the trade; a few men had accumulated considerable wealth and power; yet the developing long-distance trade had certainly not yet transformed the political economy of the region. In the late eighteenth century, men from the coastal hinterland opened commercial routes joining their home areas to settlements on the southern margins of central Kenya. Over the decades that followed, traders from Kitui increasingly entered the commerce and displaced the coastal people.[51]

The essence of the trade was straightforward: central Kenya exported ivory in return for various imported trade goods, notably cloth, beads, and copper wire. The story of the growth and transformation of this commerce is known only in general terms, having been pieced together from fragments of information about a few places at scattered intervals. The relative wealth of written evidence about Kitui has probably resulted in an exaggerated view of that area's position in the trade. In the absence of additional fact, it is impossible to say how much of the trade Kitui merchants controlled or when and how they lost that control and to whom. Kitui was clearly the prime inland destination around 1850 when Krapf traveled into the interior; it was still important during the 1870s, and it remained so through the end of the century. In 1895, the British official John Ainsworth wrote that "Kitui is on the main road to Mumoni, Meranga (Kikuyu), Thaka and Likipia Country."[52] But it is clear that even before midcentury the shortage of elephants in the areas surrounding central Kenya was driving hunters and traders far to the north and making it difficult for merchants based on the southern edge of the region to maintain a place in the ivory commerce.[53]

During the middle 1800s, with the price and demand for ivory rising, large caravans, often including hundreds of men, moved frequently between Kitui and the coast area, a journey that could last several months.[54] Major traders translated a great deal of their profits into large herds of cattle, and their villages became centers of political

51. Spear, *Kenya's Past*, pp. 119–20; Jackson, "Kamba History," pp. 221–23; and Lamphear, "Kamba and the Coast," pp. 75–81.
52. Hildebrandt, "Travels in East Africa," pp. 446–52. The quote is from PRO: Ainsworth to Pigott, 20 Feb. 1895 in IBEAC to F.O., 10 April 1895, FO 2/97.
53. Krapf, Journal, 24 Nov. 1849.
54. PRO: IBEAC to F.O., 2 Feb. 1893, FO 2/57. Spear, *Kenya's Past*, p. 117; Lamphear, "Kamba and the Coast," pp. 89–92; and Munro, *Colonial Rule and the Kamba*, pp. 68–69.

influence. But since commercial organizations rarely survived the deaths of their founders, no permanent oligarchy of trading families or houses took hold. There are signs, however, of a growing concentration of wealth and power in the hands of those lineages that had acquired large herds of livestock through trade. Descendants of men who had amassed wealth in Kitui early in the 1800s apparently formed the vanguard of later attempts to establish commercially oriented communities in the frontier areas such as Migwani and Mumoni.[55] Yet only a small segment even of Kitui's population was directly involved in or affected by long-distance commerce. Thus, while most of the leading traders happened to be Kamba-speakers, this was by no means a "Kamba trade."[56]

However limited in its social and geographical impact, the growth of the caravan trade nevertheless played a vital role in shaping the patterns of frontier settlement. Among the migrants who moved east from Ulu into Kitui during the late eighteenth century were the men who built up the commerce between central Kenya and the coast and made Kitui a hub of trade.[57] Likewise, the expansion of agricultural settlement from central Kitui reflected the subsequent development of the long-distance trade. In the early nineteenth century, the plain north of Migwani had been an important site for elephant hunting; and as the animals were killed off, traders and hunters still frequently crossed the area on the way to more remote destinations.[58] Some of these men settled down in Migwani, apparently feeling that by basing themselves to the north of Kitui's main population centers, they would gain advantages in commercial activities. In addition, the reduction of elephant herds made the plains around Migwani increasingly attractive for grazing.[59]

The establishment of settlements in the eastern sections of Mumoni came at the same time that long-distance merchants expanded their activities on the major route that ran through that area to the north. By moving into Mumoni, traders put themselves substantially closer to the places to the north, in Meru and beyond, that had become the most im-

---

55. Jackson, "Kamba History," pp. 213–14, 223–26, 233; and Neumann, *Elephant Hunting*, pp. 133–45.

56. As it has often been described, for example in Van Zwanenberg with King, *Economic History*, p. 152.

57. Jackson, "Kamba History," pp. 221–23.

58. Ibid., p. 204; and Krapf, Journal, 25–29 Aug. 1851.

59. Interviews: Nguuti s/o Ndana and Komba w/o Nzoka, Migwani.

portant centers for elephant hunting and ivory trade.[60] Merchants may also have hoped that by migrating to Mumoni they could forestall attempts by coastal merchants to consolidate their increasing dominance of trade through the region. This would explain why the most important of the Mumoni traders, Kilungya wa Mutia, established his village near the key Tana River ford.[61] But if Mumoni offered ambitious men the opportunity to amass considerable wealth, limited local agricultural resources and recurrent drought meant that basic foods would often be in short supply. Only the establishment of trade connections—and the security of food supplies that their existence implied—permitted men such as Kilungya to amass great herds of cattle and ultimately to concentrate wealth and power in their own hands. What this meant for the masses of Mumoni residents is not clear. Certainly, by settling in *mbenge* villages, people with few resources hoped to gain more. In the meantime, however, they found themselves part of a society in which a small number of men controlled much of the wealth, and many were condemned to periodic hunger.

Trends in the history of long-distance trade emerge a bit more clearly after midcentury. Although ivory supplies declined, a growing demand for livestock at the coast fueled trade in cattle, goats, and sheep. This transition from tusks to animals involved more than the replacement of one commodity with another. Ivory was relatively scarce and required a substantial mobilization of people and resources to acquire; livestock were ubiquitous and already the staple of exchange within the region. Hence, as more and more men began to take stock to the coast for sale the boundaries of long-distance and regional exchange blurred.

This extension of external trade into the regional exchange system forced a rapid commercialization of the transfer of female labor. Traders both from communities in central Kenya and from the coast manipulated the conventions of pawning to obtain women—generally refugees—who it was understood could not be reclaimed. In other words, the buyers were acquiring rights over the women themselves, not simply their labor.[62] The women—now in effect slaves—were

---

60. PRO: Ainsworth to Pigott, 20 Feb. 1895 in IBEAC to F.O., 10 April 1895, FO 2/97. Pigott, Diary, 5 May 1889; Hobley, *Kenya*, p. 205; and Jackson, "Kamba History," pp. 203–29. Interviews: Ndithio s/o Mwangi, Kele s/o Kanandu, Muli s/o Kakuru, Kaungo s/o Mutia, Kisalu s/o Kilatya, and Muasya s/o Munene, Mumoni.

61. Chanler, *Jungle and Desert*, pp. 56, 59; Neumann, *Elephant Hunting*, p. 133.

62. PRO: Ainsworth to Pigott, 20 Feb. 1895 in IBEAC to F.O., 10 April 1895, FO 2/97; Hardinge to F.O., 11 June 1896, FO 107/53; Hardinge to F.O., 24 April 1897, FO

then resold, usually to farmers within the region. Few were transported beyond central Kenya. Contemporary written accounts refer frequently to the existence of slavery and an active slave trade; but histories of the Kenya interior have generally ignored this evidence or dismissed it as either the product of European misperceptions of local institutions or attempts to rationalize conquest.[63] Similarly, the few oral records that acknowledge the existence of slave trading usually claim that it was confined to the sale of social outcasts.[64] But it stretches credulity to suggest that numerous and sometimes explicit reports of slave purchases can be explained away as either an expansionist conspiracy or alien myopia.[65] Europeans traveling through central Kenya recorded many cases of young women and girls being offered for purchase, and various private and official records describe a regular movement of slaves from Gikuyuland into Ulu and Kitui.[66] These documents are clearly not misrepresenting instances of arranged marriages or pawning agreements, since such transactions were unlikely either to have come to the attention of European observers or to have earned their condemnation. Even at midcentury, when Krapf reported that Kitui residents were beginning to buy slave women from Mbeere and from the coast, he was careful to distinguish these sales from the more common practice of acquiring women as captives or pawns.[67]

107/77. Lane, "Report on Kitui," p. 29; Perham, *Lugard Diaries*, 1:143 (14 March 1890); and Chanler, *Jungle and Desert*, pp. 488–90; and Mwaniki, *Embu Texts*, pp. 54–55. Interviews: Hussein Juma, Kitui Town; Mukusu s/o Mututhu, Migwani; Manunga s/o Nguci, Mbeere. For a broader discussion of these developments see Frederick Cooper, "The Problem of Slavery in African Studies," *Journal of African History* 20 (1979): 108–09; and Lovejoy, *Transformations in Slavery*, pp. 19, 241.

63. See Van Zwanenberg with King, *Economic History of Kenya and Uganda*, p. 178; and Richard D. Wolff, *The Economics of Colonialism: Britain and Kenya, 1870–1930* (New Haven, 1974), pp. 43–44.

64. Mwaniki, *Embu Texts*, pp. 54–55. According to one Migwani elder, "Actually slavery did not come here. It came when people started paying tax." Interview: Ngatu s/o Mauna. While misleading, his statement does point to the need of considering slavery within the larger spectrum of controlled labor. See Igor Kopytoff and Suzanne Miers, "African 'Slavery' as an Institution of Marginality," in *Slavery in Africa*, ed. Miers and Kopytoff, pp. 3–81.

65. Local British officials regularly claimed that a station was necessary in Kitui in order to suppress slave trading. PRO: Ainsworth, General Report for Jan. 1895, Machakos, 31 Jan. 1895, IBEAC to F.O., 10 April 1895, FO 2/97. Frederick Cooper has explored the relationship between antislavery and British expansion in *From Slaves to Squatters: Plantation Labor and Agriculture in Zanzibar and Coastal Kenya, 1890–1925* (New Haven, 1980), pp. 24–68. Cooper points out that British antagonism to the slave trade did not necessarily extend to slavery itself.

66. Pigott, Diary, 16 May 1889; Hall, letter, 15 March 1894; and Ainsworth, Diary, 18 Nov. 1895.

67. Krapf, *Travels, Researches and Labours*, p. 291.

The reticence of the oral records presumably reflects not only subsequent attitudes toward slavery and the relatively small scale of slave trading, but also the speed with which slaves were incorporated into local communities. Even as the trade increased at the end of the century, the position of slaves continued to be defined in kinship terms. Slave status was not inherited, and slave women were integrated into households and communities as wives. During the late 1890s a British official in Kitui noted that the large number of women from Maasai backgrounds living there were "not slaves in the true sense of the word, for the Wakamba make wives of them, and treat them like their own women."[68] As outsiders cut off from their origins, these women lacked the connections that protected local women in marriage; but there is no evidence that they occupied distinctly inferior positions in their new societies or that they or their children experienced systematic discrimination.[69] Whatever their position, alien women—with their distinctive speech and backgrounds—inevitably brought different perspectives to the families that they joined and to the children whom they raised. Moreover, the presence of substantial numbers of these "foreign" women in Gikuyuland, Ulu, and Kitui illustrates the pointlessness of discussing central Kenya societies as if they were culturally and biologically static and discrete.

Although no slave castes developed in the societies of central Kenya, slavery was not just another form of dependency. Most enslaved women presumably saw no alternative to their situation, since many had neither home nor family to return to.[70] But in central Kenya as in other parts of Africa, when recently enslaved women saw a way out of their status, they often took it. In 1894 the British official in charge of the post in southern Gikuyuland wrote in a letter home that "the number of slaves who have run away and come to my Masai kraal is beyond all count; I don't know whether I have the legal right, but I always refuse to give them up again."[71]

68. Lane, "Report on Kitui," p. 29.

69. Ibid.; and Lindblom, *Akamba*, pp. 203–04. Interview: Hussein Juma, Kitui Town. Also, Spear, *Kaya Complex*, pp. 98–101. The expansion of the slave trading is discussed further in chap. 5. Krapf claimed that by the mid-1800s wealthy Kitui merchants were buying slaves at the coast, but there is no evidence elsewhere of the existence of a distinct slave population in Kitui society. Krapf, Journal, 3 Dec. 1849; and Krapf, *Travels, Researches and Labours*, p. 259.

70. Lane, "Report on Kitui," p. 29.

71. Hall, letter, 12 Feb. 1894. Also note Chanler, *Jungle and Desert*, pp. 489–90. Lovejoy points to the importance of evidence of slave escape for assessments of slave systems. *Transformations in Slavery*, p. 247.

As the focus of central Kenya's external trade shifted away from ivory, stations along the major routes developed as centers of regional trade, and a few local merchants—including Kilungya in Mumoni—began to see their role more as brokers than long-distance traders. By the 1880s this process was only beginning, however. Wide areas continued to be isolated from the currents of international trade, and most contacts with long-distance trade and traders remained ephemeral or superficial. Despite the growth and expansion of long-distance commerce the patterns of regional exchange predominated and retained their essential structure and autonomy. Many people, especially those who lived away from the major trade routes, had only the vaguest understanding of the external forces that were beginning to reshape their region and their lives. They interpreted distant developments largely through the prophecies of local seers or through widely repeated tales like those of Mukona Uko, the mythical Arab merchant who had been pushed into the ocean by a powerful newcomer, and whose name—literally, "the person who strikes wood"—evoked the custom of hitting sticks together to signal the beginning of trade.[72]

---

72. The term varied slightly according to locality. Jackson, "Oral Traditions of Akamba," pp. 265–66.

4

The Organization
of Regional Exchange

I ndividual initiative and independent action dominated the conduct of exchange across the central Kenya region. Trade was typically informal and small in scale. In the rare instances where commercial organizations developed, they were invariably short-lived:
central Kenya had no indigenous equivalent to the corporate commercial houses that existed on the Indian Ocean coast or in many areas of
West Africa.[1] Exchange was straightforward. Most goods moved directly from producer to consumer or through a chain of small-scale
trader-consumers. Only in the natron trade, discussed later in this
chapter, was there much sign of a distinction developing between retail
and wholesale trading. If craftsmen were involved in manufacturing or
finishing the goods involved, they did not become commercial producers. In the case of the iron trade, for example, smiths made tools as re-
quested in return for a fee; the customer retained ownership of the
product itself.[2]

TRADING ORGANIZATIONS

Family-based trading parties handled most of the short-distance exchange of basic commodities; and since little or no capital was required, participation was essentially unrestricted. Family trade was an
extension of the exchange that went on among homesteads within a locality, involving a range of inexpensive domestic commodities, such as

1. For example, see A. J. H. Latham, *Old Calabar, 1600–1891* (Oxford, 1979).
2. Producers obtained raw iron through their own labor or that of family members.
Routledge, *Agikuyu*, p. 82.

74

pottery and other implements, as well as foodstuffs, small livestock, and labor. Consequently, the traffic tended to be seasonal and was especially active during times when food was in short supply. For reasons of convenience and security, traders often combined with lineage-mates or neighbors into larger groups for the trip itself, sometimes under the leadership of prominent local men. Whatever the mode of travel, however, the actual exchange transactions remained individualized.[3]

Temporary trader associations dominated trade over somewhat longer distances. Groups of five, ten, twenty, or more individuals combined and planned strategies, routes, and destinations. From the start, such enterprises were group projects: participants bound themselves together by oath. They traveled, camped, and returned as a unit. But trading associations were not partnerships. Each member brought in his or her own stock of commodities and traded individually. Traders did not pool resources or divide profits; they simply agreed to travel together for security, convenience, and companionship.[4] Males generally dominated these associations, with women included only in subordinate positions, although in some areas of Gikuyuland women organized themselves into equivalent associations, frequently making lengthy journeys into Ulu or to the settlements of Maasai pastoralists.[5] Both male and female trader associations dealt largely in local commodities: foodstuffs, livestock, ornaments, iron products (see accompanying table).[6]

Trader associations tended in practice to reproduce themselves. Each new venture ordinarily reunited people who had traveled together previously, people who were drawn together through basic lineage and marriage connections, mutual aid networks, and especially

3. Robert J. Cummings, "Aspects of Human Porterage with Special Reference to the Akamba of Kenya: Towards an Economic History, 1820–1920" (Ph.D. diss., University of California, 1975), p. 94. Interviews: Munyasia s/o Kalwe and Mulango s/o Ngusia, Migwani; Kabogo s/o Gacigua and William Muriria, Embu; Nzilu s/o Siongongo, Muli s/o Kakuru, and Mati s/o Mwinzi, Mumoni; Sarimu Njavari, Mbeere.

4. Krapf, Journal, 21 Aug. 1851; Chanler, *Jungle and Desert*, pp. 408, 470; and Jackson, "Kamba History," pp. 223–24. Interviews: Mulango s/o Ngusia, Mutia s/o Mboo, and Kasina s/o Ndoo, Migwani; Muli s/o Kakuru, Mumoni.

5. Krapf, Journal, 15 July 1851; Krapf, *Travels, Researches and Labours*, p. 317; von Höhnel, *Lakes Rudolf and Stefanie*, 1:291; Muriuki, *History of Kikuyu*, p. 107; and Clark, "Women and Power in Kikuyu," p. 363.

6. PRO: Ainsworth to Pigott, 20 Feb. 1895 in IBEAC to F.O., 10 April 1895, FO 2/97. J. W. Pringle, "With the Railway Survey to Victoria Nyanza," *The Geographical Journal* 2 (1893): 120; and Mwaniki, *Embu Texts*, pp. 204–05. Interviews: Girishom Mukono and Gatere Kamunyori, Embu.

Commodities Traded within the Region [Partial List]

Local Products
casual labor
rights over labor
cattle, sheep, goats
livestock skins
animal fat
timber
foodstuffs (including maize,
   millets, sorghum, beans,
   peas, bananas, tubers,
   sugar cane)
plant cuttings
tobacco
miraa (narcotic plant)
gourds
natron (soda)
honey
ferriferous soil
salt soil
red ochre
red and white clay
pottery clay
blue powder
monkey skins

Local Manufactures
ingots
metal tools (including blades,
   axes, hatchets, digging
   tools, knives, tweezers,
   awls)
weapons (including swords,
   shields, clubs, sheaths,
   spears, arrow tips)
hand crafts (including walking
   sticks, snuff boxes,
   straps, fiber cloth, axe
   handles, arrow shafts,
   cooking pots, grinding
   stones, leather clothes)
ornaments (many varieties
   of chains, belts, rings,
   ankle, leg and arm
   bracelets, bead and shell
   work, medallions, earrings)
honey and other beers
poisons
various medicinal and ritual
   items (medicines, amulets,
   divining stones, charms,
   "poisons")

Imports
commercial expertise
cloth sheets
rolls of cloth
ornaments
ornamental materials (including
   shells, beads, iron, brass, and
   copper wire)
iron ingots and wire
metal tools
arrow poison (or the raw material)
salt
guns
bottles, metal pots, and containers

Exports
carrier labor
ivory
rhino horns
hippo teeth
oxen
castrated sheep and goats
animal fat
tobacco
donkeys

age group affiliation. As in the organization of defense and raiding, community dance competitions provided a framework for the mobilization of men for trade. For youths, participation in trade represented variety and excitement as well as an opportunity to get ahead. As one elder commented, "When you were young and a caravan was going to Masailand, who would want to be left behind?"[7]

Associations of traders not only engaged in commerce within the region, but also traveled between central Kenya and the coast to sell livestock and occasionally ivory in return for arrow poison and various imported goods. Fragmentary evidence suggests that the groups that followed this route were structurally little different from the associations involved in regular regional trade, although apparently they were larger.[8] A contemporary account of five trading parties camped at a rest stop on the coast route in June of 1896 described groups ranging from six to fifty-eight men, all from Ulu. In each case, the traders planned to sell both small and large livestock—altogether 352 goats and 33 cattle. The ratio of men to stock and the preponderance of goats indicates clearly that these were associations of small-scale traders.[9] In the interest of greater security, the small associations of traders traveling the coast route often combined into loose caravans, with one man taking on the responsibility of maintaining order and arranging for the division or rotation of tasks.[10]

The head man or woman of a small trade expedition was generally no more than the first among equals, but in larger associations that might cover long distances through insecure country, the need for internal discipline and hence the scope for leadership increased. The leaders of trade expeditions received no specific compensation, but as such men gradually accumulated organizational skills, knowledge of commerce, and wealth, they could move into more ambitious enterprises where the possibility of profit-making was correspondingly greater.[11] The expeditions that moved between communities in Giku-

7. Jackson, "Kamba History," pp. 223–24. Interviews: Mulango s/o Ngusia and Mutia s/o Mboo, Migwani; Muruakori s/o Gacewa and Girishom Mukono, Embu; and Ikiriki s/o Masila, Mumoni. Cummings discusses the role of communal work institutions in the development of regional trade in "Akamba Trade History," esp. pp. 92–93. The quote is from Marris and Somerset, *African Businessmen*, p. 34.

8. PRO: Ainsworth, "Report on Kitwyi," 6 Feb. 1895 in IBEAC to F.O., 10 April 1895, FO 2/97. Perham, *Lugard Diaries*, 1:121 (27 Feb. 1890), 123 (2 March 1890); Neumann, *Elephant Hunting*, p. 143; and Gregory, *Rift Valley*, p. 75. Interviews: Ngatu s/o Mauna and Mbasia s/o Muliungi, Migwani; Lang'a s/o Ngile, Mumoni.

9. Ainsworth, Diary, 10 June 1896.

10. J. L. Krapf, "Excursion to the Country of the Wanika Tribe at Rabbay [near Mombasa] and Visit of the Wakamba People at Endia," journal received 22 Aug. 1845, entry for 30 Jan. 1845, Krapf Papers, Church Missionary Society Archives, London, CA5/16/166. KNA: Hildebrandt, "Ethnographic Notes of Wakamba," Machakos District Political Record Book, vol. I, pt. II, DC/MKS.4/3. Gregory, *Rift Valley*, 75. Interviews: Mulango s/o Ngusia and Nguuti s/o Ndana, Migwani; Munithya s/o Nganza, Mumoni.

11. Krapf, *Travels, Researches and Labours*, p. 232; F. Jackson, *Early Days*, p. 131; and Dundas, "History of Kitui," p. 508. Interviews: Mulango s/o Ngusia and Kasina s/o

yuland and surrounding pastoralist areas were often led by men who had gained substantial reputations for their skill. They knew the terrain intimately; they spoke the Maasai language; and in many cases they had established close personal relationships with the men in Maasailand with whom they regularly did business. In the process of becoming leaders, such men also managed to build up their wealth in livestock and personal connections. Some were rich enough to hire porters for their journeys and had sufficient capital to trade for large numbers of livestock. The lesser members of the association, however, had to make do with much less, sometimes acquiring no more than skins.[12]

A few outstanding traders managed to parlay their talents into relatively permanent commercial organizations, which operated almost exclusively in the sphere of international exchange. Known widely as *kyalo kya uvoo*, these enterprises descended directly from the grander, Kitui-based elephant-hunting and caravan system that had flourished earlier in the century.[13] A charismatic leader, with his dependents, clients, and associates formed the core of *kyalo* commercial organization, providing a degree of continuity and a model for a formal division and ranking of tasks. Many of the members of *kyalo* caravans held distinctly inferior positions, working as scouts, guards, or carriers in return for some small share of the proceeds. An expedition ordinarily included from fifty to several hundred men; but by the 1880s few if any major traders could directly command that large a following. In the late nineteenth century, most *kyalo* ventures were based on alliances among independent major traders who hired porters and made partnerships as they saw fit and retained control over their own stocks of goods.[14]

Strong and talented leadership nevertheless remained crucial to the

---

Ndoo, Migwani; Ngumu s/o Munithya, Kaungo s/o Mutia, Mathuva s/o Katui, and Ikiriki s/o Masila, Mumoni.

12. Marris and Somerset, *African Businessmen*, pp. 34–37; and Muriuki, *History of Kikuyu*, p. 107.

13. While popularly translated as "journey of peace" (*kyalo kya* meaning "journey of or to"), *uvoo* is a coastal (Kiswahili) word for a particular type of ornament. Krapf, *Journal*, 30 Jan. 1845; and Krapf, *Journal*, 15 July 1851. Interviews: Mulango s/o Ngusia, Mutia s/o Mboo, Nguuti s/o Ndana, and Kasina s/o Ndoo, Migwani; Ngumu s/o Munithya and Muli s/o Kakuru, Mumoni.

14. KNA: "Ethnographic Notes of Wakamba," Machakos District Political Record Book, vol. I, pt. II, DC/MKS.4/3. Krapf, *Journal*, 30 Jan. 1845; Krapf, *Travels, Researches and Labours*, p. 317; Hobley, *Safari Diary*, Aug. 1891; Chanler, *Jungle and Desert*, pp. 284, 406–07; and Jackson, "Kamba History," pp. 223–24. Interviews: Mulango s/o Ngusia, Nguuti s/o Ndana, Kasina s/o Ndoo, and Mutia s/o Mboo, Migwani; Munithya s/o Nganza and Lang'a s/o Ngile, Mumoni.

success of these enterprises. It was their reputations for skill and fairness, as well as their wealth, that allowed *kyalo* traders to attract and hold supporters. Unlike their counterparts in less formal trade organizations, *kyalo* leaders—both in hunting and commerce—took specific compensation for their services and controlled the apportionment of the proceeds from the exchange of commodities. Once established, *kyalo* leaders were well placed to maintain their positions. Income from trade permitted leaders to draw in more clients and dependents and thus gain greater wealth.[15] But these commercial enterprises resembled houses of cards: often large and elaborate but extremely fragile. Each *kyalo* trading organization was a reflection of the talent and charisma of an individual merchant; few if any survived the deaths of their founders.[16] During the late nineteenth century, the *kyalo* system played a progressively smaller role in international trade, even in the areas of Kitui and Mumoni where historically it was based. However, many of the system's elements did persist in the activities of the powerful merchant-brokers who established themselves across the region during the last decades of the century.

MOVEMENT WITHIN THE REGION

For those who engaged in commerce, putting together a trading party was only the beginning of a complex and often difficult enterprise. Nineteenth-century storytellers often recounted a legend of a monster that inhabited the Tana River and occasionally preyed on travelers who crossed. These tales, embellished with anecdotes of unexplained disappearances and purported sightings, frightened children and amused adults.[17] Stories told in fun nevertheless nurtured an undercurrent of fear and uncertainty that was reflected in the widely held belief that it was spiritually dangerous to drink water from the Tana.[18] A hidden and unpredictable creature evoked in inexperienced travelers

15. KNA: "Ethnographic Notes of Wakamba," Machakos District Political Record Book, vol. I, pt. II, DC/MKS.4/3. Hobley, Safari Diary, 21 Oct. 1891. Interviews: Mulango s/o Ngusia, Nguuti s/o Ndana, and Kasina s/o Ndoo, Migwani; Ngumu s/o Munithya, Muli s/o Kakuru, and Munithya s/o Nganza, Mumoni.

16. Jackson, "Kamba History," p. 228.

17. Lindblom, *Akamba*, p. 274. Interview: Muli s/o Kakuru, Mumoni; Muthura s/o Nthiga, Tharaka; and Gatema Muyovi, Mbeere. Gwyn Prins notes the existence of a similar mythical beast inhabiting the Zambezi in Bulozi. *The Hidden Hippopotamus: Reappraisal in African History: The Early Colonial Experience in Western Zambia* (Cambridge, 1980), p. 19.

18. Hitoshi Ueda, "The Power of Hunting Leaders among the Kamba," Institute of African Studies, University of Nairobi, no. 116, March 1979, p. 5.

all of the difficulties and possible dangers that even the shortest trip away from one's home society could entail.

At the very least, travel was time-consuming and arduous. Traders moved almost exclusively on foot, frequently over difficult terrain. Since pack and draught animals were still rare at the end of the century, all goods had to be carried either by the traders, members of their families, or rarely by porters. This meant slow going for men and women already burdened with livestock, weapons, and supplies.[19] Large caravans moving through open country often covered as few as fourteen miles in a day's march of seven or eight hours. Even small parties made slow progress: a group of traders walking the fifty miles that separated Mumoni from the Mount Kenya foothills required a minimum of six days of hard work to accomplish the round-trip. Progress was slower and more exhausting along the paths that twisted over the sharp ridges and through dense vegetation in the highlands.[20]

Fears of monsters aside, the major rivers often blocked or hindered free movement. Regional trade routes converged at established fords along the Athi and Tana rivers, yet people still had trouble getting themselves and their possessions from one side to the other. For most of the year the region's rivers and streams were shallow and slow-moving; nevertheless, crossing a river was often frightening for the inexperienced, and when water was high it could become quite dangerous. Travelers sometimes lost their possessions to fast currents and occasionally even their lives. At the fords along the Tana, wayfarers often paid out ornaments or measures of food for assistance. Local youths pulled people and their livestock and goods on floats; or if water levels were low, these same young men would walk through the river, keeping the loads over their heads and out of the water.[21] During November and December and again in March and April, when these streams were in flood, crossing became considerably more difficult and at times impossible. Unfortunately, high-water seasons

19. Pigott, Diary, March 1889; Neumann, *Elephant Hunting*, p. 28; Lindblom, *Akamba*, pp. 345–47; and Mwaniki, *Embu Texts*, p. 264. Interview: Ngatu s/o Mauna, Migwani. Women sometimes carried loads as heavy as 100–150 pounds. Leakey, *Southern Kikuyu*, 1:482.

20. PRO: Capt. Maycock, 19 Aug. 1906, CO 533/16. Pigott, Diary, 10 May 1889; Muriuki, *History of Kikuyu*, p. 26; and Fadiman, *Mountain Warriors*, p. 11. Interview: Ngeri w/o Ngala, Mumoni.

21. Krapf, Journal, 27 Aug. 1851; Arkell-Hardwick, *Ivory Trader*, p. 356; and Lindblom, *Akamba*, pp. 345–47. Interviews: among many, see Ngeri w/o Ngala and Kisilu s/o Katumo, Mumoni; Komba w/o Nzoka and Paul Ngutu s/o Ngutha, Migwani; and Muthura s/o Nthiga, Tharaka.

coincided roughly with the times of the year—the period just after planting—when the food trade began to intensify. In November 1849, for instance, the Tana flood prevented the Kitui merchant Kivui wa Mwendwa and his visitor Dr. Krapf from making a planned journey north toward Mount Kenya.[22]

Disease formed an additional barrier to the circulation of people and commodities. People from highlands communities—largely free of malaria—faced considerable risk if they journeyed into the hill and plains zones—where the disease was endemic. This circumstance may partly explain why men from the highlands were generally less involved in long-distance commerce.[23] In fact, any travel across ecological boundaries brought people into contact with different microorganisms, making minor illnesses a likely by-product of travel. Traders and other travelers were not merely the victims of disease, of course, but potentially the carriers of infection. Not surprisingly, people saw a clear connection between contact with strangers and ill health.[24] Finally, disease also placed seasonal and spatial constraints on the free exchange of livestock. Animals could become sick and even die when moved into unfamiliar environments, while the presence of tsetse flies in the country along the Tana made the routes that crossed the river risky for cattle traders.[25]

Any long journey within the region was thus a substantial—even dangerous—undertaking, involving many days of walking with heavy loads and sometimes uncertain supplies of food and water.[26] Travelers tried to spend nights in homesteads along the route, but more often they had to sleep in makeshift camps, where they were vulnerable to assaults from wild animals and at times human marauders. In the absence of any political institutions capable of maintaining order across a

22. Dr. J. L. Krapf to Capt. Hamerton, British Consul, Zanzibar, Mombasa, 21 Jan. 1850, quoted in *Proceedings of the Royal Geographical Society* 4 (1882): 751. Also Pigott, Diary, 29 Aug. 1889; Karl Peters, "From the Mouth of the Tana to the Source-Region of the Nile," *Scottish Geographical Magazine* 7 (1891): 118; Arkell-Hardwick, *Ivory Trader*, p. 351.

23. Bernard, *Meru Agriculture*, pp. 26–27; Muriuki, *History of Kikuyu*, p. 32; and Lindblom, *Akamba*, p. 313. Highlands people were not necessarily healthier than those from other areas, however, as reports of medical exams of First World War recruits show. KNA: Kenya Province Annual Report, 1917, PC/CP.4/1/1.

24. Jeffery Fadiman, *Mountain Warriors: The Pre-Colonial Meru of Mt. Kenya* (Athens, Ohio, 1976), pp. 8–9.

25. Porter, "Environmental Potential and Opportunity," p. 410; and Kjekshus, *Ecology Control*, pp. 53–54. Also, Mumoni and Embu testimonies.

26. Pigott, Diary, 15 May 1889; Hobley, Safari Diary, 21 Nov. 1891; and Lane, "Report on Kitui," p. 29. This was especially the case for travel beyond the region.

large territory, travelers always faced the threat of attack when they walked the paths outside settled areas. If cultural conventions did limit the extent of violence somewhat, raids against trading parties were by no means uncommon. Youths from Embu, for example, regularly attacked people traveling to the highlands for food and on occasion even disrupted markets set up to expedite the exchange of basic subsistence commodities. In 1851, when Krapf finally accompanied Kivui on a journey north, the raiders that attacked their party not only seized property but killed Kivui and a number of others, including women.[27]

THE INSTITUTIONS OF EXCHANGE

In this world of uncertainty that stretched beyond the boundaries of small societies, men and women who were traveling away from their homes used various means to provide themselves with a degree of security. Invariably, they ritually purified the routes they intended to follow and guarded themselves by carrying medicines and amulets. Some of the more active traders seem to have advertised a defiance of supernatural powers—and hence their relative immunity to the magic of others—by purposefully ignoring traditional restrictions on sexual activity or the consumption of particular foods.[28] Most travelers, however, sought to protect themselves by building up networks of personal relationships, which over generations linked individuals and families across the region. Traders depended in particular on a pervasive system of fictive kinship, called *giciaro*, to facilitate exchange and protect commercial connections.[29] Men became "blood brothers" through

27. Krapf, *Travels, Researches and Labours*, p. 269; Arkell-Hardwick, *Ivory Trader*, p. 57; and Orde-Browne, *Vanishing Tribes*, p. 160. Interviews: Mutia s/o Mboo, Migwani; Arthur Mairani, Embu; Gatema Muyovi, Mbeere; and Muthuvi s/o Mui, Mumoni. In contrast, Fadiman claims that in Meru society raiding was not permitted to disrupt society (in particular trade); that women and children were isolated from violence; and that casualties were few. *Tribal Warfare*, pp. 42, 122.

28. Krapf, Journal, 19–20 Nov. 1849; Hildebrandt, "Travels in East Africa," p. 452; and Leakey, *Southern Kikuyu*, 1:501–02. Note the similar, although far more extreme, process through which the Aro, "children of God," preserved their role in trade in eastern Nigeria. Northrup, *Trade without Rulers*, pp. 114–15.

29. Blood partnership was a vital agent of commercial interaction across precolonial Kenya. Spear, *Kenya's Past*, p. 120; and Thomas Herlehy, "Ties that Bind: Palm Wine and Blood-Brotherhood at the Kenya Coast during the Nineteenth Century," *International Journal of African Historical Studies* 17 (1984): 285–308. For a more analytical approach, see Dennis D. Cordell, "Blood Partnership in Theory and in Practice: The Expansion of Muslim Power in Dar Al-Kuti," *Journal of African History* 20 (1979): 379–94.

ritual mutual rebirth. A description from Meru in 1894 reveals some of the depth of feeling that was involved in the ceremony:

> Baikenda [a local elder] . . . came with his retinue, bringing the sacrificial sheep and we went through the ceremony of "eating blood" most solemnly and impressively. . . . Baikenda and I became, as he put it, as if born of one mother, emphasizing the relationship with expressive pantomime by squeezing suggestively his shrivelled old breast with his hand.[30]

Typically, the principals—with witnesses present—slaughtered a goat or sheep and collected the animal's blood in a gourd. By dipping sticks in this container, the two men symbolically mingled their own blood and thus declared their intention to respect all the rights, obligations, and prohibitions that would normally obtain in a relationship between siblings.[31]

Giciaro linked not only two men, but two families, theoretically in perpetuity. Men continually forged new ritual alliances and those relationships that had been left to wither were often revived by the descendants of men once "born together."[32] Thus, refugees from famine or traders seeking to open new commercial connections could exploit a moribund relationship to find assistance. Men were free to enter into numerous *giciaro* relations, limited only by an understanding that the relationships should be restricted to outside contacts. But *outside* was a concept that was vaguely defined. Blood brotherhood commonly spanned ethnic boundaries but also occurred in contacts between individuals from different small societies—for example, in Migwani and Mumoni—that were located within the boundaries of a single ethnic population. As the Meru ceremony suggests, local men also frequently entered into *giciaro* relationships with coastal or European visitors to the region.[33]

Giciaro pervaded the commercial life of the region. Men primarily

---

30. Neumann, *Elephant Hunting*, pp. 11–12. For a similar account, see Dundas, Safari Diary, 9 Sept. 1891.

31. Chanler, *Jungle and Desert*, pp. 260–61; Neumann, *Elephant Hunting*, p. 41; Boyes, *King of Kikuyu*, p. 182; Dundas, "History of Kitui," p. 547; and Orde-Browne, *Vanishing Tribes*, p. 71. Interviews: especially, Paul Ngutu s/o Ngutha and Kasina s/o Ndoo, Migwani; and Ngeri w/o Ngala, Mumoni.

32. Dundas, "Laws of Bantu Tribes," p. 286.

33. Dundas, "History of Kitui," pp. 526, 547; and Mwaniki, *Embu Texts*, pp. 304–05. Paul Ngutu s/o Ngutha, Sali w/o Mulewa, and Kasina s/o Ndoo, Migwani; Muvali s/o Kilanga, Munyoki s/o Mutui, and Kitevu s/o Ndaku, Mumoni; Muthura s/o Nthiga, Tharaka; Muruwanyamu Kathambara, Embu; Kinyatta s/o Savana, Kanake s/o Gikathi, and Njiru s/o Mutemanderi, Mbeere.

intended these links to facilitate trade, although they also acted out of friendship. The rituals themselves integrated movement and exchange, since ceremonies often involved the mutual presentation of gifts and visits to the homes of both the men involved. An outside trader was much freer to move within a community if he was known to have a local *giciaro* connection. Blood brothers also often provided practical assistance in trade, for instance, offering lodging and food or arranging for contacts in the surrounding neighborhoods.[34] For people who regularly engaged in trade or who came from areas where shortages of food or livestock recurred, *giciaro* relationships clearly represented strategic investments. The expenditure of a few goats for sacrifice and gift-giving could provide a Mumoni man with regular access to food in Embu, and his Embu blood partner the means to obtain livestock to meet bridewealth payments or other obligations. *Giciaro* played a particularly important role in small-scale trade, but the value of such connections extended into long-distance commerce as well. Major traders and hunters from Mumoni and Kitui sought *giciaro* connections with traders and brokers in the areas where they did business, as did the merchants who ventured into the region from the Indian Ocean coast. While Europeans often saw *giciaro* as a means of cementing their local contacts, they frequently and mistakenly assumed that these rituals created alliances with entire communities, rather than a relationship linking two men and their respective families.[35]

Although relationships between individuals governed most commercial transactions, communities did take some steps to regulate trade, as when Embu elders attempted to limit and control the activities of long-distance traders. Evidence suggests that communities in central Kitui made concerted use of force to protect their position in major commerce against encroachments from Mumoni competitors.[36] Community regulation of exchange commonly involved the promulgation of temporary trade treaties between neighboring areas, or especially the establishment of local market days.[37]

34. Satish Saberwal, *Political System of Embu*, pp. 44–46. See interviews cited in preceding notes.

35. F. D. Lugard, *The Rise of Our East African Empire*, vol. 1 (London, 1893): 330–31; Neumann, *Elephant Hunting*, p. 41; Chanler, *Jungle and Desert*, pp. 260–61; and Mwaniki, *Embu Texts*, pp. 304–05.

36. PRO: Ainsworth, "Report on 'Kitwyi'," 6 Feb. 1895 in IBEAC to F.O., 10 April 1895, FO 2/97. Krapf, Journal, 29 Nov. 1849; and Lamphear, "Kamba and Mrima Coast," pp. 99–100.

37. KNA: Hildebrandt, "Ethnographic Notes of Wakamba," Machakos District Political Record Book, vol. I, pt. II, DC/MKS.4/3. Chanler, *Jungle and Desert*, p. 179; Hobley, Sa-

Virtually every society made a provision for markets, but they were most common in the densely populated highland areas. Elders in the Embu area sponsored markets only sporadically, for example, when food shortages increased the demand for trade; however, in parts of Gikuyuland and Meru, markets were held much more often, possibly according to regular schedules.[38] In an account written in 1893, markets in eastern Meru

> consisted of openings in the plantations, beaten hard and bare by many feet. Thither came the women of neighboring districts of the Embe country daily, and expended many hours in exchanging their produce one with the other. One old woman would bring a large bag . . . of cassava; another manioc, another yams; while a fourth would bring bananas.[39]

Although locally oriented, these markets sometimes attracted a substantial volume of trade. In sections of Gikuyuland hundreds of people attended markets that were large enough to warrant the separation of traders according to commodity. Individual women traders in Meru still carried in as much as forty pounds of cassava or other foodstuffs for sale on a single day.[40] Domestically produced goods such as food and utensils predominated in market trade, but items imported from beyond the immediate area, including metal tools, ornaments, cosmetics, tobacco, natron, and arrow poison, sometimes circulated through small markets. Long-distance trade, however, did not penetrate community markets to any great extent. External commerce spawned its own series of ad hoc trade fairs, which drew in large numbers of people to trade foodstuffs and livestock for goods brought in from the coast.[41]

fari Diary, 8 Sept. 1891; Lambert, "Land Tenure among the Akamba," p. 141; and Leakey, *Southern Kikuyu*, 1:491. Interviews: Gatema Muyovi, Sarimu Njavari, and Ngai w/o Nthoroko, Mbeere. For the role of markets in the nineteenth-century Kenya interior, see Charles Good, *Market Development in Traditionally Marketless Societies: A Perspective on East Africa* (Athens, Ohio, 1971); Van Zwanenberg with King, *Economic History*, pp. 147–59; and Cohen, "Food Production and Food Exchange."

38. H. J. Mackinder, Typescript Diary (prepared from the original and virtually identical), entries for 2–3 Aug. 1899, Mackinder Papers, Rhodes House Library, Oxford, Mss Afr R 11-30; Chanler, *Jungle and Desert*, p. 239; Boyes, *King of Kikuyu*, p. 192; Routledge, *Agikuyu*, pp. 105–06; Orde-Browne, *Vanishing Tribes*, p. 116; Muriuki, *History of Kikuyu*, p. 108; and Good, *Market Development*, p. 7. Local markets are described repeatedly in testimonies that I collected as well as those published in Mwaniki, *Embu Texts*.

39. Chanler, *Jungle and Desert*, p. 239.

40. Ibid.; and Boyes, *King of Kikuyu*, p. 192.

41. MacDonald, *Soldiering and Surveying*, p. 56; Gregory, *Rift Valley*, p. 76; Lindblom, *Akamba*, p. 580; Hobley, *Ethnology of Akamba*, p. 56; and Lambert, "Land Tenure among the Akamba," p. 137. Interviews: Alan Kageta, Embu; Ngatu s/o Mauna and Paul Ngutu s/o Ngutha, Migwani.

Because markets were intended to ease the exchange of basic commodities, marketplaces often marked sharp ecological and economic boundaries. This was certainly the case with the markets held at Mumbumburi on the edge of the Mount Kenya foothills and with those held at most of the other sites located in and around Mbeere.[42] The logic of market placement was not always so stark, however. The market held occasionally near the Mbeere bank of the Tana River, opposite the Mumoni Hills, drew people from the surrounding and economically similar areas of Mbeere, Tharaka, and Mumoni.[43] These markets occurred irregularly. When the demand for trade in food and other consumer goods intensified, elders from the communities involved consulted with one another and set a market date. Once advertised, such markets as the one held at Mumbumburi could attract hundreds of people from a wide territory, providing men with the opportunities to make personal contacts and establish future direct trading relations.[44]

In the absence of any clearly defined controlling authority the concentration of people from diverse backgrounds could spell trouble. In circumstances where food shortages might already have created hardship and tension, disputes among young men sometimes turned to violence, and fighting and looting upset the fragile structure of exchange.[45] Nevertheless, major disruptions must have been relatively rare, since border markets were commonplace during the late nineteenth century. The fact that women carried on a considerable portion of market trade in itself imposed a degree of order, since men were generally reluctant to inject violence into activities in which women were substantially involved.[46]

42. Chanler, *Jungle and Desert*, pp. 191, 239; Orde-Browne, *Vanishing Tribes*, p. 116; Muriuki, *History of Kikuyu*, p. 107; Mwaniki, "History of Embu," p. 317; and Mwaniki, *Embu Texts*, pp. 35, 204–05, 238. Interviews: Kabogo s/o Gacigua, Mbutei s/o Mwangai, Gatere Kamunyori, and Girishom Mukono, Embu; Gatema Muyovi, Ngari s/o Matha, and Gachone w/o Rukeni, Mbeere.

43. Peters, *New Light on Africa*, p. 193; and Mwaniki, *Embu Texts*, pp. 204–05. Interviews: Nzunya w/o Mbondo, Mumoni; Muthura s/o Nthiga, Tharaka.

44. Boyes, *King of Kikuyu*, pp. 91–92; Mwaniki, "History of Embu," pp. 222, 317; and Mwaniki, *Embu Texts*, pp. 204–05, 228. Interviews: Gachone w/o Rukeni and Sarimu Njavari, Mbeere; Paul Ngutu s/o Ngutha, Migwani; Alan Kageta, Embu.

45. Chanler, *Jungle and Desert*, p. 239; Mwaniki, *Embu Texts*, pp. 204–05; and Van Zwanenberg with King, *Economic History of Kenya and Uganda*, pp. 154–55. Interviews: Nzunya w/o Mbondo, Mumoni; Muthura s/o Nthiga, Tharaka; Gachone w/o Rukeni and Ngari s/o Matha, Mbeere; Gatere Kamunyori, Embu.

46. Chanler, *Jungle and Desert*, p. 239; Boyes, *King of Kikuyu*, pp. 192–93; Clark, "Women and Power in Kikuyu," p. 363; and J. Fadiman, *The Moment of Conquest: Meru, Kenya, 1907* (Athens, Ohio, 1979), p. 10.

NETWORKS OF REGIONAL EXCHANGE

The basic structure of regional exchange—derived from the circulation of food, livestock, and labor—accommodated trades in a wide range of commodities. Each trade had its own shape and dynamic, reflecting the local configuration of supply and demand; but none could be described as autonomous. Networks overlapped and intersected in intricate patterns that defy reconstruction. Often, a community might obtain an item such as iron, for example, from several different sources. Certain goods were traded only in part of the region, and even those commodities that were carried more widely circulated through a weakly integrated series of subregional networks. In any case, few items, excepting food and livestock, were in sufficient demand to warrant trade in themselves alone. Individual traders often carried more than one type of commodity, frequently including foodstuffs or livestock. In particular, the use of small livestock in virtually every category of commercial transaction effectively blurred the boundaries of exchange. Nevertheless, it is possible to trace out some of the more important patterns of regional trade.

IRON AND IRON PRODUCTS

Every household required certain iron implements, and communities lacking deposits of raw iron had to turn to the outside for supplies. Still, a family needed only a limited range of tools, weapons, or ornaments, and these were generally quite durable.[47] Since iron deposits were widely dispersed across central Kenya, few people lived any great distance from a source of supply. As a result, the iron trade—like most regional trades—was both highly localized and limited in volume. Each of the numerous areas where iron ore was available became the center of a network through which ingots and various products such as knives, axes, digging knives, spear blades, and arrowheads were distributed to surrounding communities.[48]

To the south of Mount Kenya, sources of iron were located away from the mountain, notably in eastern Mbeere. Here as elsewhere in

47. Routledge, *Agikuyu*, pp. 81, 124b; and Hobley, *Ethnology of Akamba*, p. 20. The ornament trade is discussed in detail below in this chapter.
48. Information on local iron industries is found in KNA: Kitui District, Political Record Book, Miscellaneous Statistics (pre-1914), DC/KTI.7/2. Chanler, *Jungle and Desert*, p. 254; Gedge, "Up the River Tana," p. 525; Hobley, Safari Diary, 4 Sept. 1891; Van Zwanenberg with King, *Economic History of Kenya and Uganda*, pp. 148–49; and Mwaniki, *Embu Texts*, pp. 138–39.

the region, the raw iron was obtained from scattered deposits of ferriferous sand found in river beds. Local residents extracted iron filings from the sand through a time-consuming washing process, and then paid a local smith to smelt the iron and, if desired, shape it into a finished object.[49] The smelting technology in use permitted only a very limited output, most of which was intended for local consumption; nevertheless, eastern Mbeere supplied many of the surrounding areas, including Embu, with both finished and unfinished iron.[50] Not surprisingly, the sale of iron products was often carried on in conjunction with the far more substantial trades in food, animals, and labor that linked communities in Embu and Mbeere. But the trade in iron goods, like the exchange of subsistence commodities, was by no means confined to this pattern. Iron products were carried out of eastern Mbeere in many different directions. Moreover, communities in Mbeere also acquired some types of iron goods from the outside: ingots and wire from Migwani and Mumoni and various weapons and tools made in Gikuyuland.[51]

Most of the iron products that were brought to Mbeere from Migwani and Mumoni probably came originally from outside the region, and ultimately from outside of Africa. During the nineteenth century imported iron gradually infiltrated and ultimately undermined the established patterns of trade in iron and iron goods. Despite this increasing pressure, however, imports did not wipe out the domestic industry. In sections of Kitui and Ulu, where imports were widely available, demand for local iron continued strong, at least for certain purposes. At midcentury imported iron was already widely used in Kitui, but domestically produced iron continued to be regarded as superior.[52] The importance of the iron industry in eastern Mbeere presumably reflected Mbeere's isolation from international trade routes as

49. Routledge, *Agikuyu*, pp. 80–92; and Lindblom, *Akamba*, pp. 529–30. Interviews: Mulango s/o Ngusia and Rose Makaa w/o Mutia, Migwani; Gachone w/o Mburati, Mwageri Njuguara, Maringa s/o Maunge, and Ngari s/o Matha, Mbeere. The technology is described in Champion, "Atharaka," pp. 78–79; Van Zwanenberg with King, *Economic History of Kenya and Uganda*, pp. 111–15; and Jean Brown, "Iron Working in South Mbeere," *Mila* 2 (1971).

50. Van Zwanenberg with King, *Economic History of Kenya and Uganda*, p. 111; Mwaniki, *Living History of Embu*, pp. 138–39; and Mwaniki, *Embu Texts*, pp. 38, 289.

51. In addition to sources cited in preceding notes, see Orde-Browne, *Vanishing Tribes*, p. 153. Interviews: Gachone w/o Mburati, Maringa s/o Maunge, Ngari s/o Matha, Ruguca Nthimbu, Runji s/o Jigoya, Jimuko Ngonjo, and Mwageri Njuguara, Mbeere; Paulo Njega and Alan Kageta, Embu.

52. Krapf, Journal, 3 Dec. 1849. Also PRO: Ainsworth, Report, 1 Jan. 1894 in IBEAC to F.O., 17 March 1894, FO 2/73.

well as the relatively high cost of imports for residents of that impoverished area.[53]

ORNAMENTS

The trade in ornaments—many of which were made from iron—showed a similar resilience to competition from imports. Across the region craftsmen used a combination of local and imported materials to produce a huge variety of ornamental items, including many sorts of beads, chains, earrings, necklaces, belts, and arm and leg bracelets.[54] Virtually everyone wore some kind of jewelry, but certain pieces or types were clearly luxuries or signs of position. In Ulu and Kitui, for example, the ivory bracelet, *ngotho*, was a coveted symbol of high status.[55] While each community had individuals who made ornaments, artisans from areas of Kitui produced items that were highly prized across the region. According to one European observer, metal craftsmen from Kitui and Ulu were the most skilled in all East Africa, particularly in their use of brass and iron wire: "The patterns on their stools are most artistic; the chains they make of brass, copper, and iron wire are so regular that they might be machine made."[56] The popularity of Kitui ornaments presumably stemmed from the area's long history of involvement in long-distance trade and consequent preferential access to imported fashions and materials. Talented artisans used these advantages to develop distinctive local styles. Much of the jewelry that was produced was for personal use, but a considerable amount was eventually sold.

Ornament-making was by no means a full-time occupation; but it was nevertheless taken seriously, and craftsmen were willing to sell livestock in order to buy the materials they needed. Ownership of jewelry represented a minor form of savings, since ornaments were frequently employed in trade, especially to compensate minor services such as assistance in river crossing. However, the craftsmen themselves

53. Iron-working survived in Mbeere until the 1960s. Brown, "Iron Working."
54. Dundas, "History of Kitui," pp. 497–98; Hobley, *Ethnology of Akamba*, p. 39; Routledge, *Agikuyu*, pp. 30–56; Orde-Browne, *Vanishing Tribes*, pp. 38–39, 164; Tate, "Kikuyu and Kamba Tribes," pp. 134, 139–40. Interview: Mwige Kwigiriira, Mbeere.
55. Kennell Jackson, "Ngotho (The Ivory Armlet): An Emblem of Upper-tier Status among the 19th Century Akamba of Kenya, ca. 1830–1880," *Kenya Historical Review* 5 (1977): 35–69; Pigott, Diary, 16 May 1889; and Lambert, "Institutions of the Kikuyu," p. 255. Interviews: Kabogo s/o Gacigua and Alan Kageta, Embu; and Masila s/o Kivunza, Mumoni.
56. Hobley, "Survey of Ukamba," p. 262.

do not appear to have parlayed their skills into substantial wealth.[57] In time, the commerce that moved through Kitui spread Kitui-style ornaments across the region, in the process changing popular tastes. As a result, a demand for "Kamba" ornaments persisted long after Kitui had lost its dominant place in the commerce of the region.[58]

THE NATRON TRADE

The single commodity traded through a network that had regional scope was natron, a form of sodium carbonate in wide demand as an ingredient in snuff.[59] Iron products, ornaments, salt, and other goods came from numerous and widely dispersed sources, but most of the natron consumed in central Kenya came from a single location, the Ng'ombe Crater, at the eastern end of the Nyambeni Range in Meru. During the 1890s, the crater was described as "large and deep." According to the same observer,

> There is a small lake at the bottom whose shallow water is strongly impregnated with some mineral smelling and tasting of ammonia. It is in large white crystals. There were crowds of Embe [local Meru] women fishing quantities of this substance up from the bottom of the shallow water and carrying it up the steep path in huge loads on their backs. . . . There were also a few men with donkeys which they packed with the mineral.[60]

Men and women from surrounding communities extracted and packed most of the natron, but it was generally associations of traders from other parts of Meru and from Mumoni that handled the commerce. Most natron was distributed along routes that ran south from Ng'ombe through Mumoni, into Kitui and Ulu. The route was largely

57. Höhnel, *Lakes Rudolf and Stefanie*, 2:308; Gregory, *Rift Valley*, p. 349; Lane, "Report on Kitui," p. 29; Dundas, "History of Kitui," pp. 490, 503–04; Hobley, *Ethnology of Akamba*, p. 39; Leakey, *Southern Kikuyu*, 1:479–82; Orde-Browne, *Vanishing Tribes*, p. 164; Routledge, *Agikuyu*, p. 30; and Lambert, "Institutions of the Kikuyu," pp. 235, 255. Interviews: Kabogo s/o Gacigua, Embu; Jimuko Ngonjo, Mwige Kwigiriira, Mwageri Njuguara, and Maringa s/o Maunge, Mbeere; Kavindu s/o Ikunga, Mumoni; Rose Makaa w/o Mutia and Elizabeth Kitumba w/o Kisenga, Migwani.

58. Dundas, "History of Kitui," p. 544; Champion, "Atharaka," p. 76; Mwaniki, *Embu Texts*, pp. 92–93; and Jackson, "Kamba History," p. 232.

59. See the extended discussion of the natron trade in Ambler, "Central Kenya," pp. 235–41. Oral sources for the natron trade include the following interviews: Kilungi s/o Kithita, Nguuti s/o Ndana, Mbulwa s/o Ndoo, and Muli s/o Ndulwa, Migwani; Nzila s/o Munyoki, Manderi s/o Munzungi, Kitevu s/o Ndaku, Kiteng'o s/o Mutui, Muasya s/o Munene, Lang'a s/o Ngile, Muli s/o Sumbi, Kiliungi s/o Muuru, and Muthuvi s/o Mui, Mumoni; Ngari s/o Matha and Nthumbi s/o Gicere, Mbeere.

60. Neumann, *Elephant Hunting*, p. 82.

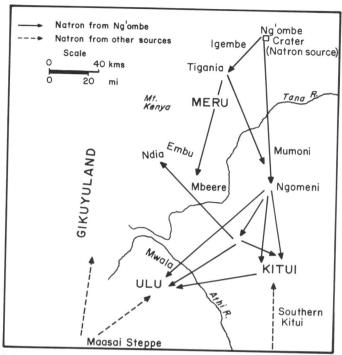

Map 10. The Natron Trade

controlled by men from Ngomeni, an area in southern Mumoni that
had long been an established center of livestock and ivory commerce.
Ngomeni's prominence in the trade probably grew out of the attempt
of established traders from that area to find an alternative commodity
to ivory, which was by then in increasingly short supply.[61]

On the several days' journey from Ng'ombe to Ngomeni, traders
moved in large, well-armed parties, but smaller associations distributed the natron to communities farther on. Association members bought
natron with goats or goatskins; they then sold the packets to local traders, who in turn broke open the packets and resold the natron in small
quantities to their neighbors in return for goats, tobacco, ornaments,
and axe blades. Although the natron commerce was fairly lucrative,
other commodities were handled along with it. In Kitui, for example,
natron traders often bought up fiber string that they could resell in
Ulu, where it was in great demand.[62]

61. PRO: Ainsworth to Hardinge, 29 Dec. 1897 in Hardinge to F.O., 14 Jan. 1898, FO
107/90. Krapf, *Journal*, 7 Aug. 1851; Pigott, Diary, 19 May 1899; Gedge, "Up the River
Tana," p. 524; and Neumann, *Ivory Trader*, p. 80.
62. Lindblom, *Akamba*, p. 21.

A less substantial trade in natron moved along routes from Meru through the Mount Kenya communities into Gikuyuland, where the use of substitute materials in snuff reduced the demand for Ng'ombe natron.[63] Some communities located in the region's southern tier did not obtain their natron from Ng'ombe at all but from the soda lakes some fifty miles to the southwest across the Maasai Steppe. This commerce was controlled by a distinct group of traders who operated in teams of husbands and wives and traveled away from their homes for months at a time.[64] The use of snuff also stimulated demand for its other ingredients, animal fat and tobacco. Most communities grew some tobacco, but it was often in short supply in dry areas. At the same time, certain places, notably in Tharaka and parts of Gikuyuland, developed reputations for producing exceptionally high quality leaf, which was cured, packed in large bundles, and sold widely. However, the circulation of these goods was generally linked closely to the exchange of food and livestock, not to the natron trade.[65]

THE CIRCULATION OF RITUAL POWER AND OBJECTS

Every locality had a number of specialists who were recognized for their talents in interpreting and influencing the supernatural forces that were assumed to permeate every aspect of life. Most of these healers, diviners, seers, and "poisoners" were known only in their immediate communities, but a few were so widely respected or feared that their reputations spread beyond their home areas, and their skills entered the sphere of regional exchange. The general tendency in central Kenya to ascribe particular supernatural powers to outsiders encouraged people to look beyond their own societies when they faced unusually difficult problems.[66] The prophetic talents of the now legendary

63. F. Hall, "The Kikuyu," draft report, 19 March 1894, p. 151, Hall Papers, Rhodes House Library, Oxford (copies at Syracuse University Library). Interviews: Jason Njigoru, Embu; Mavuli s/o Makola, Migwani; Ngari s/o Matha, Mbeere.
64. KNA: Hildebrandt, "Notes of the Wakamba," Machakos District Political Record Book, vol. I, pt. II, DC/MKS.4/3. Lindblom, *Akamba*, p. 523; Leakey, *Southern Kikuyu*, 1:501–02.
65. KNA: Kitui District, Quarterly Report, Sept. 1910, DC/MKS/1/3/3. Krapf, *Travels, Researches and Labours*, p. 255; Hobley, Safari Diary, 4 Sept. 1891; Boyes, *King of Kikuyu*, p. 271; and Lindblom, *Akamba*, p. 21. Interviews: Mwinzi s/o Kathinzi and Kimwele s/o Kyota, Mumoni; Nthumbi s/o Gicere and Ngari s/o Matha, both Mbeere; Jason Njigoru, Embu.
66. Lindblom, *Akamba*, pp. 279–81; Chanler, *Jungle and Desert*, pp. 228–29, 248; Krapf, *Travels, Researches and Labours*, p. 171.

seer Syokimau drew many people to her home in Ulu during the 1870s.[67]

Despite the emphasis on prophecy in traditions, other sorts of supernatural practice actually had far greater importance. In every section of the region, a few localities gained particular reputations as centers of supernatural arts, attracting a clientele from surrounding communities. Although occasional itinerant healers took their skills from place to place, it was the clients who generally traveled to consult specialists.[68] But such trips were not undertaken lightly. As a general rule, people did not travel any great distance to consult specialists except on very serious matters; the dangers, difficulties, and expense were simply too great.[69] Nevertheless, just as areas of Kitui and Ulu became well known across the region for the talents of their artisans, a few places acquired considerable renown for the skills of their resident experts in healing and magic.

Throughout central Kenya, people regarded the settlement of specialists at Uvariri, located on Kiang'ombe Mountain in northeast Mbeere, as a center of herbal and spiritual arts; in fact, Uvariri was thought to be the source of the most potent ritual power in the region. In contrast to the strong assimilationist theme of most oral records of migration and settlement, traditions held that the migrants who established themselves in Uvariri remained separate and aloof from surrounding communities, despite their common language and culture. People in Embu and Mbeere and elsewhere in central Kenya, saw Uvariri people as exceptional and even dangerous.[70] Nevertheless, this power had appeal. Men looked to the specialists at Uvariri to seek aid when the skills of local experts had failed or when they wished their aims to remain secret. Although visits to Uvariri carried the stigma of

67. Jackson, "Kamba History," pp. 237–38; Kenyatta, *Facing Mount Kenya*, pp. 41–51, 233; and Mwaniki, *Living History of Embu*, pp. 154–56. Interview: Muli s/o Ndulwa, Migwani.

68. KNA: Embu District, Political Record Book, Part II, DC.EBU/3/2. Hobley, Safari Diary, 4 Oct. 1891; Mackinder, Diary, 5 Aug. 1889; and Jackson, "Kamba History," p. 219. Interviews: Muli s/o Ndulwa and Komba w/o Nzoka, Migwani; Kaungo w/o Mutia and Nzila s/o Munyoki, Mumoni; Manunga s/o Nguci, Mbeere; Muthura s/o Nthiga, Tharaka.

69. Routledge, *Agikuyu*, p. 265. Interviews: Kaungo w/o Mutia, Mumoni; Anna Njira w/o Munyi and Manunga s/o Nguci, Mbeere.

70. See Map 9. KNA: Asst. District Commissioner, 1917, Embu District Political Record Book, Division III, Emberre [Mbeere], DC/EBU 3/1; and Embu District Political Record Book, Part II [1927], DC/EBU 3/2. Glazier, *Land and the Uses of Tradition*, pp. 158–59. Interviews: Thitu s/o Nzili and Muli s/o Ndulwa, Migwani; Mwageri Njuguara, Anna Njira w/o Munyi, and Manunga s/o Nguci, Mbeere.

malevolent intent, prospective clients probably went there more often to get what they thought to be particularly powerful protective medicines and amulets or powders and charms that would enhance their hunting or dancing skills.[71]

The rise of Uvariri was essentially a product of the development of regional exchange and of the consequent expansion of social and economic scale. For people who increasingly had to contend with a world beyond the narrow confines of their home communities, the Uvariri specialists offered an alternative to the parochial talents of local experts. In short, Uvariri represented a magic that was bigger and more potent and thus appropriate to the needs of people whose lives were being shaped more and more by powerful external forces.

While it would be possible to describe trades in a number of other commodities, such as pottery, dyes, weapons, and honey, the exchange of these goods generally conformed to established patterns: such items were not usually carried over great distances; trade in any type of good was generally sporadic and low in volume; much of the trade was conducted in conjunction with the exchange of basic commodities.[72] As the trade in iron products demonstrates, an increasing number of imported goods were circulating through regional trade networks by the late nineteenth century. But demand for such goods remained relatively weak. By the late nineteenth century, even so basic a commodity as imported cloth had found general acceptance only in a few areas. During the last decades before 1900, despite the intensification of external pressures, the local distribution of basic resources and the local configuration of supply and demand continued to shape the essential patterns of exchange.

71. Jackson, "Kamba History," p. 219. Interviews: Komba w/o Nzoka, wife of Kithusi, and Thitu s/o Nzili, Migwani; Kiliungi s/o Muuru, Mwinzi s/o Kathinzi, Muli s/o Kakuru, and Kaungo w/o Mutia, Mumoni.

72. See, for example, Leakey, *Southern Kikuyu*, 1:482, 499.

5

The Transformation
of Regional Exchange, 1880–1898

In the traditions of central Kenya societies, the last decades of the nineteenth century emerge as a period of prophecy, a time when community after community witnessed the rise to local prominence of men and women who were believed to possess the ability to foretell events.[1] Their visions often attributed ominous implications to the presence of outsiders in the region. According to one of the most knowledgeable of early British observers, residents of Ulu believed that whites ate children and were to blame for eclipses and for plagues of locusts and disease.[2] The content of these and other popular prophecies marked a deep unease, an uncertainty about the future that would be tragically borne out by events. As external commercial and political power steadily circumscribed the autonomy of small societies, a cycle of environmental deterioration threatened the agricultural economy of the region and reduced pastoralist groups in surrounding areas to desperate action. In the late 1890s the strands of this slowly developing crisis would merge in the catastrophe of famine and imperial subjugation.

Drought plagued central Kenya during the 1880s and 1890s. After a major famine during the late 1870s, the drier hill and plains country of central Kenya experienced twenty years of repeated seasons of poor

---

1. Jackson, "Kamba History," pp. 237–38; Kenyatta, *Facing Mount Kenya*, pp. 41–51, 233; and Mwaniki, *Living History of Embu*, pp. 154–56. Interview: Muli s/o Ndulwa, Migwani.

2. John Ainsworth, "A Description of the Ukamba Province, East Africa Protectorate, and its Progress under British Administration," *The Journal of the Manchester Geographical Society* (1900), p. 188, Great Britain, Colonial Office, East Africa Pamphlet Collection (microfilm, reel no. 1).

rainfall and failed harvests.[3] People living in southern Ulu, for instance, faced serious food shortages in the early 1880s and again in 1892, 1894, and 1896. Locust infestation exacerbated the crisis. In 1894 and 1895 clouds of these insects swept across the region, destroying crops from Meru through Ulu into Gikuyuland. The losses were particularly severe in the normally productive farmlands of southern Gikuyuland, where food supplies to the British station were interrupted.[4] The problems of drought and insect infestation were periodic and often highly localized, but their effects accumulated. Even in highland areas such as Embu, where serious crop failures were virtually unknown, farmers felt a growing demand for food from their less secure neighbors.[5]

The most serious threat to the regional economy during this period was not inadequate harvests, however, but a dramatic outbreak of cattle disease. In 1890 rinderpest spread out of the Red Sea area into eastern Africa, where herds lacked immunities. The disease swept over Kenya and the rest of eastern, central, and southern Africa with astonishing speed and appalling virulence.[6] In central Kenya, as elsewhere, cattle-owners lost as many as 90 percent of their animals during the initial outbreaks; subsequent losses were much lower but still significant. In some areas the disease virtually wiped out entire herds.[7] Traveling through eastern Mumoni in 1891, a British company representative, C. W. Hobley, recorded in his diary that "all around the [Ngomeni] rock the ground was strewn with hundreds of skeletons of oxen which had died from a disease a short time before. . . . Out of all

3. See Ambler, "Central Kenya," pp. 93–94. Dry conditions afflicted much of East Africa. Grove, "Desertification," p. 57; and John Iliffe, *A Modern History of Tanganyika* (Cambridge, 1979), pp. 165–66.
4. Ainsworth to Pigott, 30 June 1894, in IBEAC to F.O., 31 Aug. 1894, FO 2/74. Chanler, *Jungle and Desert*, p. 439; and Hall, letter, 10 June 1894.
5. PRO: Ainsworth to Pigott, Machakos, 30 June 1893, in IBEAC to F.O., 3 Aug. 1893, FO 2/95. Interviews: Maritha w/o Nthereru and Muruachuri Nyaga, Embu.
6. KNA: "History of Fort Hall," DC/FH 6/1. Berntsen, "Maasailand," p. 277; R. Brandt, "Rinderpest or Cattle Plague," *Agricultural Journal of British East Africa* 2 (1909): 705; G. Hartwig and K. David Patterson, "The Disease Factor: An Introductory Overview," in *Disease in African History*, ed. G. Hartwig and K. D. Patterson (Durham, N.C., 1978), p. 10; and Charles Van Onselen, "Reactions to Rinderpest in Southern Africa, 1896–1897," *Journal of African History* 13 (1972): 473–88.
7. Estimates of losses are highly impressionistic. See PRO: memorandum by Ainsworth, 30 Jan. 1899, in Hardinge to F.O., 22 Feb. 1899, FO 2/189. Brandt, "Rinderpest," p. 707; Hobley, *Kenya*, p. 42; Neumann, *Elephant Hunting*, p. 10; and Orde-Browne, *Vanishing Tribes*, pp. 117–18. Interviews: Mutia s/o Mboo, Migwani; Ngira Katere, Mwige Kwigiriira, and Jimuko Ngonjo, Mbeere; Munyoki s/o Mutui, Mwangangi s/o Mathenge, Mumoni. Note also, Iliffe, *History of Tanganyika*, p. 124.

their enormous herds only about 20 or 30 had survived."[8] Rinderpest was most destructive in the areas like Mumoni, where cattle-herding was extensive. In other sections of the region losses varied widely. Even the deaths of a few animals, however, could be disastrous for farmers who owned only small herds.[9]

Rinderpest had a devastating impact throughout the region. The sharp reduction in herds immediately cut an important source of nutrition, as cow's milk and blood became scarce. The consequent lack of protein must have left many children malnourished, particularly those recently weaned.[10] In the long run the loss of cattle also made it more difficult for families to compensate for inadequate harvests, since they would have fewer animals to sell.[11] Perhaps most important, the shortage of animals disrupted the web of social relations in many communities. People valued particular cattle not only as commodities but for the relationships that the animals symbolized. Without cattle, men found it difficult to meet their obligations, especially bridewealth payments.[12] Mbeere traditions convey these strains in stories of "a time when everyone was forced to marry." In very difficult circumstances—associated with the death of cattle—the elders ruled that every male down to the youngest boy had to marry immediately. Bridewealth was suspended and even marriages within clans were sanctioned.[13] Even if it is impossible to determine with objective certainty what actually occurred in Mbeere, the preservation of an account of the violation of the most basic norms of marriage reveals something of the depth of the crisis that Mbeere society faced.

In the decade that followed the rinderpest disaster, persistent dry

8. Hobley, Safari Diary, 19 Nov. 1891.

9. Perham, *Lugard Diaries*, 3:387; Hall, "Kikuyu," p. 151; and Ainsworth, Diary, 3 Aug. 1896. Interview: Mwangangi s/o Mathenge, Mumoni.

10. Iliffe, *History of Tanganyika*, p. 124; and B. Wisner and P. Mbithi, "Drought in Eastern Africa: Nutritional Status and Farmer Activity," in *Natural Hazards: Local, National, Gobal*, ed. Gilbert F. White (New York, 1974), p. 90.

11. Stanner, "Kitui Kamba," p. B-55; and Jackson, "Family and Famine," p. 201. Interviews: Munyasia s/o Kalwe, Migwani; Runji s/o Jigoya and Gachone w/o Mburati, Mbeere; Masila s/o Kivunza, Mumoni.

12. See Waller, "Maasai and British," p. 533. Calvin Martin's provocative analysis of the changing attitudes of North American Indians toward animals, while open to challenge, nevertheless points to the importance of examining phenomena like the rinderpest outbreak in relation to indigenous beliefs and values. *Keepers of the Game: Indian-Animal Relationships and the Fur Trade* (Berkeley and Los Angeles, 1978). For a critical response to Martin's work, see Shepard Krech III, ed., *Indians, Animals and the Fur Trade: A Critique of Keepers of the Game* (Athens, Georgia, 1981).

13. Interviews: Mwige Kwigiriira, Gachone w/o Rukeni; Sarimu Njavari, Konji s/o Ngai, and Kigui s/o Kithaga, Mbeere.

conditions combined with the decline of cattle herds to alter local environments and economies and push migrants in new directions. In some cases brush advanced over former pasturelands, opening the way for the spread of tsetse fly infestation. Elsewhere, fragile ground cover was destroyed as farmers compensated for cattle losses by putting more emphasis on sheep and goat raising.[14] Where the destruction of herds left people entirely impoverished, some families responded by abandoning—at least temporarily—their homesteads and moving into country where rainfall and food supplies were more reliable. The result was increased pressure on local resources in sections of the region that were already densely populated.[15] Elsewhere, people took the opposite tack. Instead of retreating into the hill country, these farming families resettled in sparsely populated frontier communities. In the end this steady movement of people into sections of the region where rainfall was low and unreliable substantially increased the proportion of the region's population that was vulnerable to drought and that depended regularly on external sources of food. Whatever their situations, farmers who had been hurt by rinderpest worked hard to rebuild their herds of cattle. For some this meant increased raiding, but for most it meant greater involvement in commerce. Perhaps the most striking result of the rinderpest outbreak was the growth and redirection of the livestock trade.[16]

Farming communities on the fringes of settlement had to contend not only with their own losses, but also with a dangerous upsurge in violence set off by the destruction of Maasai herds. For the pastoralist peoples who dominated the plains surrounding central Kenya, rinderpest came as a devastating climax to three decades in which a series of livestock diseases reduced Maasai groups from positions of strength to poverty, hunger, and endemic internal conflict. The rinderpest outbreak, coming on the heels of an epidemic of livestock pleuropneumonia, wiped out vast numbers of cattle. With the economic base

14. Mwaniki, *Embu Texts*, p. 201; Neumann, *Elephant Hunting*, p. 31; Orde-Browne, *Vanishing Tribes*, pp. 227–30; and Sir R. Shaw, Kenya Land Commission, *Evidence*, 2: 1392.

15. Pringle, "Railway Survey," p. 120; Hobley, Safari Diaries, 19 and 23 Nov. 1891. The interrelationship between population movement and ecological change is explored in Waller, "Ecology, Migration, and Expansion"; and Jeff Guy, "Ecological Factors in the Rise of Shaka and the Zulu Kingdom," in *Economy and Society in Pre-Industrial South Africa*, ed. Shula Marks and Anthony Atmore (London, 1980), pp. 102–19. Also, see Miller, "Drought, Disease and Famine," p. 22.

16. PRO: Ainsworth to Pigott, 31 Jan. 1894, in IBEAC to F.O., 16 April 1894, FO 2/73.

destroyed, thousands of people died and entire communities disintegrated.[17] In an attempt to recoup livestock losses and preserve their autonomy, warriors stepped up attacks on their cattle-owning neighbors.

This increased raiding was certainly not the product of any coordinated policy; nevertheless, attacks disrupted trade routes within central Kenya, undermined local security, and nourished a siege mentality.[18] Before the 1880s, raids by Maasai groups had occurred sporadically, but warriors generally directed their attacks against the sections of the region, largely in the southwest, that were both rich in cattle and adjacent to Maasai pasturelands.[19] As their herds declined in size, Maasai warriors expanded the scope of their raiding, hitting the areas within central Kenya, such as Migwani, Mbeere, and Mumoni, formerly too distant or insufficiently rich in cattle to have warranted much attention.[20] According to a Mbeere elder,

> *Mwenamo* [rinderpest] killed cattle all over Mbeere. Again and again. After *mwenamo*, then the *Ukavi* [Maasai] came. They came through Gikuyu and killed and raided cattle coming this way. And when they finished, then they came to Mbeere. People shouted the alarm. And when they went to see, they only saw the spears shining brilliantly in the sun.[21]

The effects of this raiding varied considerably across the region. Communities where cattle were few faced little danger of attack; but in the lower-lying areas, families were forced to pay increased attention to defense and some even found it expedient to withdraw to more easily defendable locations.[22] Even if most settlements rarely saw Maasai raiders, the extreme violence of some attacks generated an exaggerated sense of insecurity. In the words of an elder from Migwani, "People came very early to sit in *thome* [the community gathering spot] and always they sat with bows and arrows ready because of the fear of the

17. Waller, "Maasai and British," pp. 530–32; Berntsen, "Maasailand," pp. 276–79 and 283; and Alan Jacobs, "The Traditional Political Organization of the Pastoral Masai" (Ph.D. diss., Oxford University, 1965), pp. 95–99.

18. Gregory, *Rift Valley*, pp. 80–81.

19. Arkell-Hardwick, *Ivory Trader*, p. 338; Hildebrandt, "Travels in East Africa," pp. 451–52; and Berntsen, "Maasailand," p. 281. Interviews: Muthuvi s/o Mui and Muasya s/o Munene, Mumoni; Ruguca Nthimbu, Runji s/o Jigoya, and Gatema Muyovi, Mbeere.

20. Pigott, Diary, 15 May 1889; and Ainsworth, Diary, 1–6 Jan. 1897. Interviews: Muthuvi s/o Mui and Muasya s/o Munene, Mumoni; Ruguca Nthimbu, Mbeere.

21. Interview: Sarimu Njavari, Mbeere.

22. Ambler, "Central Kenya," p. 108. Note F. Jackson, "Journey to Uganda," p. 167; and J. Pigott, "Mr. J. R. W. Pigott's Journey to the Upper Tana, 1889," *Proceedings of the Royal Geographical Society* 12 (1890): 133.

Maasai who attacked us."[23] In fact, the sometimes desperate Maasai raiders did not always respect the local proprieties of warfare: they destroyed houses and property and killed many women and children.[24] C. W. Hobley's diary account from 1891 describes the immediate aftermath of a large-scale Maasai attack on a section of Mbeere:

> The cultivated country on the west of the mountain range . . . presents a sad sight after the ravages of the Masai. The [Maasai warriors] burnt villages in every direction being visible. 4 or 5 decomposing bodies were seen on our line of march, the Mbe [Mbeere] people told us the Masai arrived in Mbe at 7.00 am and swept the country as far as they reached beginning again at 7.00 am the next morning. They killed everyone they caught, old men, women and children. Numbers of children were burnt in the villages.[25]

No raiding strategy—no matter how extensive—could begin to compensate for the losses that Maasai communities had experienced. Some groups managed to preserve their identities through increased trade with neighboring farming people. Others, having lost virtually all of their animals, abandoned their established way of life and became— or were forced to become—clients, pawns, or slaves in agricultural communities.[26] In 1894 several thousand pastoralists attached themselves as clients to the newly established British post at Dagoretti on the southern edge of Gikuyu country.[27]

EXTERNAL TRADE AND THE DEVELOPMENT OF REGIONAL CENTERS

Central Kenya felt the pressures of the decline or disintegration of Maasai communities at a time when many farming societies within the region were also experiencing the impact of a rapid expansion and transformation of external trade. As the continuing high demand for ivory drove traders farther and farther into the interior, Afro-Arab traders from the coast steadily displaced Kitui merchants along the

23. Interview: Munyasia s/o Kalwe, Migwani.
24. E. J. H. Russell, Diaries, 1895–1900, 5 vols., Rhodes House Library, Oxford, Mss. Afr. s. 118–122, entry for 16 April 1896. During this entire period Russell was stationed at Dagoretti, southern Gikuyuland; and Lane, "Report on Kitui," p. 29.
25. Safari Diary, 7 Oct. 1891.
26. For example, Hall, letter, 12 Feb. 1894; PRO: Ainsworth to Hardinge, 20 Jan. 1896 in Hardinge to F.O., 10 March 1896, FO 107/50. KNA: "History of Fort Hall," CP/FH.6/1.
27. PRO: Hall to Pigott, 13 Feb. 1894, in IBEAC to F.O., 16 April 1894, FO 2/73. Lugard, *East African Empire*, 2:535–37.

routes that ran between central Kenya and the coast. Within the region the main sources of tusks for purchase shifted steadily northward, into Meru and northern Gikuyuland. The Mumoni traders who had earlier been among the major players in ivory commerce increasingly obtained their tusks from sources in Meru, rather than through locally organized hunting expeditions. At the same time, the rising costs of obtaining ivory led coast merchants to bypass middlemen and travel as near as possible to the actual sources of supply.[28] By the 1880s, Afro-Arab traders were crossing central Kenya in growing numbers, heading north toward the largely unexploited elephant country that stretched hundreds of miles toward Lake Rudolf.[29] Local men found themselves excluded from their previous roles in long-distance trade.

But the transformation of the ivory trade also opened new kinds of commercial opportunities. Locally based long-distance traders compensated for growing competition in major trade by expanding their activities within the region. At the same time, the small associations of men that typically handled regional trade became more common on the routes to the coast, as a rising demand for livestock there opened a new market to ordinary farmers. Similarly, Afro-Arab traders sometimes spent years away from the coast, moving goods among communities within central Kenya.[30] Much more significant was the fact that the caravans that were crossing the region in growing numbers could not begin to carry with them all of the provisions necessary to maintain porters for many months. For these trading caravans central Kenya was the only area between the coast and the Lake Victoria region where ample supplies could be obtained. As a result, caravan organizers came increasingly to look to the rich farmlands of Gikuyuland, Ulu, and other sections of central Kenya as vital sources of supplies.[31]

Traders traveling into the interior bought up stocks of food as well as livestock that would later be exchanged for ivory. Returning to the coast, they needed additional food to complete the journey, and some-

28. Interviews: Nzila s/o Munyoki, Ngumu s/o Munithya, and Nzilu s/o Siongongo, Mumoni.

29. Van Zwanenberg with King, *Economic History of Kenya and Uganda*, p. 173.

30. PRO: Hall, "Report on Kikuyu," 19 March 1894, in IBEAC to F.O., 11 May 1894, FO 2/74; and several reports by Ainsworth in IBEAC to F.O., 10 April 1895, FO 2/97. Ainsworth, Diary, 10 June and 13 Nov. 1896; Perham, *Lugard Diaries*, 1:260 (2 Sept. 1892); Gregory, *Rift Valley*, p. 350; Munro, *Colonial Rule and the Kamba*, p. 27; and Jackson, "Kamba History," pp. 232–34. Interviews: Thitu s/o Nzili, Ngatu s/o Mauna, Nguuti s/o Ndana, Migwani; and Mulatya s/o Mutia, Mumoni.

31. Gregory, *Rift Valley*, p. 76. Also Van Zwanenberg with King, *Economic History of Kenya and Uganda*, p. 172.

times additional porters to replace those who had died or deserted. For ambitious local men, the chance to profit from an expanding ivory trade lay more and more with providing supplies, trade goods, and workers. The boundary between regional and external commerce steadily blurred, as traders concentrated on meeting an external demand for ordinary foodstuffs and livestock—items that dominated regional exchange, and which were produced on every farm in central Kenya.

The emergence of central Kenya as a supply zone for a rapidly expanding long-distance trade system led, during the last decades of the century, to the development of a series of established collection and distribution centers where passing caravans could obtain provisions. These centers generally grew up around the homesteads of the local hosts and middlemen who handled the supply trade for the alien merchants who increasingly controlled the most profitable segments of long-distance commerce.[32] Acting as translators and intermediaries, brokers arranged for the purchase of trade goods, supplies of food, and labor services. In return, brokers gained preferential access to imported goods and monopolies over local dealings with visiting caravans. Coastal traders often returned repeatedly to the same broker's settlement, building a personal relationship that was often cemented with the rituals of blood partnership.[33]

Brokers established their provisioning stations at places where established trade routes entered or ran close to densely settled areas. The settlements of Sila wa Ivuli and Ngulu wa Siviri in Migwani were located on the edge of the dry Yatta Plain, close to the path that ran through Kitui toward northern Gikuyuland and Mount Kenya. Likewise, Kilungya wa Mutia's village in northern Mumoni was situated on the Meru route, the last outpost before the hard trek across the Tana River to the Nyambeni Range. As the impromptu trade fairs held at the homesteads of these and other brokers became increasingly common-

32. This statement is based on evidence drawn from a wide range of sources, a partial listing of which may be found in Ambler, "Central Kenya," pp. 283–85. A similar argument is made for the Meru area in Frank E. Bernard, "Meru District in the Kenyan Spatial Economy, 1890–1950," in *The Spatial Structure of Development: A Study of Kenya*, ed. R. A. Obudho and D. R. F. Taylor (Boulder, Col., 1979), pp. 266–67.

33. PRO: Ainsworth to Hardinge, 10 Jan. 1896, in Hardinge to F.O., 12 April 1896, FO 107/51. Jumea bin Makame, Kenya Land Commission, *Evidence*, 1:945. Interviews: Mulango s/o Ngusia, Mutia s/o Mboo, Ngatu s/o Mauna, Komba w/o Nzoka, Nguuti s/o Ndana, and Mbasia s/o Muliungi, Migwani; Nzila s/o Munyoki, Mumoni; and Alan Kageta, Embu.

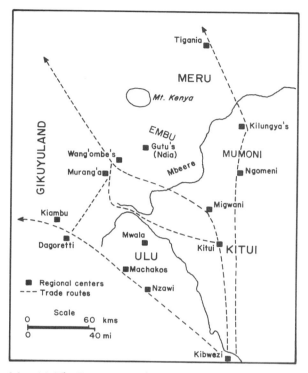

Map 11. The Emergence of Regional Centers

place, the settlements of such men grew into hubs of local trade.[34] By the 1880s many localities in Gikuyuland, Ulu, and Kitui regularly provided supplies to caravans.[35] In a few cases these villages, or groups of villages, became the centers of wide-ranging trade networks.

During the late nineteenth century, as Mumoni developed into an important staging point in ivory commerce, local men also made the area the center of regional trades in natron and especially livestock. Because local traders resolutely refused to give up stocks of ivory except in return for cattle, a series of complicated trading arrangements developed to bring livestock into Mumoni from distant parts of the region. Imported trade goods were used to obtain sheep or goats in Ulu, which

34. PRO: Ainsworth, "Report on 'Kitwyi'," 6 Feb. 1895, in IBEAC to F.O. 10 April 1895, FO 2/97. Chanler, *Jungle and Desert*, pp. 56–59; and Neumann, *Elephant Hunting*, p. 27. Interviews: Rose Makaa w/o Mutia and Muli s/o Ndulwa, Migwani; Muli s/o Kakuru and Muthuvi s/o Mui, Mumoni; see also the testimonies of informants listed in the previous note.

35. Von Höhnel, *Lakes Rudolf and Stefanie*, 1:286–90, 2:310.

in turn were exchanged in southern Gikuyuland for rights over dependent women. These rights could then be resold in Ulu again or Kitui for cattle, which were ultimately traded in Mumoni for ivory or other livestock.[36] While Mumoni experienced rapid and substantial change as a consequence of the expansion of external trade, many parts of the region remained essentially unaffected. Some areas of Mbeere, for instance, were drawn into trade networks emanating from regional centers in Mumoni or in eastern Gikuyuland, but most of Mbeere, like most of the Mount Kenya societies, had little involvement in major trade. Even in sections of the region that were heavily involved in long-distance trade, many of the communities that were relatively distant from trade routes and trade centers remained isolated from the impact of commercial growth.[37]

By the 1890s a few of the broker settlements began to show signs of the more complex division of labor that marks the emergence of commercial centers.[38] On the northeastern margins of the Gikuyu highlands, the broker and warlord Wang'ombe parlayed a strategic site and a talent for leadership into a position of wealth far overshadowing that of the big men of Migwani.[39] Located astride the major route into northern Kenya, Wang'ombe's village commanded access both to pasturelands and to rich agricultural communities. The village also served as a base for bands of hunters who brought in ivory from the open plateau to the north. Wang'ombe protected his position with an armed force of Maasai client-warriors. In central Kitui, the region's longest established trading center, various settlements, families, and individuals specialized in particular activities related to commerce: long- or short-distance trade, brokerage, porterage, and various kinds of artisanry. In addition, many families undoubtedly produced foodstuffs

---

36. Krapf, Journal, 28 Nov. 1849; and Pigott, Diary, 17 May 1889. PRO: Ainsworth to Pigott, 20 Feb. 1895, in IBEAC to F.O., 10 April 1895, FO 2/97. Interviews: Nguli s/o Kinuva, Migwani; Muli s/o Sumbi and Kalundu s/o Ndai, Mumoni.

37. PRO: Lane, P.C., 14 Nov. 1907, CO 533/33, no. 507. Peters, *New Light on Africa*, p. 182; Boyes, *King of Kikuyu*, p. 151; and Bernard, "Meru in the Kenyan Spatial Economy," pp. 266–67. Interviews: Muthuvi s/o Mui, Kavindu s/o Ikunga, Muvali s/o Kilanga, and Kisalu s/o Kilatya, Mumoni; Muthura s/o Nthiga, Tharaka.

38. In the language of spatial theory, "central places." See Allen Howard, "The Relevance of Spatial Analysis for African Economic History: The Sierra Leone-Guinea System," *Journal of African History* 17 (1976): 373–76.

39. For Wang'ombe's career see Boyes, *King of the Kikuyu*, pp. 22, 32, 39, 165; Jomo Kenyatta, *My People of Kikuyu and the Life of Chief Wangombe* (Nairobi, 1966 [1942]), pp. 27–29; Mackinder, Diary, 28 Aug. 1899; Chief Njega wa Gioko, Kenya Land Commission, *Evidence*, 1:252; and Muriuki, *History of Kikuyu*, pp. 89–90, 159–60. PRO: Jackson to Ainsworth, 8 Aug. 1899, in Crauford to F.O., 18 Sept. 1899, FO 2/197.

and livestock for the caravan market. During the 1880s and 1890s the leading broker in Kitui, Simba wa Mutyauvyu, managed to acquire substantial political influence in the area.[40]

The growth of such personal political power was the critical element in the development of regional centers during the last decades of the nineteenth century. Men like Simba, Wang'ombe, and Ngulu wa Siviri from Migwani used their positions in a rapidly changing commercial system to make their influence felt in surrounding settlements.[41] While principles of self-sufficiency continued to rule household economies, trade increasingly governed the distribution of power in many localities. Thus, even if a Migwani household satisfied most of its own needs within the immediate neighborhood, family members nevertheless felt the growing political weight of Ngulu or Sila wa Ivuli, local leaders who derived their own wealth and position from their roles as brokers and traders in long-distance and regional commerce.[42]

THE PENETRATION OF BRITISH CAPITAL AND POWER

The most conspicuous of the regional centers in the 1890s were those that developed at Machakos and Dagoretti as a consequence of the expansion of British power into the Kenya interior. Beginning in the 1880s, a small number of Europeans competed with Afro-Arab merchants for the profits of the ivory trade; but this initial entry of whites into the commerce of the interior made little real impact. To the peoples of central Kenya the actions of these newcomers were scarcely distinguishable from those of other alien traders based on the Indian Ocean coast. After 1890, however, the rapid penetration of European economic and political power substantially altered the patterns of exchange and the concentrations of wealth and influence within the region. In an agreement reached in 1886, the major European nations

40. PRO: Ainsworth, "Report on 'Kitwyi,'" and Ainsworth to Pigott, 20 Feb. 1895, in IBEAC to F.O., 10 April 1895, FO 2/97; and Ainsworth to Hardinge, 10 Jan. 1896, in Hardinge to F.O., 12 April 1896, FO 107/51. Hildebrandt, "Travels in East Africa," p. 451; and Munro, *Colonial Rule and the Kamba*, p. 26. Interview: Hussein Juma, Kitui Town. F. Bernard describes similar developments in Meru in "Meru in the Kenyan Spatial Economy," p. 268.

41. Allen Howard discusses the importance of political power in the development of central places in "Relevance of Spatial Analysis," p. 373.

42. Interviews: Muli s/o Ndulwa and Nguuti s/o Ndana, Migwani. J. L. Krapf noted the political importance of major traders in Kitui around 1850. *Travels, Researches and Missionary Labours*, p. 355.

recognized a British sphere of influence in the northern sections of East Africa. Two years later, a still cautious British government granted a charter to the Imperial British East Africa Company (IBEAC) to manage and exploit the vast territory that would ultimately become Uganda and Kenya. For the IBEAC, as for its Afro-Arab competitors, the societies of central Kenya held relatively little interest. In the company's view, the prize was Buganda and all of its imagined wealth and possibilities. But to secure that prize the IBEAC had first to guarantee safe and efficient passage from Mombasa, on the Indian Ocean Coast, to Lake Victoria.

After 1889, IBEAC officials set up a series of permanent stations along the main caravan track from the coast into the interior, with the two most important located along the section of the route that traversed the southern margins of the central Kenya region: at Machakos in southwestern Ulu, and forty miles farther west at Dagoretti on the southern fringe of Gikuyuland. Initially, both were little more than small, well-fortified trading posts, isolated from surrounding settlements. Indeed, local opposition forced the British to withdraw from Dagoretti for a time, and neighboring communities periodically refused to provide supplies of food to the station.[43] In 1892 the Machakos fort had a "six-foot ditch guarded with barbed wire all round. Inside the four sides are houses and stores all round. . . . The garrison consists of about 50 men who are used as police, dispatch runners or porters as occasion requires."[44] From these small posts, and with these few men, the company hoped to regulate and protect travelers and provide caravans with the large quantities of supplies needed for the journey west across the Rift Valley or east toward the coast. Both of the stations were close to rich farming and grazing country, and both were located in areas that were already deeply involved in long-distance trade. In fact, the British called their station Machakos after the broker Masaku, who had dominated trade in the area during the 1880s.[45]

The IBEAC policy of establishing its supremacy along the main

43. Hall, letter, 28 May 1893. For convenience, Dagoretti is used here, although the station was known by different names and during the 1890s was moved to a new location a short distance from the old.
44. Hall, letter, Machakos, 10 Oct. 1892.
45. Wolff, *Economics of Colonialism*, p. 48; von Höhnel, *Lakes Rudolf and Stephanie*, 1:286; and Munro, *Colonial Rule and the Kamba*, p. 101. PRO: Ainsworth to Pigott, Machakos, 30 June 1893, in IBEAC to F.O., 31 Aug. 1893, FO 2/59.

caravan route was intended not only to provide security for company traffic, but also to guarantee an IBEAC monopoly over the most profitable kinds of trade, notably in ivory. Consequently, the 1890s were years of growing and bitter competition between Afro-Arab merchants and the British. British regulation and harassment pushed coastal traders to develop commerce in other sections of the region and become more involved in commodities other than ivory, thus encouraging the existing trend toward broader local involvement in external exchange.[46]

The initial entry of British capital into the East African interior was a conspicuous failure. Lacking adequate financial resources and being poorly managed from the start, the IBEAC was incapable of coping with what were, in any case, virtually insurmountable economic and political obstacles to success.[47] In 1893 the company abandoned its tenuous position in Uganda; as the IBEAC slid further into bankruptcy, the British formally declared their hegemony over Uganda in 1894, and what would ultimately become Kenya in 1895. In central Kenya, as throughout the newly designated Uganda and East African Protectorates, this transition passed virtually unnoticed. Until the end of the 1890s, former company men—John Ainsworth at Machakos and Francis Hall at Dagoretti—continued to direct British affairs in central Kenya. Moreover, the British remained preoccupied with the problem of securing control over Uganda and thus saw their presence in central Kenya almost exclusively in terms of ensuring free and efficient movement of traffic through the region—and not in terms of the assertion of territorial control.

British officials acquired influence essentially as the by-product of the development of the Machakos and Dagoretti stations as centers of supply and commerce.[48] They planned raiding expeditions against areas where attacks had interrupted trade, and the fines or tribute payments they imposed on recalcitrant communities were demanded in the

46. Wolff, *Economics of Colonialism*, pp. 36–45; F. Jackson, *Early Days*, pp. 182–83; D. A. Low, "British East Africa: The Establishment of British Rule, 1895–1912," in *History of East Africa*, vol. 2, ed. V. Harlow and E. M. Chilver (Oxford, 1965), p. 10; Munro, *Colonial Rule and the Kamba*, pp. 31–37; Orde-Browne, *Vanishing Tribes*, p. 232; Lane, "Report on Kitui," p. 29; Chanler, *Jungle and Desert*, pp. 402, 461; Hobley, Safari Diary, 3 Sept. 1891.

47. Marie de Kieweit Hemphill summarized her research into the history of the IBEAC. in "The British Sphere, 1884–94," in *History of East Africa*, vol. 2., ed. R. Oliver and G. Mathew (Oxford, 1963), pp. 391–432.

48. The most complete record of the development of the British stations is found in F. Hall's correspondence and J. Ainsworth's diaries.

form of food supplies.[49] In yet other localities, the British rewarded cooperative elders with payments and military assistance. Throughout the 1890s, the British Foreign Office resisted most attempts by its agents in Kenya to expand their hegemony beyond Machakos and Dagoretti. Hall, in particular, would have liked to demonstrate British power more forcefully, but he was restrained by the precariousness of his position in southern Gikuyuland: "There is only one way of improving the Wakikuyu, & that is to wipe them out; I should be only too delighted to do so, but we have to depend on them for food supplies."[50] Indeed, officials spent a great portion of their time arranging for the purchase of food and livestock and the hiring of labor to supply caravans and eventually railway construction camps. Only in 1900, with the establishment of a station at Murang'a in northern Gikuyuland, did the direction of British policy shift toward the assertion of direct control over the Kenya interior. Even then, officials still felt obligated to argue a need for new food collection centers.[51]

Despite Foreign Office reluctance to extend imperial authority, by the mid-1890s extensive networks of trade and patronage spread in every direction from each of the British stations, drawing surrounding communities within the commercial and political spheres of these British-controlled centers.[52] Officials expanded their influence through a combination of force and diplomacy, building a series of alliances with local notables. By the late 1890s the British at Machakos had managed to assert some degree of authority over most of Ulu and had begun to extend their reach into Kitui. A meeting of elders called by John Ainsworth in 1897, for example, easily drew some eight hundred men to the Machakos station.[53] The expansion from Dagoretti followed a similar course, although British influence spread more slowly there.[54] During the 1890s the European presence also numbered an occasional independent trader and some missionaries, including German Luther-

49. Hall, letters, 2 April 1893, 30 May 1893, and 14 Jan. 1894.

50. Hall, letter, 5 July 1894.

51. G. H. Mungeam, *British Rule in Kenya, 1895–1919: The Establishment of Administration in the East African Protectorate* (Oxford, 1966), p. 43.

52. For a thorough description of the gradual expansion of British influence and authority from Machakos during the 1890s see Munro, *Colonial Rule and the Kamba*, chap. 3.

53. Ainsworth, Diary, 10 April 1897, and see also entries for 15 Feb. 1895 and for Aug. and Sept. 1896. Also, Great Britain, Parliamentary Papers, "Report by John Ainsworth on the Progress of the Ukamba Province, Feb. 1905," in "Reports Relating to the Administration of the East African Protectorate," Oct. 1905, London, 1906 (Cd 2740). Perham, *Lugard Diaries*, 1:158 (24 March 1890).

54. Hall, letter, 4 Nov. 1896. Also Muriuki, *History of the Kikuyu*, p. 155.

ans in Kitui and American Baptists in Ulu. Their stations in Ulu and Kitui became local centers of supply and patronage, but otherwise they made little impact on surrounding communities.[55] After three years' residence in southern Ulu, one departing missionary wrote, "It is so hard for us to know that we have been here so long and yet they do not know why we have come to their country."[56]

The amount of traffic moving into the interior increased rapidly during the 1890s, and with it the demand for supplies of food and labor.[57] Like the IBEAC, the British government rapidly concluded that a railroad was the key to establishing an inexpensive and secure communications and supply link between the coast and Uganda. Unlike the IBEAC, the British state had the resources to undertake such a project. Construction began in 1895; by 1898, trains reached as far as central Kenya, following a route that skirted the southern edge of the region. The steady progress of the rail line vastly expanded the demand for foodstuffs and labor and substantially increased the volume of movement into the interior. In particular, thousands of unskilled workers imported from India had to be fed and otherwise provided for.

During the 1890s officials at Dagoretti and Machakos were able to buy steadily increasing amounts of supplies from surrounding communities. The numbers of Europeans in central Kenya remained small, but the British presence in Kenya and Uganda generated a steady expansion in the number of African workers—most of whom were from outside central Kenya—who in various capacities traveled through the region or were stationed there. In January of 1895, for instance, more than one thousand porters were staying at Dagoretti, all of whom had to be provided for.[58] Hall complained in 1892 about the work involved in obtaining 20 tons of food within several days, yet still managed to find all he needed within fifteen miles of the station. Soon such demands became commonplace. By 1894, in addition to serving the Uganda caravans, the station was providing 5,000 pounds of grain each month just to maintain the route between Dagoretti and the coast. Two years later that amount had risen to 33,000 pounds, as railway

55. PRO: J. Hofman [missionary in Kitui] to Ainsworth, Ikutha, 27 July 1897, in Hardinge to F.O., 30 Oct. 1897, FO 107/81. Ainsworth, Diary, 7 Dec. 1895; Perham, *Lugard Diaries*, 3:392–93 (18–19 Aug. 1892); Boyes, *King of Kikuyu*, p. 77; Chanler, *Jungle and Desert*, pp. 487, 493; Neumann, *Elephant Hunting*, p. 143; and *Hearing and Doing* (April 1896), supplement, p. 11.

56. Mrs. Thomas Allen, Kilungu (southern Ulu), 19 March 1898, *Hearing and Doing* (6 June 1898), p. 6.

57. Mungeam, *British Rule*, p. 19.

58. Russell, Diary, 9 Jan. 1895.

construction moved forward. Still, in addition to these regular requirements, officials bought 112,000 pounds of food in a sixteen-day period of 1897 and supplied the upsurge in caravan traffic in the aftermath of the mutiny of forces in Uganda. Even at Machakos officials managed to obtain some 400,000 pounds of food annually from the relatively less productive countryside surrounding that station.[59]

The British found it easier to acquire food supplies than to attract laborers; nevertheless, by the end of the decade substantial numbers of men from central Kenya were going out to work for wages. As early as 1894 the British were able to attract more than a hundred local women to the Dagoretti station to grind maize. During 1896 between fifty and one hundred laborers were hired each week at Machakos, primarily as porters or for work at railway construction sites. In Ulu, at least, this steady movement of men out of their communities undermined existing patterns of labor mobilization, replacing the patronage of local brokers with that of the British and their agents.[60]

The rising trade in food and labor at Machakos and Dagoretti— reproduced on a smaller scale at broker centers across the region— generated commercial networks that rapidly expanded into other commodities and beyond the control of station officials. According to Hall, many of his former police and other employees had "blossomed out into traders, & though they stick to the old District, they are not in my garrison."[61] At the same time, traders ranged out from Machakos into the outlying country; and men and women from communities as far away as Gikuyuland, Kitui, and Mwala in eastern Ulu brought their produce to the station area for sale.[62] The evidence of shifting commercial patterns was apparent in the growing use of imported goods in the Machakos and Dagoretti hinterlands. John Ainsworth recalled that when he first arrived at Machakos "nearly all the natives" wore goatskins, but by 1895 an estimated half of the residents of Ulu and Kitui

59. PRO: Ainsworth Report to Pigott, Machakos, 30 June 1893, in IBEAC to F.O., 3 Aug. 1893, FO 2/95. Hall, letters, 22 Oct. 1892, 5 July 1894, 8 Oct. 1896, and 28 Feb. 1898; and Report by a correspondent from Kikuyu, 19 Dec. 1892, *The Times* [London], 3 March 1893. For a thorough discussion of the importance of the supply trade at Dagoretti, see Rogers, "The British and the Kikuyu," esp. p. 262.

60. Hall, letters, 12 May 1894, also 10 Sept. 1896; Ainsworth, Diary, 30 April 1896, 6–9 Dec. 1896, and 15 Feb. 1898; Herbert H. Austin, *With MacDonald in Uganda* (London, 1973 [1903]), p. 253; A. Clayton and D. C. Savage, *Government and Labour in Kenya* (London, 1974), pp. 13–15. Also Robert J. Cummings, "Aspects of Human Porterage," chaps. 3–5.

61. Hall, letter, 1 April 1899.

62. Ainsworth, Diary, 18 and 28 Sept. 1896, 12 Jan. 1898, 29 March 1898.

were wearing some imported cloth. Before the end of the 1890s, large numbers of men in southern Gikuyuland had also adopted cloth dress, and people living in the country surrounding both stations were said to be making regular use of coin currency.[63]

As the British spheres of influence expanded, the Machakos and Dagoretti posts evolved into active market centers. In 1896 the firm of Smith Mackenzie and Company opened stores near the British stations, and within two years a number of Indian merchants were also well established.[64] In 1897, a visitor reported that one could buy "anything, from a darning needle to a saddle" at the shops and bazaar in Dagoretti. Basic food supplies were also readily available from local people, "who crowded around our camp in hundreds all day during our stay."[65] The small permanent settlements that grew up adjacent to the stations were central Kenya's first towns, and the signs of occupational specialization that marked the villages of major brokers were even more evident in Dagoretti and Machakos. Although many of the residents of these towns did some farming, they were primarily merchants, petty traders, craftsmen, and laborers. They were also almost exclusively outsiders, including Indians, Europeans, coastal people, Ugandans, and a few local converts to Islam. The fledgling towns that grew up at Machakos and Dagoretti were clearly set apart by their cultural diversity and isolation. Even those few people from Ulu who settled down in Machakos during the 1890s largely cut their ties with their home areas and became what officials would later call detribalized natives—members of an Islamic, Swahili-speaking community.[66]

The gradual settlement of large numbers of pastoralist refugees near the Dagoretti station very much complicated relations between that station and nearby farming communities. In late 1893, as growing numbers of Maasai families congregated in the area, British officials were gradually drawn into the conflicts among various herder groups and local farmers.[67] Early in 1894, Francis Hall offered direct protection to a group of destitute pastoralists, arguing that if he did not act they would be forced into slavery. This original group swelled rapidly

63. Ainsworth, "Description of the Ukamba Province, 1905," p. 189; and Austin, *MacDonald in Uganda*, p. 273.

64. Ainsworth, "Report on Ukamba," p. 189.

65. Austin, *MacDonald in Uganda*, pp. 24–25.

66. Ainsworth, Diary, 15 May 1896. PRO: Hardinge to F.O., 18 March 1899, FO 2/190; D. C. Brumage, Kenya Land Commission, *Evidence*, 2: 1328. Interviews: Hussein Juma, Zura w/o Muhammad, and anonymous male elder, Kitui Town.

67. Waller, "Maasai and the British," pp. 536–38, 544–55.

into a huge camp of several thousand people, dependent on station patronage and increasingly in conflict with nearby farming communities.

British officials saw this tension as the inevitable consequence of entrenched tribal animosities; but the leaders of the farming communities had in fact initially made no objection to the Maasai settlement, presumably seeing the refugees as a labor resource.[68] After all, a long history of intermarriage, migration, and trade in the area around the Dagoretti station had built up a dense network of kinship and commercial ties among the various local hunting, farming, and herding societies, and many of the elders of Gikuyu-speaking farming communities could themselves claim some Maasai ancestry.[69] Local agricultural settlements had in any case already absorbed large numbers of Maasai refugees. Nevertheless, to the leaders of the farming communities the creation of a large refugee settlement adjacent to their communities yet beyond their control represented an intolerable threat.

Once established at Dagoretti, Maasai warriors were soon regularly taking part in British raids into Gikuyuland. With relatively few soldiers at their disposal, British officials increasingly relied on Maasai forces in their military actions in central Kenya.[70] This use of mercenaries generated precisely the kind of generalized ethnic antipathy that the British assumed was the product of ancient tribal antagonism. Farmers in central Kenya gradually came to view pastoralist society in monolithic terms, as the violent and aggressive agent of alien power. Not surprisingly, oral accounts of nineteenth-century relations between farming and herding communities came increasingly to reflect this growing hostility.[71] In fact, the Dagoretti and Machakos stations were themselves microcosms of future ethnicity. In these small colonies, officials carefully separated the various groups who competed for patronage under British hegemony. By 1894 Francis Hall in Dagoretti already feared the violent potential of a situation that he had helped engineer: "For what with Swahilis, Nubians, Masai, & Wakikuyu, all of whom

68. Hall, letters, 12 Feb. 1894 and 5 July 1894.

69. See the testimony in Kenya Land Commission, *Evidence*, 1:266–67, and Ainsworth's written submission in the same volume on p. 495.

70. Waller, "Maasai and the British," pp. 535–36.

71. Hall, letter, 5 July 1894. Russell, Diary, 14 April 1896. PRO: Hardinge to F.O., 1 Aug. 1898, FO 107/95. Interviews: Kabogo s/o Gacigua, Embu; Mulango s/o Ngusia, Migwani. In 1911 British officials in Kitui reported a rumor that an alliance of the British, Gikuyu, and Maasai (the latter two by that time conceived of as discrete and cohesive tribes) would soon attack and destroy Kitui communities. KNA: Kitui District, Annual Report, 1911, DC/KTI/1/1/1.

cordially hate each other, it takes me all my time to prevent a grand hurroosh."[72]

The British-organized raids on farming communities only intensified the violence and disorder that accompanied the expansion of international trade across central Kenya. During the 1880s and 1890s alien travelers often relied on guns rather than persuasion to press their objectives in a region where firearms were largely unknown. Caravans of European and Afro-Arab merchants and adventurers regularly used force to obtain supplies. The accounts of travelers are filled with tales of men killed, hostages taken, livestock stolen, and foodstuffs seized in areas where residents were reluctant to trade or had the temerity to demand higher prices. Like British officials, these visitors intervened in local politics—with or without the consent of local allies.[73] In one extreme case, the British freebooter John Boyes set himself up in central Gikuyuland as a warlord, attracting a variety of local clients to his compound.[74] Boyes and his European contemporaries—both official and unofficial—imagined that their actions had a stabilizing effect; the actual result was precisely the opposite. As commercial competition intensified and aliens increasingly resorted to force, local people retaliated by attacking caravans and resisting imposed trade terms.[75]

The rapid shifts in long-distance trade and the collapse of pastoralist economies also created opportunities for ambitious local men to acquire considerable personal power. In an uncertain and often dangerous time, these new leaders could offer relative physical security and economic possibilities to their followers. The most powerful of these men became small-scale warlords, acquiring substantial military forces, as they raided widely for cattle and other booty. The Gikuyuland broker Wang'ombe (described earlier) not only built a large local power base, but attracted groups of client hunters, acquired numbers of refugee women, and made effective use of contingents of Maasai warriors.[76]

72. Hall, letter, 15 April 1894.

73. Hobley, Safari Diary, 8 Oct. 1891; Ainsworth, Diary, 14 June 1897; Peters, *New Light on Africa*, p. 182; Chanler, *Jungle and Desert*, p. 431; von Höhnel, *Lakes Rudolf and Stefanie*, 1:342–43; and Gregory, *Rift Valley*, 158.

74. Boyes, *King of Kikuyu*; Muriuki, *History of Kikuyu*, pp. 157–61; and F. Hall, Evidence Collected Against John Boyes, Nov. 1900, Hall Papers, vol. 3.

75. Hall, letter, 14 Jan. 1894; Ainsworth, Diary, 21 July 1897; Chanler, *Jungle and Desert*, pp. 198–200; von Höhnel, *Lakes Rudolf and Stefanie*, 1:342–43.

76. PRO: Jackson to Ainsworth, 8 Aug. 1899, in Crauford to F.O., FO 2/197. Mackinder, Diary, 28 Aug. 1899; and Ngatunyi Wanjohi, Kenya Land Commission, *Evidence*, 1:254.

The most prominent of all these warlords and brokers was Mwatu wa Ngoma, from Mwala in eastern Ulu. Alone among the leaders of nineteenth-century central Kenya, he developed a reputation that encompassed the entire region.[77] As a young man, Mwatu had left the densely populated Ulu hills to settle just to the east in the open country of Mwala, attracted by the area's ample grazing land and strategic location for raiding and trade. There, he gradually built up large herds of livestock, which he drew on to contract numerous marriages and attract clients. During the 1880s he became the wealthiest and most powerful man in the area.

In the decade that followed, Mwatu developed close tributary ties to the new trade center at Machakos, including resident British officials. Using this connection, as well as his contacts with the coastal traders who often passed through or near Mwala, he rapidly expanded his influence and military strength. With forces augmented by Maasai client warriors and strengthened by a few—essentially symbolic— firearms, he increased his raiding, striking in every direction at settled communities and commercial traffic. As he acquired more and more cattle, he further enlarged his immediate following and extended his influence over a wider circle of lineage villages. By the mid 1890s, if not before, Mwatu had in effect made himself the head of a small, predatory state in Mwala.[78] His rise put into relief the destructive impact on local societies of the growth and transformation of international trade during the late nineteenth century. But because these developments came relatively late to central Kenya, the residents of the region escaped the extended period of predatory violence that so disrupted societies elsewhere in East Africa during the same period.[79]

77. Tate, "Kikuyu and Kamba Tribes," p. 136; Lambert, "Institutions of the Kikuyu," p. 255. Interviews: Ngatu s/o Mauna and Ngavi s/o Mwanzi, Migwani; Njiru s/o Ngonjo and Abedinego Kagundu Njangaruko, Mbeere.

78. For Mwatu's career, see PRO: Ainsworth, General Report for the Month ending 28 Feb. 1894, Machakos, and Ainsworth to Pigott, 16 March 1894, in IBEAC to F.O., 11 May 1894, FO 2/74; Ainsworth, General Report for Jan. 1895, Machakos, in IBEAC to F.O., 10 April 1895, FO 2/97; Report on the East African Protectorate, April 1903, in Eliot to F.O., 18 April 1903, FO 2/712. Note the many references to Mwatu in Ainsworth's Diary, notably 11 Nov. 1895 and 29 March 1898. Munro, *Colonial Rule and the Kamba*, p. 42; and Decle, *Three Years in Africa*, p. 488. Interviews: Ngavi s/o Mwanzi, Komba w/o Nzoka, and Nguuti s/o Ndana, Migwani. According to oral traditions, Mwatu had more than twenty-five wives, Cummings, "Akamba Local Trade History," p. 109n45. Mwatu was made a colonial chief, but he never came entirely under British control. With the rapid expansion of British power during 1900, Mwatu's position declined; he died in 1901. Ainsworth, Diary, 18 Jan. and 4 Feb. 1899. Munro, *Colonial Rule and the Kamba*, pp. 42, 58–59.

79. See Iliffe, *History of Tanganyika*, pp. 52–66. During the late nineteenth century few central Kenyans possessed firearms.

TOWARD FAMINE

In an atmosphere of growing violence and political instability, farming families in many sections of central Kenya showed a remarkable capacity to meet external demand for supplies and trade commodities.[80] The rapid expansion of caravan traffic stimulated a substantial production of foodstuffs and livestock for sale not only in the official and unofficial markets of Machakos and Dagoretti, but in various other regional centers as well. While the development of the supply trade beyond the British spheres of influence is not well documented, it is evident that the new brokers of long-distance commerce—men like Sila wa Ivuli and Ngulu wa Siviri in Migwani—owed their positions in large part to their success in obtaining provisions for visiting caravans.[81] The existence of well-established supply centers is clear from various travelers' accounts. Visitors making their way through the region were often surprised to find areas in which people were indifferent to trade adjacent to communities that were prepared to provide foodstuffs in large quantities on short notice and that apparently did so frequently. On the dry eastern fringes of Meru, for example, settlements regularly supplied caravans traveling to the north of Mount Kenya. But given that area of Meru's limited agricultural resources, much of the food that local traders sold was actually produced in the neighboring Nyambeni highlands.

Little is known about the organization of the supply trade. Even for the areas immediately surrounding the British stations, it is impossible to estimate the scale of food sales for the external market and difficult to assess their impact on domestic economies. It can be said that during a decade marked by drought and cattle disease, the development of commercial agriculture clearly left the region as a whole more vulnerable to natural disaster.[82]

80. For discussion of the same phenomenon in Uganda, see John Tosh, "Lango Agriculture During the Early Colonial Period: Land and Labour in a Cash-Crop Economy," *Journal of African History* 19 (1978): 423.

81. PRO: Ainsworth, "Report on 'Kitwyi,'" 6 Feb. 1895, in IBEAC to F.O., 10 April 1895, FO 2/97. Chanler, *Jungle and Desert*, pp. 56–59; and Neumann, *Elephant Hunting*, p. 27. Interviews with numerous Migwani informants, including Mulango s/o Ngusia, Rose Makaa w/o Mutia, Nguuti s/o Ndana, Muli s/o Ndulwa, and Nguli s/o Kinuva. The means by which such men accumulated wealth and influence and maintained and wielded power is considered in the final section of chap. 1, above.

82. Von Höhnel, *Lakes Rudolf and Stefanie*, 2:310–12; and Chanler, *Jungle and Desert*, p. 218. Michael Lofchie has investigated the political and economic sources of famine for the recent past in "Political and Economic Origins of African Hunger," *Journal of Modern African Studies* 13 (1975): 551–67.

In order to take advantage of the growing external market, many farmers expanded production, especially in the country near the British stations. A missionary who first visited Dagoretti in 1895 noted that when he next returned in 1898, "I found the country very much changed." In the three-year interim, a great deal of forest had been cleared, and cultivation and settlement had expanded substantially.[83] With the growth of alien traffic through the region, a consistent and seemingly insatiable demand for farm products replaced the previous sporadic demand for surplus. In these circumstances it made sense for farming households to expand their output, but it is by no means clear how families achieved this. There is no evidence, for example, that farmers adopted new tools, such as hoes, to any appreciable extent; but some farmers did expand cultivation of new crops, notably maize. Maize, however, remained a minor crop, despite the fact that—in some areas—it promised relatively higher yields and demanded less attention than traditional grains.[84]

In most cases households probably increased surplus simply by increasing labor. The apparent underutilization of land and labor resources in nineteenth-century Kenya meant that communities had the capacity to expand production substantially when demand for agricultural products developed. Farmers who wanted to take advantage of new commercial possibilities either pushed their wives, daughters, or other female dependents to do more work, or drew more women— and hence more workers—into their households. Males could have taken on much of the labor involved in market production, as would later occur, but this did not happen.[85]

During the 1890s, the rapid development of new markets for agricultural produce converged with the flood of female refugees sent into farming communities, especially in southern Gikuyuland, by the collapse of surrounding pastoralist economies. Their new guardians came

83. John Patterson, Kenya Land Commission, *Evidence*, 1:745.

84. On the infrequent use of hoes, see PRO: Agricultural Report by Mr. Linton on the Kenya District, 12 June 1904, in Stewart to F.O., 1 Sept. 1904, FO 2/839. Also, Lindblom, *Akamba*, p. 278; and Hobley, *Ethnology of Akamba*, p. 20. It was claimed that women resisted the adoption of metal hoes. Orde-Browne, *Vanishing Tribes*, p. 76; and Dundas, "Laws of Bantu Tribes," p. 303. On the spread of maize see Miracle, *Maize in Africa*, pp. 93–100, 209–15; and Bernard, *East of Mount Kenya*, p. 41. By this time maize was much more widespread along the Kenya coast and inland as far as Taita. E. Hollis Merritt, "A Brief History of the Taita of Kenya to 1900" (Ph.D. diss., Indiana University, 1975), pp. 128–29.

85. Like many contemporary European observers, Francis Hall believed women in central Kenya were overworked. "Kikuyu," p. 158. However, Gavin Kitching has argued convincingly that both male and female labor was underutilized. *Class and Economic Change in Kenya: The Making of an African Petite Bourgeoisie, 1905–1970* (New Haven, 1980), pp. 14–16. Supporting evidence is found in Routledge, *The Agikuyu*, p. 123.

increasingly to see recently arrived dependent women as commodities for which there was demand in other parts of the region.[86] Many of the women were sold as slaves. Trading parties led by local and coastal men regularly moved between southern Gikuyuland and Ulu or Kitui, taking with them not only various goods but women as well. In some cases, raids were organized to seize captives who could later be sold.[87] A visitor to central Kitui in the early 1890s was told that

> this place was a slave-trading centre, and that caravans which had been trading in Kikuyu, and had acquired slaves, sold them here for goats and cattle. The Wakamba were the purchasers, and they employed them in work upon their plantations. The price of a good-looking Masai or Kikuyu girl was three goats.[88]

The push to expand production for the market pressed not only on the labor resources of the region, but on the land resources as well. The growth of the trade in livestock to caravans and to the coast encouraged increased settlement in the drier areas of the region where extensive pasturelands were available but where rainfall was unreliable, soils were poor and subject to erosion, and agriculture was marginal at best. The profits to be made may also have led farmers during good years to build up their herds beyond the carrying capacity of the land.[89] By 1890 the Nzaui section of southern Ulu had become well known as a provisioning stop and livestock area, and the neighborhood was described as "one mass of cultivation of all kinds."[90] Beginning in 1892, however, caravans found it difficult to obtain supplies there. Later, in

86. The less time that slaves had spent with owners, the more likely it was that they would be resold. Lovejoy, *Transformations in Slavery*, pp. 126–28. Marcia Wright has examined how nineteenth-century commercial and political developments in the central African interior left women vulnerable to exploitation. "Women in Peril: A Commentary on the Life Stories of Captives in Nineteenth Century East Central Africa," *African Social Research* 20 (1979): 819.
87. PRO: Ainsworth to Pigott, 20 Feb. 1895, in IBEAC to F.O., 10 April 1895, FO 2/97; Hardinge to F.O., 11 June 1896, FO 107/53; and Hardinge to F.O., 24 April 1897, FO 107/77. KNA: D. Crampton, "Early History of Chuka and Mwimbe," Embu Political Record Book, EBU/45 A1. Perham, *Lugard Diaries*, 1:143 (14 March 1890); Ainsworth, Diary, 18 Nov. 1895; Hall, letter, 15 March 1894; Russell, Diary, 15 April 1895; Chanler, *Jungle and Desert*, pp. 488–90; Decle, *Three Years in Africa*, p. 496; Muriuki, *History of the Kikuyu*, p. 106. Interviews: Hussein Juma, Kitui Town; Ruguca Nthimbu, Mbeere.
88. Chanler, *Jungle and Desert*, p. 488.
89. This seems to have been the case in Migwani and in Mwala. PRO: Ainsworth, "Report on 'Kitwyi,'" 6 Feb. 1895, in IBEAC to F.O., 10 April 1895, FO 2/97. Pigott, "Tana Diary," 20 May 1889; and Hobley, Safari Diary, 23 Nov. 1891. Miller argues that recent climate history has often led farmers into what seem to have been disastrous economic decisions. "Drought, Disease and Famine," p. 31.
90. Austin, *MacDonald in Uganda*, p. 276. Also von Höhnel, *Lakes Rudolf and Stefanie*, 2:314.

the aftermath of the rinderpest epidemic, a traveler reported that many resident families had temporarily abandoned Nzaui because the area had become "practically a desert."[91]

At the same time, many accounts of central Kenya during the 1890s noted high densities of population and cultivation. In his account of his trip through central Gikuyuland in 1887, von Höhnel recalled "districts so carefully and systematically cultivated that we might have been in Europe."[92] A European traveler described Embu in 1900 as being "most densely cultivated. [It] seemed to be prodigiously rich in food. We saw thousands of acres planted with [grain], stretching as far as the eye could reach. There were no boundaries between the shambas [fields]."[93] Intensive cultivation was by no means confined to the agriculturally richer highlands sections of the region. In their tour reports, British officials noted that Ulu and central Kitui were both thickly populated.[94] Although the authors of these accounts demonstrated little awareness of the subtleties of local ecologies, the accumulation of their sporadic reports points to trouble in some of the heavily populated areas. Population was also building up in some of the less densely settled—and drier—sections of the region. By the early 1890s the Migwani countryside was being intensively farmed and population there was increasing: "There are large tracts unoccupied by natives, but still the Wakamba cultivation is much closer than formerly."[95] The supposedly unoccupied land was presumably used as pasture.

These descriptions of densely settled farming communities suggest that the pressure to extend cultivation had led farmers into dangerous agricultural practice. Planting on steep hills and along watercourses

91. Gregory, *Rift Valley*, p. 81. The quotation comes from MacDonald, *Soldiering and Surveying*, p. 44.

92. *Lakes Rudolf and Stefanie*, 1:315. For a similar description of the same general area, see Hall, letter, 11 Jan. 1897. D. W. Cohen argues that the extensive cultivation reported in the Lake Victoria region during the nineteenth century was more the product of state exploitation than evidence of rural abundance. "Food Production and Food Exchange," p. 12.

93. Arkell-Hardwick, *Ivory Trader*, p. 70.

94. PRO: Ainsworth, "Report on 'Kitwyi,'" 6 Feb. 1895, in IBEAC to F.O., 10 April 1895, FO 2/97. Ainsworth, Diary, 19 Dec. 1897. Also, Pigott, "Tana Diary," 28 May 1889; Hobley, Safari Diary, 24 Nov. 1891; Chanler, *Jungle and Desert*, p. 486; Perham, *Lugard Diaries*, 1:142 (14 March 1890); and Hall, letter, 22 Oct. 1892.

95. Hobley, Safari Diary, 24 Nov. 1891. Archeological research may throw more light on the region's ecological history. David Brokensha and Bernard Riley examine the interplay between social and ecological change in "Mbeere Knowledge of their Vegetation and its Relevance for Development: A Case Study from Kenya," in *Indigenous Knowledge Systems and Development*, ed. D. Brokensha, D. M. Warren, and O. Werner (Lanham, M.D., 1980), pp. 113–29, and in their forthcoming larger study of the ethnobotany of Mbeere.

promoted erosion; reducing fallow periods depleted soil fertility; and cutting down trees for fuel led to serious deforestation. Scattered records suggest that wide areas of Ulu and Kitui had in fact been denuded of trees, eliminating wind breaks and leaving topsoil vulnerable.[96] A visitor to Kitui in the early 1890s wrote that "as one travels northwards [the land] rises and becomes more open and hilly, and a good deal of it is densely populated. Here we get among granite hills, bare of wood, and even firewood is scarce; what bush there may in former times have been, having been used up."[97] While this and similar accounts suggest strongly that by the late 1800s a number of communities faced significant pressures on local resources, there is no indication that these pressures had as yet produced substantial social division or serious conflict over land. But growing population densities did circumscribe economic opportunities. Oral records show quite clearly that the great engine of agricultural expansion in the nineteenth century was the perception among residents of established communities that land resources at home were limited or in decline and that future opportunities therefore lay on the frontier.

Central Kenya farmers met the rising external demand for foodstuffs and livestock not only by increasing their production, but also by redirecting existing surplus. Unfortunately, the resulting interruption of existing exchange relationships had dire implications for the poorer members of the population in general as well as for those communities, notably in Kitui and Ulu, that regularly imported food to offset inadequate local harvests. By the late 1890s, many of the areas of southern Gikuyuland and Ulu that had often sold off surplus to farmers in other, less favored sections of the region had become much more oriented toward providing produce for the external market. Clearly, the possibility that poor harvests would translate into serious hunger increased when communities in the drier zones could no longer depend on their traditional sources of supply in the highlands.[98] Expanded cultivation of maize was a clear sign of this shift in exchange patterns, since people from outside the region generally preferred maize over established lo-

---

96. PRO: Ainsworth, 6 Feb. 1895, in IBEAC to F.O., 10 April 1895, FO 2/97. Pigott, "Tana Diary," 20 May 1889; Hall, letter, 22 Oct. 1892; C. R. W. Lane, Kenya Land Commission, *Evidence*, 1:400.

97. Neumann, *Elephant Hunting*, p. 143.

98. Hall, letter, 28 Feb. 1898; Hotchkiss, letter, Kangundo [northwestern Ulu], 1 Aug. 1898, printed in *Hearing and Doing* (Oct. 1898), p. 10; Mackinder, Diary, 15 July 1899; and J. Patterson, Kenya Land Commission, *Evidence*, 1:746. Kershaw, "Land is the People," pp. 146–47, 168.

cal grains such as millet or sorghum. Maize cultivation represented labor and land given over to production of food explicitly for export,
rather than to crops that could be consumed locally. Worse, levels of
rainfall that might yield marginal harvests of traditional crops could
lead to the failure of a maize crop, as was the case in Ulu in 1894.[99]

At the same time that farmers in these areas were finding themselves cut off from their established sources of food, they were also
finding it more difficult to obtain the livestock that ultimately protected them from hunger. The combination of increased external demand for stock and the decline in herds caused by rinderpest drove
up prices. By 1894, in some areas of Ulu demand for livestock from
coastal traders had reportedly forced a tripling of cattle prices.[100]
Those communities—located in Ulu and Kitui—most actively involved in exporting livestock during this period would also be those
most disrupted by the famine of 1897–1900.[101] This coincidence suggests that opportunities for profit sometimes led farmers to sell off reserves of foodstuffs and livestock that might otherwise have been circulated within their own communities or consumed within their own
households.

James Scott and others have argued that the subsistence and redis-
tributive ethics of precapitalist societies made such actions unlikely.
According to Scott, farming households zealously preserved a margin
of security in their economic calculations.[102] Presumably, farmers did
not consciously sell off supplies of food and livestock that their families
might need to survive; however, it is less clear that their concern extended to others—in their own communities or beyond—who might
previously have counted on the availability of this same surplus. Many
of the men, women, and children living in the societies of central Kenya
were, moreover, in no position to make rational economic calculations
at all; the disposition of their labor and its product was decided for

99. Von Höhnel, *Lakes Rudolf and Stefanie*, 1:297. PRO: Ainsworth to Pigott, 31 Jan.
1894, in IBEAC to F.O., 16 April 1894, FO 2/73. Also Bernard, *East of Mount Kenya*, p. 41.
For the implications of similar developments to the south, see Iliffe, *History of Tanganyika*,
pp. 69–71; and Kjekshus, *Ecology Control and Development*, chap. 2.

100. PRO: Ainsworth to Pigott, 31 Jan. 1894, in IBEAC to F.O., 16 April 1894, FO
2/73.

101. PRO: Ainsworth, memorandum, 30 Jan. 1899, in Hardinge to F.O., 22 Feb. 1899,
FO 2/189.

102. J. C. Scott, *The Moral Economy of the Peasant: Rebellion and Subsistence in
Southeast Asia* (New Haven, 1976), pp. 4–9. Michael Watts draws on Scott's interpretation
in "The Demise of the Moral Economy: Food and Famine in the Sudano-Sahelian Region in
Historical Perspective," in Scott, *Life Before the Drought*, p. 127.

them, by patrons, masters, husbands, and parents.[103] Certainly, the growth of the supply trade permitted a small group of brokers to accumulate substantial coercive power.

On balance, the legacy of the commercial expansion of the 1880s and 1890s was an erosion of the autonomy of the central Kenya region. By the late 1890s, the combination of rising production and recurrent drought pressed limited local resources, accentuating the growing differences in wealth among and within communities. Even for those who profited substantially, however, the material benefits of this trade were meager. The acquisition of imported cloth and ornaments did represent an improvement in standards of living, and—if durable—such commodities could constitute savings. But ownership of imported goods rarely if ever facilitated an expansion or diversification of production.[104] As long-distance trade increasingly penetrated domestic economies, competition for economic resources and political control created disorder, undermining the capacity of the region—as a whole—to sustain itself in the coming crisis of famine and epidemic.

103. See Frederick Cooper, "Africa and the World Economy," *African Studies Review* 24 (1981): 5.

104. For example, accumulated trade goods were used to purchase food during the 1897–1901 famine. Lane, "Report on Kitui," p. 29. Imported metal did support the expansion of some craft industries. Jackson, "Kamba History," p. 232; and Bernard, "Meru in the Kenyan Spatial Economy," p. 267.

6

The Great Famine, 1897–1901

Beginning in late 1897, drought and hunger spread across central Kenya. For much of eastern Africa, the 1890s was a period of erratic and inadequate rainfall—a time of troubles.[1] A legacy of economic upheaval and environmental deterioration left central Kenya particularly vulnerable. In the region's hill and plains sections, a succession of failed harvests brought massive death and social turmoil. By early 1899 central Kenya was in the grip of a famine more serious than any recalled in living memory. Much of the highlands escaped drought, but no area remained beyond the famine's reach. Thousands of refugees poured into communities where food was available, often carrying with them deadly smallpox contagion. Not surprisingly, Kitui traditions recall these years as *Yua ya Ngomanisye*, "the famine that went everywhere." Elsewhere, it was simply called the Great Famine, a plain testament to the scale of suffering.[2] The drought did not begin to ease until the end of 1899, and it would be many months before communities began to recover from the combined impact of hunger and disease. The lingering effects of disorder and depopulation would

1. PRO: Hardinge to F.O., 7 Jan. 1900 and 5 Feb. 1900, FO 2/284. Marcia Wright, "Societies and Economies in Kenya, 1870–1902," and Peter F. B. Nayenga, "Busoga in the Era of Catastrophes, 1898–1911," both in *Ecology and History in East Africa (Hadith 7)*, ed. B. A. Ogot (Nairobi, 1979), pp. 179–94, and pp. 153–78, respectively; Iliffe, *History of Tanganyika*, pp. 123–25; and Kjekshus, *Ecology Control and Development*, pp. 134–43.

2. *Ngomanisye* was the name most commonly used by informants in Kitui District. See J. B. Carson, ed., *Life Story of a Kenya Chief* (London, 1958), p. 16; and J. A. Stuart Watt, "Recollections of Kenya, 1895–1963," typescript, Rhodes House Library, Oxford, Mss. Afr. s. 391, p. 1.

prove a critical element in the subsequent rapid advance of imperial authority and the early evolution of colonial society.[3]

The drought hit first and with greatest force in Kitui, in those sections that had experienced several years of marginal rainfall and rising external demand for food. By late 1897 even those farmlands that typically produced surplus were yielding little or nothing. During the early months of 1898, drought spread across the region's entire southern tier, from Mumoni west through Kitui and Ulu, into southern Gikuyuland, with locust infestation and a serious outbreak of rinderpest cattle disease exacerbating the effects of inadequate rainfall.[4] Livestock losses did not approach the levels of the disastrous rinderpest outbreak of 1891, but some communities saw as much as 50 percent of their herds destroyed. Whatever the number, farmers already hard-pressed by repeated crop failures could scarcely afford to lose even a few animals to disease, especially when the extreme dry conditions were already killing off considerable numbers of animals.[5] Crop failures had particularly devastating effects in the parts of Kitui and Ulu where severe drought was rare, the highest hill country.[6] As early as the middle of 1898 large numbers of people were dying in these areas.

Across the southern sections of the region, people who had not yet lost hope and fled their homes looked to the November 1898 season of rains to revive the land and replenish their granaries. Food was still available in some localities in Ulu and southern Gikuyuland, but it was

3. Munro makes this point succinctly, *Colonial Rule and the Kamba*, pp. 46–47. Until recently largely ignored, the historical causes and impact of hunger are examined in a number of recent studies. See Iliffe, *History of Tanganyika*; Miller, "Drought, Disease and Famine"; Watts, *Silent Violence*; Gerald Hartwig, "Social Consequences of Epidemic Disease: The Nineteenth Century in Eastern Africa," in *Disease in African History*, ed. G. Hartwig and K. David Patterson (Durham, North Carolina, 1978), pp. 25–45; and Jill R. Dias, "Famine and Disease in the History of Angola, ca. 1830–1930," *Journal of African History* 22 (1981): 349–78.

4. PRO: Ainsworth to Hardinge, 9 April 1898, in Hardinge to F.O., 27 April 1898, FO 107/93. Lane, "Report on Kitui," p. 28.

5. PRO: Ainsworth, Memorandum, 30 Jan. 1899, in Hardinge to F.O., 22 Feb. 1899, FO 2/189. Hotchkiss, letter dated Kilungu [southern Ulu], March 1898, in *Hearing and Doing* (Sept. 1898), p. 8; and Hotchkiss, letter, Kangundo [northwestern Ulu], *Hearing and Doing* (Oct. 1898), p. 7. Also see Wisner and Mbithi, "Drought in Eastern Africa," pp. 90–93.

6. Lane, "Report on Kitui," p. 28. Interviews: Mutia s/o Mboo and Elizabeth Kitumba w/o Kisenga, Migwani. According to the "climate of hunger" argument, peasant farmers do not prepare to cope with extreme droughts that occur at wide intervals, hence the relatively greater stress experienced in Kitui and Ulu as opposed to Mumoni. Miller, "Drought and Famine," p. 31. Also Mbithi and Wisner, "Drought and Famines in Kenya," pp. 115, 143; and Porter, *Food and Development*, pp. 38–40. Interviews: Muvali s/o Kilanga and Muli s/o Kakuru, Mumoni.

clear that if conditions did not soon improve, massive famine threatened.[7] In an attempt to get harvests as quickly as possible, many farmers risked planting early. Unfortunately, the rain in 1898 was both late and inadequate. Across Kitui, Ulu, and southern Gikuyuland crops failed to germinate or died stunted in the fields for lack of moisture. In another year, farmers might have recouped their losses by replanting, but in 1898 seeds were in short supply, as was labor. Many men and women were either too weak from hunger to work or were away from home altogether. Thus, the harvest season of early 1899 brought little of the usual celebration. Many families had no crops whatsoever, while others, desperately hungry, stripped their fields bare before plants had a chance to mature. Worse yet, renewed drought ended any hope that the famine might ease. Describing the entire famine area, a British official wrote, "The natives have suffered so long that they have reached the stage where they are past any kind of work."[8] With their resources depleted by a year of shortages, people in Kitui, Ulu, and Gikuyuland began to die in large numbers. "These are days," a missionary wrote home, "in which we are witnessing scenes almost too horrible to narrate."[9]

In the face of crisis, people sought out ritual healers; they bought amulets, poured libations, and sacrificed livestock. Their lack of success only reinforced a perception that larger forces had profoundly disturbed the cosmological balance. Many felt that the growing power of Europeans, however vaguely understood, lay behind these destructive forces. People viewed the construction of the Uganda railway, which was only then reaching the region's southern extreme, with a mixture of apprehension and awe. This same confusion of emotions colored attitudes toward most of the activities of Europeans in the region. Thus, in the midst of famine in Gikuyuland, local people simultaneously blamed the British adventurer John Boyes for their misfortunes and called on him to aid them with whatever powers he might possess.[10]

7. Hotchkiss, letters, Kangundo, *Hearing and Doing*, Oct. 1898–Jan. 1899; and Hall, letter, 1 April 1899.

8. PRO: Crauford to F.O., 30 May 1899, FO 2/196. Also Mackinder, Diary, 13 July 1899; and R. Blayden-Taylor, Kenya Land Commission, *Evidence*, 1:759.

9. Bangert to Hurlburt, Kangundo, 8 April 1899, *Hearing and Doing* (May 1899), p. 7. Also PRO: Hardinge to F.O., 18 Feb. 1899, FO 2/189; Hardinge to F.O., 18 March 1899, FO 2/190; Crauford to F.O., 30 May 1899, FO 2/196; and Ainsworth to Crauford, 22 Aug. 1899, in Crauford to F.O., 19 Sept. 1899, FO 2/198. Missionary letters in *Hearing and Doing*; and Ainsworth, Diary, 19 Jan. and 24 Feb. 1899.

10. Boyes, *King of Kikuyu*, pp. 167, 247. For evidence of attitudes regarding external forces, see PRO: Ainsworth to Acting Commissioner, 10 May 1899, in Crauford to F.O., 18

The first appearance of the sandflea, or jigger, in the region just as the famine was beginning was for many people a bizarre confirmation of the external origins of catastrophe. In a pattern strangely analogous to the advance of Europeans, this pest quietly spread across central Kenya, burrowing in the feet of unsuspecting victims. For people unfamiliar with jiggers and their habits, the results were often crippling and sometimes even deadly.[11]

THE STRATEGIES OF SURVIVAL

Following well-rehearsed strategies, families looked initially to local trade to relieve shortages. Even within the most affected sections of the region, hunger spread in an irregular pattern; neighboring localities and even homesteads felt the impact of drought with varying speed and intensity. Consequently, those people whose crops had failed could often find some food nearby. As drought burned the lower reaches of Kitui and Ulu in 1898, local trade networks moved produce from plots located in the wetter valleys and hillsides and along riverbeds to homesteads where food was in short supply, but where farmers had livestock to sell off.[12] Similarly, in early 1898, when the situation in southern Ulu was already being described as desperate, fields elsewhere in Ulu were reportedly flourishing, and farmers still had food to sell. Some of this surplus flowed into the external market. In northern Ulu, for instance, a few farmers went on exchanging food for cloth, despite the fact that some of their neighbors were already starving.[13] This continuing external flow of local agricultural produce undermined the capacity of societies to withstand food shortages, accelerating the progress toward famine. Around Machakos and in southern Gikuyuland,

Sept. 1899. Mackinder, Diary, 4 Aug. 1899; Lindblom, *Akamba*, p. 25; Glazier, "Generation Classes," pp. 320–21; and J. Fadiman, "Mountain Witchcraft: Supernatural Practices and Practitioners among the Meru," *African Studies Review* 20 (1977): 87–101. Interviews: Mwangangi s/o Mathenge, Mumoni; Muruangerwe, Embu.

11. Hall, letter, 29 Aug. 1893; and Kjekshus, *Ecology Control and Development*, pp. 134–36. The arrival of jiggers was noted in numerous interviews.

12. KNA: Kitui District Political Record Book, 1868–1946 [entry written 1918], DC/KTI.7.1. Bangert to Hurlburt, Kangundo, 27 July 1899, *Hearing and Doing* (Aug.–Sept. 1899), p. 8; Lane, "Report on Kitui," p. 28; Stanner, "The Kitui Kamba," p. B–55; and Mwaniki, *Embu Texts*, p. 205. Interviews: Mutia s/o Mboo, Elizabeth Kitumba w/o Kisenga, Mukusu s/o Mututhu, and Wamui w/o Munyasia, Migwani; Mwangangi s/o Mathenge and Musyoka s/o Ndeto, Mumoni. The concept of famine strategies is discussed in Watts, *Silent Violence*, pp. 140–41.

13. Hotchkiss, letter, Kilungu, 16 June 1898, *Hearing and Doing* (Oct. 1898), p. 10; and Hotchkiss, letter, Kangundo, 23 Sept. 1898, *Hearing and Doing* (Jan. 1899), p. 7.

rapidly growing demands for food to supply railway construction crews and the increased caravan traffic to Uganda depleted the reserves that might have protected some farming families in those areas from the worst effects of the deepening drought. As one early missionary recalled,

> The terrors of this [famine] were greatly intensified by the fact that about that time an enormous *safari* with Nubian troops marched right through the Kikuyu country. The agents of the food contractor . . . bought up quantities of grain . . . for what seemed to the unfortunate sellers magnificent returns of brass wire, Amerikani [cloth], and beads. But it spelt disaster for them because when at last after two futile plantings if not three, a sufficiency of rain did come to produce crops, there was hardly any grain left in the granaries to put in the soil.[14]

With crops withering in the fields and few reserves remaining, the key to survival was livestock. The milk and blood provided some immediate nourishment, but more important, the animals could be sold off gradually to obtain foodstuffs. Thus, people did everything they could to maintain or expand their herds. Many turned to litigation: compensation was demanded for forgotten crimes; rents were required for the use of farming plots; payments were abruptly called in on bride-wealth obligations that might otherwise have remained outstanding almost indefinitely. In some cases junior wives were returned to their fathers in hopes of recouping bridewealth payments that had already been paid.[15] In others, poor people arranged for the marriages of their young daughters to obtain advance marriage payments: "When one had a daughter he could give her to someone who had many goats. Then he could take goats from there that could be used to get food."[16] Even during famine, animals were rarely slaughtered for meat. To European observers, the fact that people sometimes died of the effects of malnutrition when they still possessed cattle, sheep, or goats spoke of an irrational attachment to livestock, but local men understood full well that killing off a herd could seal an entire family's fate.[17]

14. H. Leakey, Kenya Land Commission, *Evidence*, 1:865.

15. Hotchkiss, letter, Kangundo, 24 March 1899, *Hearing and Doing* (May 1899), pp. 4–5; Dundas, "History of Kitui," p. 517; J. Ainsworth, "Report on Ukamba, 1905"; and Stanner, "Kitui Kamba," p. B–55. Interviews: Njuguna Kivuli, Mbeere; Muito s/o Muthamba, Migwani.

16. Interview: Gachone w/o Mburati, Mbeere. Also Stanner, "Kitui Kamba," p. B–55. Interview: Njuguna Kivuli, Mbeere.

17. Tate, "Kikuyu and Kamba Tribes," p. 135; Lindblom, *Akamba*, p. 350; and Stanner, "Kitui Kamba," p. B–55. Interviews: Kikwae w/o Nthambu, Migwani; Runji s/o Jigoya, Mbeere; Munithya w/o Nganza, Mumoni.

As drought turned into famine, the poor suffered first and most severely. They lacked food reserves to carry them over a season of shortage and animals to sell to make up the shortfall. In many areas poor people were reduced to a daily and desperate struggle for existence, relying on wild plants and game for food. Old men and boys hunted animals such as gazelles and large lizards that could be found close to home; younger men absented themselves from their families for extended periods, forming hunting parties that traveled far to the north and east, surviving on what they could kill and forage and on what they garnered through occasional raiding and trade.[18] Some residents of the surrounding areas of Mbeere, Kitui, and Ulu moved into camps along the Tana River, where they collected plants that grew along the banks and hunted for hippopotamuses.[19] For those remaining at home, various wild fruits, grasses, and tubers became the staff of life. One man recalled, "We had to eat the leaves of trees, as if we were goats."[20] Weak from hunger, small children with their mothers spent long days searching out roots and berries that could be cooked into an unappetizing gruel, if they weren't eaten on the spot. In Ulu, according to a missionary report, local people were "existing entirely on a little root berry about the size of a pea, which they dig out of the sand. . . . Where these are to be found you will daily see hundreds of the most pitiable specimens imaginable, . . . with mouths besmeared with dirt, squatting about digging out these roots and eating them as fast as found."[21] For the desperately hungry, bedding skins, arrow quivers, and even the urine-soaked leather slings that were used to carry babies became the raw materials of spare meals.[22]

The oral records of Migwani describe in painful detail the desolation of empty and dispirited communities. Men and women who were children then vividly recalled eighty years later the trauma of villages and homesteads breaking up and family members dying and disap-

---

18. PRO: Hardinge to F.O., 27 June 1900, FO 2/288. Tate, "Kikuyu and Kamba Tribes," p. 136; Jackson, "Family and Famine," p. 201; and *The Taveta Chronicle* [publication of Church Missionary Society Mission in Taita-Taveta] (Oct. 1899), p. 167.

19. Interviews: Nguuti s/o Ndana, Migwani; Kanguru s/o Kirindi, Mbeere.

20. Interview: Nguli s/o Mbaluka, Migwani. Also Mackinder, Diary, 13 July 1899; and Lindblom, *Akamba*, p. 350. Interviews: Munyasia s/o Kalwe and Komba w/o Nzoka, Migwani; Syanderi w/o Muivia and Mutinda s/o Ruanyaki, Mbeere; Munithya s/o Nganza, Munyoki s/o Mutui, and Mwangangi s/o Mathenge, Mumoni.

21. Bangert to Hurlburt, Kangundo, 20 Sept. 1899, *Hearing and Doing* (Nov. 1899), p. 5.

22. Boyes, *King of Kikuyu*, p. 247. Interviews: Munyasia s/o Kalwe, Migwani; Gachone w/o Rukeni, Mbeere.

pearing. Small bands of hungry people living by their wits moved from place to place in search of something to eat. A woman remembered, "Some people were unable to survive. They were too weak. They just lay there along the roads, helpless. . . . Vultures would come and peck out their eyes."[23] Elsewhere, conditions were no less appalling. In Ulu, homeless men and women, fearful that they would be eaten alive by hyenas as they slept, took to sleeping in trees. Some did not live through the night.

By September 1899 American missionaries in the Kangundo section of northern Ulu were reluctant to leave their compound, because to do so was to confront pervasive suffering and death: "Go in any direction and you are bound to stumble on dead bodies. . . . The shambas [fields] and paths are litterly strewn with corpses and thousands have died and scores are dying daily."[24] Two months later one of these missionaries described the scene he encountered on a twenty-mile walk across Ulu:

> On our way over the hills . . . we passed three bodies lying right in the path, as though they had but recently dropped out of sheer exhaustion; and as we passed the huts along the way gaunt, emaciated figures crouched beside them, sometimes extending a boney hand in mute appeal for a morsel to eat.[25]

Along the same route another missionary soon thereafter encountered more than a dozen bodies rotting by the wayside. A British resident of the area recalled that "no matter where one went corpses strewed the tracks. Little skeleton babies were found crying by the dead bodies of their mothers."[26] In southern Gikuyuland, the countryside around the Dagoretti station was so dry that streams had dried up and drinking water, normally abundant, had become difficult to obtain. In the hills around Nairobi, miles of dusty fields turned normally verdant scenes to dull red.[27] An early white settler later recalled, "In 1899, when I went up the line, I could not get quite as far as Limuru. The railway line was a mass of corpses."[28]

23. Interview: Komba w/o Nzoka, Migwani.

24. Bangert to Hurlburt, Kangundo, 20 Sept. 1899, *Hearing and Doing* (Nov. 1899), pp. 5–7.

25. Johnson to Hurlburt, Kangundo, 30 Nov. 1899, *Hearing and Doing* (Jan. 1900), p. 3.

26. Rachel S. Watt, *In the Heart of Savagedom* (3d ed., n.p., n.d. [ca. 1920]), p. 309. Also, Bangert, letter, Kangundo, 17 Nov. 1899, *Hearing and Doing* (Jan. 1900), p. 5.

27. John Patterson, Kenya Land Commission, *Evidence*, 1:746.

28. R. Blayden-Taylor, in ibid., p. 759. For corroboration, PRO: Ainsworth to Hardinge, 28 Dec. 1899, in Hardinge to F.O., 7 Jan. 1900, FO 2/284. Hall, letter, April 1899.

During early 1899 the situation across the southern section of central Kenya steadily worsened, but conditions in most of the rest of the region were considerably less severe. Although Mumoni experienced serious drought and many families faced hardship, communities there seem to have escaped disaster. Large herds of cattle and relative proximity to areas in Meru where food could be found generally held off the extreme deprivation that was common in adjacent areas of Kitui.[29] In Mbeere, the availability of food in the nearby Mount Kenya highlands allowed people to avoid serious hunger, despite severe drought and crop shortages. Similarly, in the settlements on the eastern margins of central and northern Gikuyuland, residents who lacked adequate food could find supplies in areas reasonably close by. Parties of hundreds of men, women, and children regularly trekked into the neighboring highlands to buy or work for surplus produce. But according to the account of John Boyes, even many of these relatively fortunate people were so weak that they died along the route from the effects of hunger.[30]

The deepening drought pushed residents of famine-stricken communities into a steadily widening search for available food. The men and women who traveled beyond their home areas to obtain food drove the frontiers of famine ahead of them, buying up surplus from farmers who would themselves soon face the difficulties of drought and inadequate harvests. During the first half of 1898 starving Kitui men and women regularly obtained food in northern Ulu, but by August it was impossible to buy foodstuffs in Ulu, and by September it was reported that some people there were actually dying of starvation. In turn, many families from Ulu then looked to southern Gikuyuland for food, but within a few months that area too would face famine.[31] In Mbeere, tradition records that a local seer had warned, "If Akamba come here, do not exchange anything with them, because if you do, all of you will sleep in Embu."[32] This prediction proved all too accurate. In the early stages of the drought, hungry people from Migwani and

29. Interview: Masila s/o Kivunza, Mumoni.

30. Boyes, *King of Kikuyu*, pp. 248–250. Also, PRO: Hardinge to F.O., 18 Feb. 1899, FO 2/189; and Ainsworth to Crauford, 22 Aug. 1899, in Crauford to F.O., 19 Sept. 1899, FO 2/198. KNA: "History of Fort Hall, 1888–1944," DC/FH.6/1. Mackinder, Diary, 1 Aug. 1899. For Mbeere, see interviews: Jimuko Ngonjo, Maringa Maunge, Sarimu Njavari, Manunga s/o Nguci, and Nthumbi s/o Gicere, Mbeere; Elizabeth Kitumba w/o Kisenga, Migwani.

31. Lane, "Report on Kitui," p. 28; Hotchkiss, letters, Kangundo, 1 Aug. 1898 and 8 Sept. 1898, in *Hearing and Doing* (Oct. 1898), p. 7, and (Nov. 1898), p. 5.

32. Interview: Nthumbi s/o Gicere, Mbeere.

Mumoni depleted granaries in many parts of Mbeere; when rainfall failed in Mbeere as well, local people had few reserves to fall back on and were forced to depend for subsistence on food from communities on the Mount Kenya slopes.[33]

Each month of drought made people in the famine zone more dependent on purchased food, available increasingly only in the highlands. By early in 1899 conditions had become so difficult in Mumoni, Kitui, Ulu, and southern and eastern Gikuyuland that a large proportion of families relied continuously on supplies obtained from the outside to maintain even marginally adequate diets.[34] Some men, acting as professional traders, carried food into the famine zone to sell, but most of the trade was carried on directly between consumers and producers. Large makeshift caravans traveled continually into the highlands, where individuals exchanged ornaments, imported goods, livestock, and livestock products for foodstuffs, which they carried home to children and other family members who had been left to look after the homestead and remaining livestock.[35] Following well-established trade routes, Mumoni people generally went north and west into the Nyambeni and Mount Kenya highlands of Meru; those from Migwani and the rest of Kitui as well as some from Ulu generally headed to communities on the southern slopes of Mount Kenya; and families from Ulu and southern Gikuyuland ordinarily went to the high country of central and northern Gikuyuland. These trade patterns blurred, however, as hunger intensified and men and women went off in every direction seeking food where they could find it.[36]

Highland farmers welcomed the opportunity to acquire livestock in exchange for their surplus crops, but few families from the famine zone owned herds large enough to sustain themselves indefinitely through trade. The rising demand for grain and other foodstuffs, coupled with declining supplies, drove up prices: "As the food became less,

33. Interviews: Manunga s/o Nguci, Muturi s/o Ruveni, and Sarimu Njavari, Mbeere; Mutia s/o Mboo, Migwani.

34. PRO: Crawshay to Ainsworth, Kitui, 20 Jan. 1899, in Hardinge to F.O., 18 Feb. 1899, FO 2/189. KNA: Kitui Political Record Book [entry written 1919], DC/KTI.7/1. H. Leakey, Kenya Land Commission, *Evidence*, 1:865; and Boyes, *King of Kikuyu*, pp. 248–50.

35. Lane, "Report on Kitui," pp. 28–29; and Ainsworth, Diary, 3 March 1899. Interviews: Sarimu Njavari and Cigana s/o Karere, Mbeere; Thitu s/o Nzili and Komba w/o Nzoka, Migwani.

36. PRO: Crawshay to Ainsworth, Kitui, 20 Jan. 1899, in Hardinge to F.O., 18 Feb. 1899, FO 2/189. Lane, "Report on Kitui," p. 28; and Mackinder, Diary, 5–6 Aug. 1899. Interviews: Ngeri w/o Ngala, Ndithio s/o Mwangi, Nzunya w/o Mbondo, and Munyoki s/o Mutui, Mumoni; Kilungi s/o Kithita, Kasina s/o Ndoo, Komba w/o Nzoka, and Ngatu s/o Mauna, Migwani.

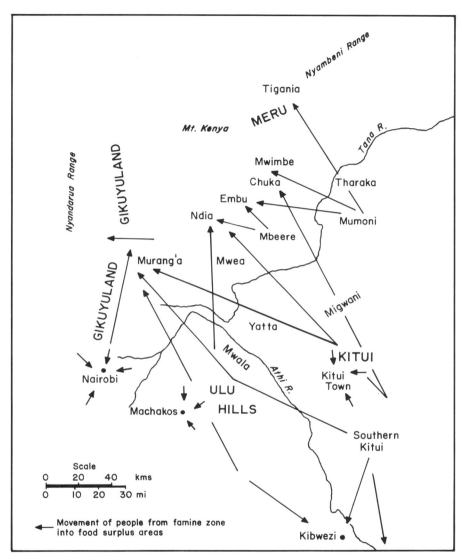

Map 12. The Great Famine

the measures got smaller."[37] With resources dwindling, more and more people survived by selling their labor or that of their dependents. Unfortunately, short-term work brought relatively small return. It also lengthened the overall time involved in a journey to the highlands and sapped the strength needed for long days of walking with heavy loads. Given the amount of time required for travel and the limited amount of produce that could be carried back, people had to be on the move almost continually if they were to keep their families supplied.[38] A Migwani woman recalled, "My father went there to the highlands alone and he worked for food. When he was returning, the Tana River was in flood and they could not cross. As a result, all the food was used up over there."[39] Men and women returning to Ulu from Gikuyuland were dropping and dying along the paths from hunger and exhaustion.[40] In most famine-stricken communities residents simply had neither the property nor the strength to continue supplying their families through trade.[41]

FAMINE AND MIGRATION

An elder from the Mount Kenya society of Ndia recalled that during the famine, "Kamba first brought their livestock to exchange for foodstuffs. Later, they brought their wives and children."[42] As this reminiscence attests, persistent and intense food shortages led destitute families to turn increasingly to the transfer of rights over female labor under their control—the pawning of female dependents. For the fathers, husbands, or guardians of the women and girls involved, pawning represented a practical means of obtaining desperately needed food. By transferring their rights over dependents, men were able to supply the remaining members of their families while at the same time reducing the number of mouths that had to be fed. Consequently, during the years from 1898 to 1900 thousands of females found themselves thrust into unfamiliar communities in areas separated from their homes not only by many miles but by considerable cultural and linguis-

---

37. Quote from interview with Sarimu Njavari, Mbeere. Also, Interviews: Nthumbi s/o Gicere, Mbeere; Manderi s/o Munzungi, and Mukungi s/o Masila, Mumoni.
38. Interviews: Jason Njigoru, Embu; Mwalimu Charley, Kitui Town; Paul Ngutu s/o Ngutha and Mbulwa s/o Ndoo, Migwani.
39. Interview: Kikwae w/o Nthambu, Migwani.
40. Bangert to Hurlbert, Kangundo, 14 Aug. 1899, *Hearing and Doing* (Oct. 1899), p. 5.
41. Lane, "Report on Kitui," p. 28; and Boyes, *King of Kikuyu*, p. 247. Interviews: Komba w/o Nzoka, Migwani; Masila s/o Kivunza, Mumoni.
42. Mwaniki, *Embu Texts*, p. 304.

tic distance as well. The transition could involve considerable trauma, but many scarcely looked back. They were grateful to exchange the insecurity and hunger that famine had forced on them for the material and psychological certainty offered by their new guardians.[43]

If pawning was not intrinsically inhumane, the rapid expansion of the practice during the famine years encouraged men to view female labor as a commodity, a trend already evident in the growth of slave trading. As communities weakened and travel became increasingly dangerous, female refugees in general were left extraordinarily vulnerable to exploitation. Some men from highland communities apparently attempted to use "gifts" of food and shelter offered to young women in order to create obligations and thus extract payments from the families of the girls involved. Women who had intended only to trade or work for brief periods found themselves held in households permanently or at best until they escaped or relatives secured their release. Others became the victims of marauders who captured and detained female migrants.[44] In Ndia, just west of Embu, the broker and later colonial chief Gutu wa Kibetu enriched himself by assisting coastal traders who were profiting from an active commerce in dependent women.[45]

In the long run, the transfer of large numbers of women from communities in Ulu and Kitui to the highlands created a simmering resentment over the loss of vital reproductive and labor resources. Once relative prosperity had returned, men from these areas began to feel considerable anger at what they saw as the unwillingness of highland farmers to relinquish their former dependents. As time passed and the young women who had been pawned married and had children, the possibility that they would be repatriated became increasingly less likely. In some parts of Kitui and Ulu, men presumably found their marriage opportunities restricted by a shortage of partners. In a few cases, men hired coastal traders to kidnap and return pawns to their families of origin.[46] In the years following, the continued presence of daughters and wives in distant highland communities remained a sore

43. Jackson, "Family and Famine," pp. 205–06. Interview: Mbatia w/o Mukumi, Mbeere.

44. PRO: Crawshay to Ainsworth, Kitui, 20 Jan. 1899, in Hardinge to F.O., 18 Feb. 1899, FO 2/189. Lane, "Report on Kitui," p. 29; and Ainsworth, Diary, 7 and 25 Oct. 1898. Interviews: Komba w/o Nzoka, Paul Ngutu s/o Ngutha, and Nguuti s/o Ndana, Migwani. Also see Wright, "Women in Peril," pp. 188–89.

45. KNA: Central Province, Embu District Political Record Book [entry written 1911], PC.CP 1/5/1.

46. PRO: Hardinge to F.O., 7 Jan. 1900, FO 2/284. Interviews: Meri daughter of Pereira and Hussein Juma, Kitui Town; Ngavi s/o Mwanzi and Nguuti s/o Ndana, Migwani; Nzunya w/o Mbondo and Ngeri w/o Ngala, Mumoni; Muruakori s/o Gacewa and Kabogo s/o Gacigua, Embu.

point in Ulu and especially in Kitui, an issue that came to be defined in ethnic terms—as the question of "Kamba" women held in "Gikuyu" territory.[47]

During 1899, as sources of food supplies became increasingly remote and travel to and from the highlands more difficult, a steadily growing stream of refugees fled the famine zone. Relocation was a well-established response to drought, but now movement occurred on an unprecedented scale. Some wealthy men were able to keep a part of their family and livestock at home, but most people had no choice but to move with all of their property and dependents. People fled Ulu by the thousands, leaving the countryside "practically deserted on account of famine."[48] Many areas of Kitui and Ulu were left virtually unpopulated. An elder from Migwani recalled that "by the time the famine was over, all of the Akamba [people of Migwani] were in Gikuyu or Mwimbe."[49]

Refugees—traveling for the most part in small family parties—generally had little trouble establishing connections with prospective hosts. Migrants from Kitui communities sometimes made their initial arrangements at resting points or at markets located outside the settled areas. The highlands farmers who sold their produce in these places often directed famine victims to their own or other homesteads, where refugees would be welcome. For a fee, men from Mbeere occasionally acted as guides and intermediaries for families from Mumoni who wished to find refuge in Embu.[50] As a rule, however, famine refugees simply traveled directly into the highlands and negotiated their own agreements, often returning to communities where they had already come to buy food or where they had long-standing trade connections. Men frequently drew on established blood-partnership relationships (*giciaro*) to find places for their families.[51]

47. KNA: Kitui District, Annual Report, 1915, DC/KTI/1/1/1; Minutes of a Meeting between the P.C. and Kitui Chiefs, 14 June 1912, Kitui District Political Record Book, Miscellaneous Statistics (pre-1914), DC/KTI 7/2. Interviews: Paul Ngutu s/o Ngutha, Migwani; Ngeri w/o Ngala, Mumoni; Tirisa Kanyi w/o Mbarire, Embu.

48. Bangert, undated letter, Kangundo, *Hearing and Doing* (June 1899), p. 7. For evidence of migration, see PRO: Ainsworth to Hardinge, 28 Dec. 1899, in Hardinge to F.O., 7 Jan. 1900, FO 2/284. Bangert to Hurlburt, Kangundo, 8 April 1899, *Hearing and Doing* (May 1899), p. 6; Lane, "Report on Kitui," p. 28; H. Leakey, Kenya Land Commission, *Evidence*, 1:865; and Dundas, "History of Kitui," p. 485. Interviews: Nguuti s/o Ndana, Ngatu s/o Mauna, and Munyambu s/o Ngindo, Migwani; Manunga s/o Nguci, Mbeere.

49. Interview: Mutia s/o Mboo, Migwani.

50. Interviews: Ngatu s/o Mauna, Paul Ngutu s/o Ngutha, and Komba w/o Nzoka, Migwani; Gitavi s/o Kunyira and Cigana s/o Karere, Mbeere.

51. Interviews: Munyoki s/o Mutui, Lang'a s/o Ngile, and Kavindu s/o Ikunga, Mumoni; and Komba w/o Nzoka, Migwani.

Refugee families typically settled down for a period of months or even years. They lived within their host's compound and were assigned plots where they could raise a portion of the food they consumed. Following this pattern, one man from Mumoni took his family to Tigania in Meru to the homestead of his blood-brother, a former trading partner. The Mumoni family stayed in Tigania for several seasons, working with their host's family as well as in the separate fields they had been allocated. Many families had similar experiences of being well cared for and protected in the homes of friends or acquaintances, and when the famine eased these families—like the one from Mumoni—returned home essentially intact.[52] Although feelings of friendship and compassion no doubt motivated some of this generosity, hosts clearly had much to gain from housing and feeding refugee families. In the short term, they received payments of livestock and access to additional labor; in the long run, they might draw some of the refugees into their own families or communities as well as build a potentially valuable personal relationship with individuals and lineages in distant sections of the region.

In a few cases leaders like Nzambu wa Ndove from Migwani attempted to organize large groups of migrants. In negotiations with elders in Mwimbe on eastern Mount Kenya, Nzambu obtained permission to establish his followers in the lower country, at the edge of more densely settled areas. They built settlements there on the model of cattle camps and survived by trading, foraging, cultivating small plots, and working for neighboring Mwimbe farmers.[53]

Not surprisingly, those with little wealth had a more difficult time finding refuge. Because they were unlikely to have accumulated the connections that smoothed the way for others, they were often forced to go into homesteads where they were unknown, places chosen by appearances or from bits of intelligence. Lacking livestock or other property, poor people had little bargaining power, and as a result sometimes found themselves exploited for the convenience of their hosts. The members of refugee families were frequently dispersed among a number of homesteads in a neighborhood, with often disastrous consequences. For many poor people the integrity of the family was practi-

52. Interviews: Kavindu s/o Ikunga, Mumoni; Rose Makaa w/o Mutia, Ngatu s/o Mauna, and Komba w/o Nzoka, Migwani.

53. Nzambu's move to Mwimbe is discussed above in the Introduction, and his return to Migwani below in chap. 7. For the experience of the Migwani refugees, see Interviews: Mutia s/o Mboo, Wamui w/o Munyasia, Kikwae w/o Nthamba, and Musungu Kalola, Migwani. See also Arkell-Hardwick, *Ivory Trader*, p. 331. Interviews: Nzunya w/o Mbondo, Mumoni; Mbatia w/o Mukumi, Mbeere.

cally the sole source of strength. Numbers of these refugees never made it back to their original homes: women married into local lineages; men often saw permanent relocation as an alternative preferable to the uncertainty and insecurity of return, alone, to their places of origin.[54]

The steady stream of migrants placed a heavy social and economic burden on highland societies. Even in sections of the Mount Kenya highlands where farmers continued to produce adequate crops, traditions describe the 1898–1901 period as a famine (*yura*), a term which evokes the sense of crisis caused by the arrival of large numbers of hungry outsiders.[55] In some instances this onslaught exacerbated deeply held suspicions of outsiders.[56] In Mwimbe, the settlements of refugees from Migwani and neighboring areas created considerable tension. Because they were settled in separate hamlets, Nzambu and his followers had a measure of security and independence; but this autonomy was in itself provocative, especially as the flood of outsiders created growing competition for limited resources. Disputes over women, work arrangements, and trade sometimes erupted into violence. Considerable conflict marred the relations between Nzambu's people and their neighbors. Thefts were committed on both sides; some Migwani women and children were kidnapped; and several male refugees were murdered. The refugees had little recourse. These settlements of strangers had no clearly defined place in Mwimbe society. For their basic survival, Migwani people simply had no choice but to maintain the goodwill of their hosts.[57]

While migrants who lived in the compounds of local families were generally insulated from community hostility, many nevertheless felt exploited by the arrangements they were forced to make and humiliated by their sudden poverty and powerless dependency. Those who lacked even this element of protection were likely to find themselves victimized and in physical danger. In the later stages of the famine, for

54. Dundas, "History of Kitui," p. 485. Interviews: Meri daughter of Pereira, Kitui Town; Mukusu s/o Mututhu, Ngatu s/o Mauna, and Komba s/o Nzoka, Migwani; Nzunya w/o Mbondo and Ngeri w/o Ngala, Mumoni; Mbatia w/o Mukumi, Mbeere; Tirisa Kanyi w/o Mbarire, Embu.

55. Mwaniki, *Embu Texts*, pp. 167, 290, 304.

56. Interviews: Kilungi s/o Kithita, Migwani; Mwalimu Charley, Kitui Town; Ngeri w/o Ngala, Mumoni; Manunga s/o Nguci, Mbeere.

57. Ainsworth, Diary, 7 and 25 Oct. 1898. Interviews: Mutia s/o Mboo; Wamui w/o Munyasia, Mulango s/o Ngusia, and Musungu Kalola, Migwani; Kisilu s/o Katumo, Mumoni; Nthumbi s/o Gicere, Mbeere. See Niara Sudarkasa, "From Stranger to Alien: The Socio-Political History of the Nigerian Yoruba in Ghana, 1900–1970," in *Strangers in African Societies*, ed. William Shack and Elliot Skinner (Berkeley and Los Angeles, 1979), pp. 146–47.

instance, there were reports of massacres of refugees from Ulu in the Gikuyu highlands.[58] Nevertheless, relationships between local people and famine refugees were seemingly more often characterized by cooperation than discord. Even the conflicts that troubled contacts between Nzambu's followers and their Mwimbe neighbors never became sufficiently severe to threaten the existence of the refugee hamlets.[59]

EXTERNAL FORCES IN THE HISTORY OF THE FAMINE

Traditional accounts of the famine years in Ulu often describe the period as *Yua ya Mapunga*, "the famine of rice," or *Yua ya Magunia*, "the gunny sack famine." The assignment of these names reflects a local perception of the role that external forces played in shaping the famine. The rice that was imported and distributed to the hungry by Europeans was then largely unfamiliar in central Kenya, as were the bags used to transport it. In a deeper sense, these and other new products were seen to have engendered the disequilibrium that led inexorably to catastrophe.[60] Of course, it was by no means unreasonable for central Kenyans to trace their troubles to external causes. In southern Gikuyuland and in Ulu, many famine victims must have been painfully aware that recent increased external trade had drained off local reserves. In any case, by the last months of 1898 few if any farmers in Ulu, Kitui, or southern Gikuyuland had food to sell anyone.[61]

In the midst of disruption, the regional centers that had gradually emerged during the previous two decades generally retained their influential place in the region's political economy. Those men who had accumulated wealth and influence as middlemen in external trade for the most part held on to their positions. In the areas where surplus food remained available, traders and refugees provided local brokers with ready and inexpensive supplies of both labor and livestock. Thus, men like Gutu wa Kibetu from Ndia or Wang'ombe, the warlord-broker discussed in chapter 4, who had bases of wealth to build from, often

58. Hotchkiss, letter, Kangundo, 18 Dec. 1898, *Hearing and Doing* (Feb. 1899), p. 7. Interviews: Mulango s/o Ngusia and Nguli s/o Kinuva, Migwani; Meri daughter of Pereira, Kitui Town; Mbatia w/o Mukumi, Mbeere.

59. PRO: Crawshay to Ainsworth, Kitui, 20 Jan. 1899, in Hardinge to F.O., 18 Feb. 1899, FO 2/189. Interviews: Wamui w/o Munyasia, Elizabeth Kitumba w/o Kisenga, Paul Ngutu s/o Ngutha, Komba w/o Nzoka, Migwani; Mbatia w/o Mukumi, Mbeere.

60. KNA: Kitui District Political Record Book, 1868–1946 [entry written in 1919], DC/KTI 7/1. Lindblom, *Akamba*, p. 339; and Munro, *Colonial Rule and the Kamba*, p. 48.

61. See Hall's letters for this period. Chapter 5 explores some of the ways that the penetration of external forces created the conditions for famine.

emerged from the famine years with their personal wealth and power much enhanced. Even in the most devastated areas of Kitui and Ulu, many local brokers managed to retain their positions. During the seasons of hunger, men like Nzambu wa Ndove acquired a host of personal debts that they would turn to their advantage when the famine eased and they set about rebuilding their fortunes. The warlord Mwatu wa Ngoma apparently saw the famine in particularly opportunistic terms. Although his home base of Mwala endured severe drought, Mwatu maintained his strength right through these years by preying on the parties of traders and refugees that continually moved along the nearby routes to the highlands.[62]

European-controlled trading, administrative, and mission centers, with their access to imported goods, were particularly well placed to expand their scope. The completion of the railway to the burgeoning settlement at Nairobi not only brought a flood of outsiders into the region, but permitted British officials to import supplies of food relatively easily to replace those which they had previously obtained locally. The growth of the various towns, stations, and missions generated a rapidly increasing demand for local labor. At the same time, access to imported food gave European merchants, administrators, and missionaries the means to secure workers.

Before 1898, the American mission at Kangundo in northern Ulu had found it impossible to attract any laborers from the immediate locality, but by the middle of the year some had to be turned away. At the same time, the German Protestant missionaries in southern Kitui were able to build a second station with labor that they bought with food. Quite a few youths found casual jobs as messengers or porters at the British posts at Kitui and Machakos and at the new administrative center at Nairobi. The absolute numbers involved were still small; the Kangundo mission, for example, regularly employed no more than twenty men.[63] Moreover, European officials were largely frustrated in their attempts to recruit workers for permanent jobs that paid cash

62. PRO: Ainsworth to Hardinge, 29 Dec. 1897, in Hardinge to F.O., 14 Jan. 1898, FO 107/90. KNA: Central Province, Embu District Political Record Book [entry written 1911], PC.CP 1/5/1. Ainsworth, Diary, 12 Jan. 1898; and Mackinder, Diary, 28 Aug. 1899. During the famine Mwatu was captured while on a raid into Kitui and was released only after British intercession. Ainsworth, Diary, 18 Jan. and 4 Feb. 1899. Interview: Ngatu s/o Mauna, Migwani.
63. PRO: Ainsworth to Hardinge, 24 Jan. 1900, in Hardinge to F.O., 5 Feb. 1900, FO 2/284; and Ainsworth to Hardinge, 9 April 1898, in Hardinge to F.O., 27 April 1898, FO 107/93. Hotchkiss, letter, Kangundo, 1 Aug. 1898, *Hearing and Doing* (Oct. 1898), p. 6; Hardinge, "Report on British East Africa, 1898–99," p. 9; Lane, "Report on Kitui," p. 28; and Boyes, *King of Kikuyu*, pp. 252–53.

wages. Despite the extreme famine conditions, few men were willing to sign up with the single major employer—the railroad. The idea of working for a month before being paid on a job that was several days' journey from home made little sense to men whose relatives required continuous supplies of food. In Migwani and other similar communities, only a few young men whose families had disintegrated or who were willing to cut their family ties left to work on the rail line or occasionally in jobs as far away as Mombasa.[64]

The magnitude of the crisis soon forced missionaries and British officials to overcome their antipathy to the free distribution of food and to institute a relief campaign for the starving. The program began at the coast in 1898 and expanded inland, paid for by contributions and by various government funds.[65] A series of relief camps in Kitui, Ulu, and at Nairobi offered adults a pound of rice each day and children half that. In Machakos, by August of 1899 British officials were feeding five hundred people a day, and by December more than fifteen hundred; the camp at Nairobi fed similar numbers. By late 1899, at least five thousand people in central Kenya were living on the dole of food provided by officials and missionaries.[66] However paltry in comparison to the overall scale of suffering and death, this relief effort was significant in the areas where it was concentrated—in communities surrounding missions and stations. The distribution of food entrenched the increasingly dominant position of these centers in commercial, political, and ideological terms. Officials who only a few years earlier had complained of the autonomy of local people now decried their dependence.[67]

As refugees and workers swarmed into Machakos, Kitui, and Nairobi, the "Swahili towns" that had grown up beside the markets in these centers grew in size and importance. Lacking the support and protection of family or lineage, numbers of unattached men, women, and children settled down permanently, becoming part of these small Muslim societies.[68] A song about the famine that Gerhard Lindblom

64. Hardinge, "Report on British East Africa, 1898–99," p. 9; and Clayton and Savage, *Government and Labour in Kenya*, pp. 13–15. Interviews: Mutia s/o Mboo and Komba w/o Nzoka, Migwani.

65. A selection of press clippings on the relief efforts is in E. J. H. Russell's Diaries.

66. PRO: Ainsworth to Crauford, 22 Aug. 1899, in Crauford to F.O., 19 Sept. 1899, FO 2/129; and Ainsworth to Hardinge, 24 Jan. 1900, in Hardinge to F.O., 5 Feb. 1900, FO 2/284. Also Lindblom, *Akamba*, pp. 350–51.

67. Ainsworth, Diary, 16 July 1899; Hall, letter, Machakos, 26 Nov. 1899; and Bangert to Hurlburt, Kangundo, 9 Feb. 1900, *Hearing and Doing* (April 1900), p. 6.

68. PRO: Hardinge to F.O., 18 March 1899, FO 2/190. Ainsworth, Diary, 15 May 1896. Interviews: Zura w/o Muhammad and anonymous male, Kitui Town.

heard performed in 1912 by an itinerant Kitui minstrel lamented this movement of women into the towns:

> When it rains very little, we are deprived of
>   the wives. . . .
> It is then it has caused to be lost Mweli, child
>   of e-Mulinga.
> It is then it has caused to be lost Mweke . . . and
>   Niki and Nthansi.
> You have caused to be lost by the rice.
> They have gone to wash leso [cloth],
> to dig with the back [an allusion to sexual
>   intercourse].
> May they pass.[69]

At the same time, the town markets assumed a much greater role in external commerce. The railroad quickly challenged caravan routes for domination of commerce moving between the coast and the interior and thus channeled trade along official routes. As a result, a growing proportion of the commodities bound to or from the coast moved through the new administrative and market centers. With market-places expanding and British influence on the rise, a number of the coastal traders who had previously ranged widely in the region established permanent bases in one or the other of these towns.[70] Whatever their long-term significance, these developments made little impact on most of the people who were struggling to cope with famine. The British still had only tentative control in areas beyond the immediate neighborhood of their few fortified posts, along the region's southern edge. The establishment of a new station at Kitui marked a move into the settled heart of the region, but in the late 1890s the entire British presence there consisted only of a single administrator supported and protected by a force of thirty-eight African soldiers and policemen and a series of alliances with local elders. In Mumoni and Migwani, which theoretically fell within the confines of the vast Kitui District, people were aware of the British presence, but they certainly did not comprehend, let alone accept, the absolute nature of British claims to their land.[71]

In these areas, as in most of central Kenya during the famine, it was

69. Lindblom, *Kamba Folklore*, 3:42. The women who had moved into the towns were often regarded as prostitutes by people from rural areas. Ibid., p. 44.
70. PRO: Hardinge to F.O., 18 March 1899, FO 2/190. KNA: Kitui District Political Record Book, 1890–1948 [entry written 1919], DC/KTI.7/1. Lane, "Report on Kitui," p. 29.
71. PRO: Ainsworth to Hardinge, 29 Dec. 1897, in Hardinge to F.O., 14 Jan. 1898, FO 107/90. Ainsworth, Diary, 19 Dec. 1897 and 7 March 1899.

the established institutions and patterns of regional exchange that governed the struggle for survival. Indeed, British officials themselves made regular attempts to encourage the circulation of food within the region. With an exaggerated confidence that their actions would facilitate trade, they issued chits to groups of hungry people traveling to the highlands; and on at least one occasion, an official personally led a relief caravan from Kitui to Mount Kenya.[72] But such intervention may well have undermined established exchange relationships. The tendency of both official and unofficial Europeans (as well as traders from the coast) to coerce trade presumably provoked hostility and made it more difficult for future parties of hungry people to obtain food. Similarly, when British officers took it upon themselves to release Kitui women held in Gikuyuland, these actions had the effect of weakening confidence in pawning contracts, thus partly closing off an important avenue of famine relief.[73]

EPIDEMIC AND DISORDER

Hunger created enormous hardship, but disease rather than starvation was responsible for death on a massive scale. The major killer was smallpox. Beginning in early 1899 an epidemic swept over the region, attacking the hungry and the well fed without discrimination.[74] For nearly a year, the disease ravaged communities weakened by a year of famine. The contagion spread along a profusion of routes, carried in every direction by the traders and refugees whom the famine had forced into a continual search for food.[75] Sparing no area of the region, smallpox hit hardest in the highlands, where unusually dense concentrations of impoverished refugees eliminated the natural defense that dispersed, rural societies ordinarily have against general epidemic.[76]

72. Lane, "Report on Kitui," pp. 28–29; and Mackinder, Diary, entries for Aug. 1899.

73. PRO: Crawshay to Ainsworth, Kitui, 20 Jan. 1899, in Hardinge to F.O., 18 Feb. 1899, FO 2/189. Lane, "Report on Kitui," pp. 28–29; Mackinder, Diary, 5 and 7 Aug. 1899; and Boyes, *King of Kikuyu*, pp. 248–50.

74. Miller, "Drought, Disease and Famine," p. 23; and Marc H. Dawson, "Smallpox in Kenya, 1880–1920," *Social Science and Medicine* 13B (1979): 245. Of course, mortality rates were higher among malnourished people.

75. The development of the smallpox epidemic is outlined in Marc H. Dawson, "Socio-Economic and Epidemiological Change in Kenya, 1880–1925" (Ph.D. diss., University of Wisconsin, Madison, 1983), pp. 36–39. Also Ambler, "Central Kenya," pp. 364–65.

76. For estimates of death rates, see Dawson, "Smallpox in Kenya," pp. 245–47, and the sources cited therein. Also Hartwig, "Social Consequences of Epidemic," p. 27. Some contemporary accounts of the epidemic include PRO: Ainsworth to Hardinge, 28 Dec. 1899,

Families and communities sought to build barriers against disease by protecting themselves against the outsiders they saw as carriers. With appropriate rites, they purified the gates to their homesteads and the paths leading into their neighborhoods. When they left their home areas, they made offerings, performed rituals, and carried special charms to protect themselves from the disease. In Embu and in neighboring Chuka, areas already isolationist in outlook, elders had considerable success in blocking the epidemic's advance simply by discouraging most contact with outsiders.[77] Those who contracted smallpox elsewhere were often isolated, sometimes in special camps for the sick, where they were cared for by people who had acquired immunity through previous infection. Refugees in Gikuyuland were occasionally forced to nurse the sick, so that local people could avoid contact with the disease.[78] Given the pervasive danger of infection, it is hardly surprising that fear of smallpox increasingly translated itself into a general antagonism toward outsiders. Itinerant refugees came to be seen more as a source of disease than as a source of livestock and labor. A European trader witnessed a group of some seventy such people who, having fled famine conditions in their homes in Ulu and Kitui, were attempting to cross the Tana River on their way to the Gikuyu highlands.

> They were extremely emaciated, and so weak that three or four . . . were drowned. Suddenly the Maranga [people from central Gikuyuland] who were watching them raised the shrill cry of "Ndui! Ndui!" (smallpox), and rushing at those of the Wakamba who had already landed, then drove them into the water and across the river again.[79]

This incident suggests that people in the highlands were coming increasingly to define the spread of epidemic in ethnic terms, as the result

in Hardinge to F.O., 7 Jan. 1900, FO 2/284; and Ainsworth to Hardinge, 24 Jan. 1900, in Hardinge to F.O., 5 Feb. 1900, FO 2/284. Boyes, *King of Kikuyu*, pp. 243–44; and Arkell-Hardwick, *Ivory Trader*, pp. 59, 354. Interviews: Kavindu s/o Ikunga and Nzunya w/o Mbondo, Mumoni; Paul Ngutu s/o Ngutha and Wamui w/o Munyasia, Migwani; Sarimu Njavari, Mutinda s/o Ruanyaki, and Cigana s/o Karere, Mbeere.

77. Arkell-Hardwick, *Ivory Trader*, p. 59. Interviews: Gideon s/o Mwea wa Methumu, Embu; Mwalimu Charley, Kitui Town; Ngatu s/o Mauna, Migwani; Nzunya w/o Mbondo, Mumoni. In comparison to those of neighboring societies, Embu traditions contain little information on the epidemic.

78. Leakey, *Southern Kikuyu*, 2:899–900; and J. Patterson, Kenya Land Commission, *Evidence*, 1:146. Interviews: Paul Ngutu s/o Ngutha, Migwani; Sarimu Njavari and Mutinda s/o Ruanyaki, Mbeere. Dawson disputes claims that inoculation was practiced in some areas of central Kenya. "Socio-Economic and Epidemiological Change," pp. 43–44.

79. Arkell-Hardwick, *Ivory Trader*, p. 354.

of the movement of Kamba-speaking refugees and traders.[80] Such attitudes were portentous for refugees dependent on the surplus production of highland societies. In fact, basic regional exchange relationships were showing the strain of more than a year of crisis. Coercion and violence made travel more and more dangerous, as fears of disease grew and competition over scarce resources intensified. Despite often desperate circumstances, men and women from Kitui and Ulu became reluctant to leave the relative safety of their homes; at the same time, attacks against refugees, including women and children, were reportedly provoking a considerable exodus from Gikuyuland back to Ulu. But as a local missionary noted, this was "only a case of 'out of the frying pan into the fire,' as they come back here to starve."[81]

By the close of 1899 the combined effects of starvation and disease had killed many thousands of people, although most of the contemporary estimates of the scale of death were basically guesswork. The one systematic attempt to reconstruct the mortality rate for a single community revealed that in one neighborhood in southern Gikuyuland twenty-four of seventy-one adult males died.[82] But this and other evidence also makes plain that the extent of death varied substantially even between neighboring areas. The movement away from famine areas also led some observers to conclude that the former inhabitants of depopulated localities had died. Suggestions that the death rate reached as high as 90 percent—however speculative—did convey the sense of horror that people felt at the grisly scenes they often witnessed. The dead and dying certainly became commonplace sights along central Kenya's paths.[83] Several decades later a missionary recalled that on a tour through Ulu in the immediate aftermath of the famine he found many deserted villages: "Evidently they had died, because the villages were all there; you could go in and find their things undisturbed. . . . It looked as though these people were away for the day, and then, of course, there were skeletons all over the place."[84] Oral testi-

80. Ibid., pp. 60–61; and Mwaniki, *Embu Texts*, p. 304. Interviews: Paul Ngutu s/o Ngutha, Migwani; Mutinda s/o Ruanyaki, Mbeere.

81. Bangert to Hurlburt, Kangundo, Aug. 1899, *Hearing and Doing* (Oct. 1899), pp. 4–5.

82. Kershaw, "Land is the People," p. 171. Mortality estimates are summarized in Ambler, "Central Kenya," pp. 381–82. Also Ainsworth, "Report on Ukamba, 1905," p. 25. The daily death rate in the Machakos relief camp in late 1899 was 2 percent (of total numbers over one thousand). Johnston to Hurlburt, Kangundo, 3 Nov. 1899, *Hearing and Doing* (Jan. 1900), p. 3.

83. See, for example, Hardinge, "Report on British East Africa, 1897–98," p. 9; Mackinder, Diary, 13 July 1899; and excerpted missionary letters in *Hearing and Doing*.

84. C. Johnston, Kenya Land Commission, *Evidence*, 2:1438.

monies provide repeated and similarly stark substantiation of death occurring on an appalling scale. Despite wide local variation in death rates, the region as a whole clearly experienced a devastating loss of life.

During the hard months of 1899 this rising tide of death increasingly threatened the moral order in those sections of the region hardest hit by hunger and disease. Men and women found themselves engaged in grim and often lonely struggles for existence, as depopulation weakened the bonds of community. Desperate people concentrated on the preservation of their immediate families, retreating from the wider networks of kin that ordinarily dominated small societies. Leaders like Nzambu wa Ndove, who managed to stem the process of social fragmentation, were exceedingly rare.[85] Instead, patrons cut loose their clients; and men retreated from their traditional responsibilities to in-laws, lineage-mates, and members of their extended families. One Migwani man who had found refuge in Mwimbe agreed to accommodate his daughter when she followed him there but turned away her husband. Missionaries in Ulu took in one woman who had been driven away by her family because she had become lame and another—described as a slave—who had also been left to fend for herself. In Mumoni, an orphan found himself abandoned by a guardian who absconded with the boy's small inheritance of livestock.[86]

By the closing months of 1899—the climax of the famine—even the most intimate family bonds were dissolving. Husbands deserted their wives and children, mothers their babies. On one occasion, twenty-four homeless children were found dead, huddled together inside a small, abandoned house.[87] It is difficult for us, after nearly a century, to comprehend how people adapted emotionally to the spectacle of death, suffering, and cruelty that enveloped them. For many, the memories of the famine remained vivid and painful; as late as the 1950s, people in southern Gikuyuland were reluctant to describe the

---

85. There were apparently a few other Kitui leaders who attempted to organize famine victims from other areas. Ainsworth, Diary, 23 Oct. 1898.

86. PRO: Extract of a letter from Ainsworth in Crauford to F.O., 30 May 1899, FO 2/196. Bangert, letter, Kangundo, 24 March 1899, *Hearing and Doing* (May 1898), p. 6. Interviews: Nguuti s/o Ndana, Wamui w/o Munyasia, and Mukusu s/o Mututhu, Migwani; Masila s/o Kivunza and Muvali s/o Kilanga, both Mumoni.

87. PRO: Extract of a letter from Ainsworth in Crauford to F.O., 30 May 1899, FO 2/196. Hotchkiss, letter, Kangundo, 24 March 1899, *Hearing and Doing* (May 1899), pp. 4–5; and Bangert, letter, Kangundo, 17 Nov. 1899, *Hearing and Doing* (Jan. 1900), p. 5.

specific experiences of their families or to mention those who had died.[88]

When relatives died or fled, the remaining husbands, wives, and children were often left defenseless and in desperate straits. One woman recalled how, as a child, she and her sister wandered from place to place in Migwani searching for food and shelter. The country was lifeless and so dry that homes easily caught fire and burned. People with food or livestock were continually threatened by thieves, while those with nothing had to protect themselves against attacks from increasingly brazen and vicious hyenas. To that young girl it seemed as if society itself had ceased to exist.[89] A Migwani man echoed her feelings when he recalled that "if someone met another weak person he could take all his possessions and leave him to die."[90] Communities in drought-stricken areas were near collapse, and much of the rest of the region seemed on the edge of chaos. The struggle for basic existence took precedence over the established codes of behavior; one witness later remembered that "during the famine it was a question of the survival of the fittest."[91]

Across the southern sections of the region, desperation bred lawlessness, and violence became commonplace. According to a British official, "In Kitui, thefts, robbery and murder are becoming daily occurrences. In Ulu, cattle thefts, etc. are being reported daily."[92] Administrators complained that their casual workers openly stole everything they could: "They even steal loads of Famine Relief food when carrying it from the station to the camp. They steal the horse blankets & any mortal thing they can see. . . . They won't carry a load without breaking it open."[93] The missionaries in northern Ulu were kept awake at night by shouting, as local people tried to keep thieves away from the few crops in their fields. Increasingly, violence sur-

88. Kershaw, "Land is the People," pp. 170–74. The same reluctance was still evident among some of the people whom I interviewed.

89. Interview: Wamui w/o Munyasia, Migwani.

90. Interview: Mutia s/o Mboo, Migwani.

91. J. Patterson, Kenya Land Commission, *Evidence*, 1:150. Also Hall, letter, 15 Aug. 1899. Despite the breakdown in community bonds and even occasional—perhaps apocryphal—references to cannibalism in the sources, central Kenya had certainly not disintegrated to the point of southern Africa during the *Mfecane*. For comparison see Leonard M. Thompson, "Co-operation and Conflict: The High Veld," in *The Oxford History of South Africa*, vol. 1, ed. Monica Wilson and Leonard Thompson (Oxford, 1969), pp. 391–405.

92. PRO: Ainsworth to Crauford, 23 June 1899, in Crauford to F.O., 10 July 1899, FO 2/197.

93. Hall, letter, Machakos, 20 Dec. 1899.

rounded them, with local factions fighting one another over food and livestock. In Mumoni, raiders from the eastern sections near Ngomeni launched a series of unusually destructive assaults against their marginally more prosperous brethren to the west near the hills. On the region's southern edge, local men often attacked the construction camps along the railroad line, setting off a violent cycle of retribution.[94]

Worn down by months of starvation, people turned their anger against isolated individuals, often abandoned women who were believed to be thieves or witches.[95] Rather than risk such attacks, men, women, and children who had been left alone often banded together for mutual protection. Some famine victims formed outlaw organizations, known as *muthakethe*, and maintained themselves through banditry. Ignoring the accepted strict limits on the use of violence, these bands preyed on the most vulnerable members of society, including children, the elderly, and the sick. Ranging out from makeshift bush camps, outlaw raiders attacked poorly defended herds and homesteads, seizing not only cattle and goats, but whatever food and property they could lay their hands on. Bandit gangs based in the haphazard settlements that Kitui people had established along the Tana River hit regularly at the groups of travelers that moved along the nearby routes to the highlands.[96] Parties of refugees were routinely attacked from every side, victimized by warriors who carried off property, foodstuffs, and female hostages. Youths from some of the highland areas saw this kind of raiding as an opportunity to acquire the wealth and dependents that would permit rapid advancement.[97]

Meanwhile, the refugees themselves increasingly disregarded law and custom in their search for food. With growing regularity, they took food from granaries and fields by force, sometimes going so far as

94. Bangert to Hurlburt, Kangundo, 17 and 27 July 1899, *Hearing and Doing* (Aug.–Sept. 1899), pp. 7–8; Ainsworth, Diary, 5 Oct. 1898, and passim; Hall, letter, 5 Aug. 1899; Carson, *Life Story of a Chief*, p. 16; and Mungeam, *British Rule in Kenya*, p. 62.

95. Hotchkiss to Hurlburt, Kangundo, 9 April 1899, *Hearing and Doing* (May 1899), p. 5.

96. PRO: Ainsworth to Crauford, 23 June 1899, in Crauford to F.O., 10 July 1899, FO 2/197. *Taveta Chronicle* (Oct. 1899), p. 167. Interviews: Mutia s/o Mboo, Ngavi s/o Mwanzi, and Munyasia s/o Kalwe, Migwani; Manderi s/o Munzungi, Lang'a s/o Ngile, Masila s/o Kivunza, and Munithya s/o Nganza, Mumoni; Mwige Kwigiriira, Mbeere.

97. PRO: Hardinge to F.O., 12 Aug. 1898, FO 107/95. Ainsworth, Diary, 29 March, 9 June, and 11 June, 1898; Lane, "Report on Kitui," p. 29; Boyes, *King of Kikuyu*, p. 248; and Carson, *Life Story of a Chief*, p. 16. Interviews: Mwalimu Charley, Kitui Town; Munyasia s/o Kalwe, Kilungi s/o Kithita, Itali s/o Mwethya with Mumbi w/o Itali, Nguuti s/o Ndana, Nguli s/o Kinuva, and Kasina s/o Ndoo, Migwani; Manunga s/o Nguci and Mwige Kwigiriira, Mbeere.

to repudiate the supposedly sacrosanct obligations of blood partnership.[98] From the perspective of the victims of theft, these acts represented a violation of civilized behavior. Seventy-five years after the fact, a woman in Mbeere still recalled the transgressions of Kitui refugees with outrage. In her words, "They stepped on the feces of the children."[99]

THE END OF FAMINE

In the last months of 1899 abundant rainfall brought an end to the drought that had devastated central Kenya for two years, but brought no immediate end to hunger. In fact, for many in Ulu and Kitui this would be the worst period of suffering. Despite the rain, fields remained choked with weeds, their owners dead, absent in the highlands, or lacking the energy or seeds to plant. One observer described famine-stricken communities as still chaotic and demoralized.[100] Even those farmers who had crops in the ground had to endure the long weeks until harvest. Indeed, hunger drove many farming families to eat plants before they matured, leaving them without sufficient grain to provide seed and food for the next season. With harvests still meager, livestock herds much depleted, and labor in short supply, it would be several seasons before agricultural production recovered and food became available in adequate amounts and variety.[101]

In this early period of recovery, raiders from Mumoni, northern Kitui, and Ulu bent on sating their immediate hunger and recovering some of their lost wealth descended on Mbeere communities. In an uncoordinated mass assault, waves of armed groups—including both men and women—repeatedly crossed the Tana River, seizing food, livestock, and hostages and gradually moving across Mbeere toward Mount Kenya. One man recalled, "Our warriors could not resist the force of these hungry people."[102] Eventually, in fighting that is dra-

---

98. Interviews: Manunga s/o Nguci, Syanderi w/o Muivia, and Maringa Maunge, Mbeere.

99. Interview: Syanderi w/o Muivia, Mbeere.

100. PRO: Hardinge to F.O., 7 Jan. 1900, including Ainsworth to Hardinge, 28 Dec. 1899, FO 2/284; and Ainsworth to Hardinge, 21 Jan. 1900, in Hardinge to F.O., 5 Feb. 1900, FO 2/284.

101. Johnston, letter, Kangundo, 13 Dec. 1899, *Hearing and Doing* (March 1900), p. 4; and Ainsworth, "Report on Ukamba, 1905," p. 26. Also see Wisner and Mbithi, "Drought in Eastern Kenya," p. 90.

102. Mwaniki, *Embu Texts*, p. 191. Traditions for these raids are among the most complete in the whole body of oral evidence for the eastern sections of central Kenya. The earliest

matized in oral records from both sides of the Tana, warriors from Ndia and Embu repulsed the ragtag horde of invaders and forced them home. Embu traditions celebrate this action as their victory, yet many of the defeated raiders had in fact captured considerable stocks of food and livestock in the early assaults. In truth, the clearest losers were families in Mbeere, many of whom were left thoroughly impoverished.[103] For Embu, victory was a mixed blessing. Although the attacks themselves scarcely touched Embu communities, the episode reinforced an intransigent, defensive unity. Particularly among the warrior class, the experience of combat seems to have encouraged an unrealistic confidence in Embu military strength, setting the stage for the disastrous confrontation with the British in 1906.[104]

The booty that raiders from Mumoni and Migwani captured in Mbeere not only helped them through the last months of hunger, but provided the chance for a few men to build up their positions of wealth and influence.[105] Most of those who organized and profited from the raids came from lineages that had managed to hold on to some wealth during the famine. In general, the famine accentuated the distance between rich and poor. One observer noted, "The poor people simply died and the rich survived."[106] These processes of accumulation reflected a gradual redistribution of wealth and authority across the region. Many of those leaders who emerged from the famine had built their wealth and influence as brokers in regional and long-distance commerce, but the success of others was the product of their close association with new institutions.[107] Men who had attached themselves to missions during the famine were sent back to their homes with a supply of seeds as well as a critical set of contacts. From the mission point of view, the famine represented a "marvelous opportunity for . . .

---

published mentions are H. R. Tate, "Account of a Journey from Rendille to Nairobi," *East African Quarterly* 3 (1904): 175; Orde-Browne, *Vanishing Tribes*, p. 54; and Jumea bin Makane, Kenya Land Commission, *Evidence*, 1:945. For a fuller description of the raids, and for the oral sources, see Mwaniki, "History of Embu," pp. 350–55; and Ambler, "Central Kenya," pp. 376–80.

103. Mwaniki, *Embu Texts*, p. 203. Interviews: Nguku s/o Kuliria, Ngai w/o Nthoroko, and Benjamin Kau s/o Kimwele, Mbeere; Mwinzi s/o Kathinzi and Mwangangi s/o Mathenge, Mumoni; Mwalimu Charley, Kitui Town.

104. PRO: Hardinge to F.O., 7 Jan. 1900, FO 2/284. Interview: Johana Kavuru s/o Muruanjuya, Embu.

105. Mwaniki, *Embu Texts*, p. 195. Interviews: Mulango s/o Ngusia, Ngatu s/o Mauna, Muito s/o Muthama, Muli s/o Ndulwa, Migwani; Muli s/o Kakuru, Kimwele s/o Kyota, and Mwinzi s/o Kathinzi, Mumoni; Sarimu Njavari, Mbeere.

106. J. Patterson, Kenya Land Commission, *Evidence*, 1:150.

107. Interviews: Nguuti s/o Ndana and Wamui w/o Munyasia, Migwani.

getting the gospel into the hearts of these people, who, when the famine is over, will return to their homes, which are located over a good share of Ukambani [Ulu]."[108] Even more striking was the way that the individuals whom the British recognized as "chiefs" were able to accumulate power during the famine. Despite sometimes violent local hostility, a number of such men were able to expand substantially both their livestock herds and their circles of dependents and clients.[109]

With society in turmoil, men who had been able to hold on to some livestock and maintain their families were often in the position to ignore the rule of law. There were reports, for example, of local leaders who stole livestock and even killed poor men in order to seize their herds.[110] As the famine wound down, a legacy of unresolved disputes and unsettled scores provided such "big men" the opportunity to confirm and entrench their wealth and influence. In early 1900, when he was shutting down the Machakos relief camp, Francis Hall noted that the "Chiefs . . . are only too glad to adopt any orphans we have to spare."[111] One woman from a poor background pointed to this process of accumulation with some bitterness: "When the people who had gone away came back those rich men who had remained tried to keep those returning from owning anything."[112]

108. Bangert to Hurlburt, Kangundo, 8 April 1899, *Hearing and Doing* (May 1899), p. 7. Also Bangert to Hurlburt, Kangundo, 9 Feb. 1900, *Hearing and Doing* (April 1900), p. 6.

109. Johnston, letter, Kangundo, 5 Nov. 1899, *Hearing and Doing* (Jan. 1900), p. 5.

110. J. Patterson, Kenya Land Commission, *Evidence*, 1:150. Also PRO: Hardinge to F.O., 18 March 1899, FO 2/190; and Ainsworth to Hardinge, 28 Dec. 1899, in Hardinge to F.O., 7 Jan. 1900, FO 2/284. Merritt, "History of Taita," p. 124.

111. Hall, letter, Machakos, 12 Jan. 1900.

112. Interview: Wamui w/o Munyasia, Migwani.

7

Redefining the Region

THE AFTERMATH OF THE GREAT FAMINE

In late 1899 or early 1900, Nzambu wa Ndove left the refugee settlement he had established in Mwimbe to return home to Migwani.[1] The group that traveled with him was certainly not the same as the one that he had led to Mwimbe a year or more earlier. The numbers were smaller. Of the original party, many were dead from smallpox or the effects of hunger; and others—young women—had married into Mwimbe communities and would remain there permanently. Within the group returning to Migwani there were also new people—men, women, and children largely from northern Kitui who had made their way to Mwimbe and had found security in Nzambu's refugee community. Nzambu and his followers, like other refugees leaving the highlands, returned to the arduous and painful task of rebuilding a society devastated by famine and death. With little food available until the next harvest, they had to prepare fields, plant crops, and construct new homesteads. For many, the lingering effects of hunger and disease made physical work difficult. Worse, the heavy death toll made the individual burden of work that much heavier.[2]

The survivors who returned to Migwani—like others across Kitui, Ulu, and southern Gikuyuland—not only had to rebuild local economies, but also to reassemble or reconstitute families and lineages that had been reduced, fragmented, or dispersed by death and migration.

1. See the sources cited for the discussion of Nzambu's career, above in the Introduction.
2. Wright, "Societies and Economies in Kenya," p. 188.

Because such large numbers of livestock had died or been sold off, the material means to accomplish this were often lacking. Many families thus found themselves even more dependent than before for assistance and protection on those local men like Nzambu who had managed to preserve or increase their wealth despite—or because of—the famine.

Survivors could not hope to recreate the communities that had existed before the famine, notwithstanding the remarkable resiliency of local institutions. For a Migwani woman, even after the pain of hunger subsided, the stench of death persisted:

> After the famine, a season came when people planted millet and it came up very well. But you could not walk in the fields because of the corpses of those who had died. You would see a pumpkin or a gourd but you couldn't get to them because they were on top of the bodies of people.[3]

The hyperbole of this remembrance conveys both a child's horror at the parched bones that littered the central Kenya.landscape and an adult's understanding of the profound impact that the famine had on those who survived.[4] In itself the famine altered patterns of settlement, exchange, and wealth, but the experience of disaster also changed perceptions of the environment and how best to exploit it. Farmers withdrew from some of the low-lying areas in southern Gikuyuland, resettling in forest areas, which offered more secure rainfall but less opportunity for grazing. Across the famine zone, in fact, the decline in both human and livestock populations made the plains zone less attractive for settlement. In the long term, the resulting movement into the hills opened some grasslands areas to the advance of tsetse fly infestation, making it difficult for farmers to revive local cattle economies.[5]

In Mumoni, the famine set in motion a rapid decline in the fortunes of the large *mbenge* villages that had been such a conspicuous element of local society in the 1880s and 1890s. Families moved into smaller hamlets, perhaps aware of the heavy pressures that population concentration placed on fragile resources. At the same time, the reduction in herds and the disruption and redirection of major trade eliminated both the means and purpose of village concentration.[6] In both Mu-

3. Interview: Wife of Kithusi, Migwani.

4. Severn to Hurlburt, Kangundo, 13 May 1900, *Hearing and Doing* (June 1900), p. 6; and Lindblom, *Akamba*, p. 24.

5. PRO: Dickson, "Report on the Country between Nairobi, Mbirri and Kitui," 12 Nov. 1901, in Eliot to F.O., 8 Dec. 1901, FO 2/451. Tate, "Journey from Rendille to Nairobi," p. 228. White settlers occupied some of the abandoned lands in southern Gikuyuland. Muriuki, *History of Kikuyu*, p. 173.

6. Arkell-Hardwick, *Ivory Trader*, p. 59. Interview: Mwinzi s/o Kathinzi, Mumoni. Iliffe discusses population dispersion in *History of Tanganyika*, pp. 163–66.

moni and Migwani, population dispersal was already well under way before colonial authority was established and was not therefore a product of the imposition of colonialism. On a journey across Migwani in 1891, C. W. Hobley described numerous large villages and dense cultivation, but when he returned there in 1908—when British rule was barely established—he reported that the local population lived in widely scattered homesteads.[7] The experience of Mumoni and Migwani, however, was not the experience of the region as a whole. In northeastern Gikuyuland, in Ndia, and in eastern Ulu, men such as Mwatu wa Ngoma actually consolidated and expanded their villages and the extent of their influence.

If the local patterns of change were diverse, in a broader sense, the period that culminated in famine clearly saw an expansion of social scale. The rapid upsurge in trade generated a mass of connections among individuals, families, and communities that would persist in subsequent decades. The experience of contact in turn forced people to look beyond the boundaries of their small home localities and see themselves as part of a much wider world. More than half a century later, this expansion of perspective was still clearly evident in the recollections of women, many of whom scarcely left their home areas again. In sum, the famine left contradictory legacies. On one hand, the massive movement of people and commodities strengthened the basic structures of regional interchange and regional economic autonomy. But on the other, the famine so weakened the individual societies and economies of central Kenya that they were vulnerable to political subjugation and economic penetration.

THE IDEOLOGY OF TRIBE

In the decade that followed the famine, the British rapidly extended their control across the entire central Kenya region. British representatives made a series of alliance agreements with local leaders—often extracted with demonstrations of force—which rapidly evolved into the apparatus of administration. In some of the Mount Kenya societies, notably in Embu, the population organized concerted resistance, but most was extinguished within months.[8] Important traders and war-

---

7. Hobley, Safari Diary, 23 Nov. 1891; and Hobley, "Nairobi to Fort Hall," p. 262.

8. For the details of establishment of British authority, see Mungeam, *British Rule in Kenya*; Munro, *Colonial Rule and the Kamba*, pp. 31–50; and for the communities discussed in detail in this book, Ambler, "Central Kenya," pp. 395–400. The outstanding analysis of the transition to colonial rule in Kenya is John Lonsdale and Bruce Berman, "Coping

lords, like Kilungya wa Mutia from Mumoni, Gutu wa Kibetu from Ndia, and Mwatu wa Ngoma from Mwala, rapidly evolved from British allies to clients to "chiefs" in the colonial service. Nzambu wa Ndove became a minor functionary, eclipsed by other Migwani men.[9] During this period of the rapid expansion of colonial authority, a great many local leaders claimed to represent British interests, their profusion reflecting the dispersion of power to myriad autonomous communities. Often these men staked their claims on possession of a *barua*, literally, a "letter," but often no more than a small scrap of paper.[10] The British soon moved to establish a clear hierarchy among these men, reducing many to distinctly subordinate status. This classification of chiefs was part of a larger process in which the new rulers of central Kenya sought to devise a rational administrative structure, consistent with their view of the nature of "primitive" societies.[11]

Consumed themselves by notions of national character and mission, Europeans made mental maps of an Africa comprised of neatly bounded, homogenous tribes, units in which physical, cultural, and even psychological attributes would find neat correlation.[12] If the British agents who were stationed in central Kenya before 1900 often misunderstood local societies, the reports they wrote at least betray an appreciation of the autonomy and fluidity of small communities. For these officials success required the accommodation of an existing political and commercial order. Their successors, having gained military and economic dominance over African societies, were free to devise a colonial system that conformed to the prevailing European conception of Africa.[13] What they envisioned ultimately was a constellation of ethnically exclusive districts that incorporated deeply rooted, isolated, and mutually antagonistic tribes.[14] The gradual assertion of this

with the Contradictions: The Development of the Colonial State in Kenya, 1895–1914," *Journal of African History* 20 (1979): 487–506.

9. He was appointed a subheadman in 1916. KNA: General list of Kitui Headmen, DC/KTI.7/5.

10. KNA: Kitui District, Quarterly Report, June 1910, DC/MKS.1/1/2.

11. See Iliffe, *History of Tanganyika*, p. 318.

12. See Douglas A. Lorimer, *Colour, Class and the Victorians: English Attitudes to the Negro in the Mid-Nineteenth Century* (New York, 1978), p. 202. The extreme South African manifestation of this view is discussed in Leonard M. Thompson, *The Political Mythology of Apartheid* (New Haven, 1985), p. 197.

13. For an interesting exception, see Norman Leys, *Kenya* (London, 1924), pp. 32–33, 87–89.

14. This shift in outlook can be traced clearly in the evolving attitudes of several pioneer representatives of British interests. See Ainsworth, "Report on Ukamba, 1905," p. 1; and Hobley's written memorandum to the Kenya Land Commission, *Evidence*, 1:125. Also

framework involved not only the creation of a neatly segmented administrative order, but the redirection of the flow of commodities and labor to reinforce this order. In other words the commercial development of each outlying district increasingly focused on its relationship to the emerging capitalist economy of the center—Nairobi and the white-owned agricultural estates.[15]

Against this trend, the entrenched structures of regional exchange persisted. For several decades a large volume of livestock, food, and labor continued to move between the highlands and communities in the hill and plains zones, but eventually the opportunities for cash crop agriculture and wage labor, the construction of a road network, and the imposition of a series of restrictions on free trade made the new patterns of commerce predominant. Yet seventy years after the great famine the logic of ecological and economic complementarity still drove men and women from Mumoni to seek work in Embu when food was in short supply. In the 1970s, however, these workers no longer followed the 40-mile direct route to Mount Kenya. No road had ever been constructed linking the two areas, and the remaining paths were obscured by weeds. The only bus route ran from Mumoni—defined as Kamba territory—through other Kamba-speaking districts to the towns and estates of Kenya's economic and political center and only then to Embu—a distance of 150 miles.[16]

If British policies provided the impetus for ethnic exclusivity, it was local men and women who created and refined the new concepts of tribe.[17] For them the construction of the colonial state and economy demanded a redefinition of identity. Gradually, the overlapping, large identities that had shaped interaction in the regional context gave way to a more exclusive identification with ethnic groupings such as Kamba, Gikuyu, Embu, or Meru. In a period of rapid social, economic, and political change, tribes were seen as the vehicles of individual and community progress.[18] The competition for the resources of the state

see Hall, "Kikuyu," p. 156; Tate, "Kikuyu and Kamba Tribes," p. 256; and Dundas, "History of Kitui," p. 74.

15. See Bernard, "Meru in the Kenya Spatial Economy"; and Ambler, "Central Kenya," pp. 400–17.

16. Wisner and Mbithi, "Drought in Eastern Kenya," pp. 88, 94.

17. For illustration of this process, see the comments of J. Kenyatta in Kenya Land Commission, *Evidence*, 1:123; and Harry Thuku (with the assistance of Kenneth King) in *An Autobiography* (Nairobi, 1970), pp. 2–3. Also Iliffe, *History of Tanganyika*, p. 318; and C. S. Lancaster, "Ethnic Identity, History, and 'Tribe' in the Middle Zambezi Valley," *American Ethnologist* 1 (1974): 707–30.

18. Ambler, "The Renovation of Custom in Colonial Kenya."

increasingly pitted tribe against tribe, with predictably inflammatory results.[19] Although ethnic identities became steadily more visible and divisive, the emergence of tribes was only one aspect of a more complex process of social and cultural redefinition. The small locality—variously conceived—continued to dominate the outlook of most people at most times.[20]

By the advent of independence, popular, official, and scholarly views had essentially converged, with increasingly virulent ethnic conflicts seen as the direct product of centuries of tribal divisions.[21] From this perspective precolonial history became the record of the migration and resettlement of coherent tribes—the direct ancestors of contemporary ethnic groups—and their occasional collision with equally exclusive "enemies." While the scholarly assault on the concept of tribe dates back to the 1960s, history continues to be written in ethnic terms, especially in the form of popular histories of particular ethnic groups.[22] Likewise, the elders of Mumoni, Migwani, Mbeere, and Embu have increasingly defined the histories of their communities in

19. See, for example, Brian du Toit, ed., *Ethnicity in Africa* (Boulder, Colorado, 1978); Leo Despres, ed., *Ethnicity and Resource Competition in Plural Societies* (The Hague, 1975); and Donald Horowitz, *Ethnic Groups in Conflict* (Berkeley and Los Angeles, 1985).

20. See the useful discussion of the continuities and discontinuities of village response to incorporation within a colonial system in William B. Taylor, *Drinking, Homicide and Rebellion in Colonial Mexican Villages* (Stanford, 1979), pp. 152–70.

21. In a recent article concerning conflict in Uganda, a Kenya businessman is quoted: "You are dealing with hundreds of years of tribalism in that country." *New York Times*, 28 Jan. 1986, p. 4. Wim Van Binsbergen has explored the emergence of "tribal consciousness" in central Africa in "From Tribe to Ethnicity in Western Zambia: The Unit of Study as an Ideological Problem," in *Old Modes of Production and Capitalist Encroachments: Anthropological Explorations in Africa*, ed. W. Van Binsbergen and Peter Geschiere (London, 1985), pp. 181–234.

22. See Aidan Southall, "The Illusion of Tribe," in *The Passage of Tribal Man in Africa*, ed. Peter C. W. Gutkind (Leiden, 1970), pp. 28–50; A. Mafeje, "The Ideology of 'Tribalism,'" *Journal of Modern African Studies* 9 (1971): 253–61; and M. Godelier, *Perspectives in Marxist Anthropology*, trans. Robert Brain (Cambridge, England, 1977), pp. 70–96. Robert Tignor's study of colonial Kenya has an explicitly tribal framework. *The Colonial Transformation of Kenya: The Kamba, Kikuyu and Maasai from 1900 to 1935* (Princeton, 1976). See F. Cooper's review of that work in *African Economic History* 5 (1978): 99–101. One recent survey of modern African history reduces the second half of the nineteenth century in the interior of Kenya to one brief statement of "tribal conflict": "From the mid-nineteenth century the feared Maasai pastoralists lost their grip on the plains of central Kenya while the Kamba people, who traded extensively with the coast, became stronger as did the Kikuyu agriculturalists south of Mount Kenya." Bill Freund, *The Making of Contemporary Africa: The Development of African Society since 1800* (Bloomington, Indiana, 1984), p. 69. One example of such a popular history is Mwaniki, *Living History of Embu*. Leonard Thompson has examined some of the same issues in the South African context in *Political Mythology*, pp. 204–05.

terms of a larger ethnic past. In their repetition of traditions, they describe a region of tribes and a system of tribal interconnection.[23] At
the very least, this study of the late nineteenth century in central Kenya
demonstrates that such a vision of the past—however commonplace—seriously distorts a complex historical experience.

IDENTITY IN HISTORICAL PERSPECTIVE

Despite their strong affinities of language and culture, the people of
nineteenth-century central Kenya lived out their lives in worlds dominated by numerous, distinctive small societies. Within any area, com-
plexes of kinship and territorial relationships bound people into amor-
phous and highly autonomous localities. Few of these societies were at
all precisely bounded, however, and none possessed a unified political
structure. But if communities were overwhelmingly local in outlook,
they were not exclusively so. People identified with others beyond their
lineages, neighborhoods, and sections. The movement of commodities,
individuals, and ideas broke down insularity, drawing communities
into the larger region and beyond.

Movement took two basic forms. Within central Kenya a series of
deeply entrenched trading relationships among communities reproduced the long-term structures of regional interchange.[24] But at the
same time, the movements of migrants and traders continually altered
the patterns of exchange and ultimately the shape of the region itself.
In particular, by the last decades of the nineteenth century, the expansion of long-distance trade into central Kenya had brought fundamental change. Not only were the lines of regional trade sometimes interrupted, but in some areas, where leaders like Mwatu wa Ngoma and
Wang'ombe had established themselves, the emergence of centers of
trade and influence brought an enlargement of scale. These processes
were clearest in the hinterlands of the British posts at Machakos and
Dagoretti, and they were evident if less pronounced in the development
of new settlements in Mumoni and Migwani as well. But Embu's in-

<hr>

23. In this regard the interview transcripts in the volumes on Embu prepared for the
Human Relations Area File, Cross Cultural Study of Ethnocentrism Series make interesting
reading, although conceptually the series begins with the assumption of the centrality of ethnic affiliation. S. Saberwal, *Embu of Kenya*, 2 vols. (New Haven, 1972).

24. I refer advisedly to F. Braudel's concept of "the long term." J. Vansina drew directly on Braudel's historical framework in *The Tio Kingdom of the Middle Congo, 1880–
1892* (London, 1973). The point regarding movement owes much to my discussions with
Robert Harms.

Jul 1 — Aug 30
240

139/2010 5577778

5424 1800 4558 5871

1065 15AUG87 31JUL88
JAMES F SEARING

PRINCETON
UNIVERSITY STORE 031888
PRINCETON NJ
2294823141

(215) 592 7547

PURCHASER SIGN HERE
X

Cardholder acknowledges receipt of goods and/or services in the amount of the Total shown hereon and agrees to perform the obligations set forth in the Cardholder's agreement with the issuer.

3607   GENERAL CREDIT FORMS ST. LOUIS 63045

SAFE PERF® U.S. Pat. 4,403,793

QUAN.	CLASS	DESCRIPTION	PRICE	AMOUNT
1	170-300-0385-4-3			27 00
			SUB TOTAL	
			TAX	1 65

DATE 5/18/88
AUTHORIZATION 9501
REFERENCE NO.
CLERK/DEPT. 0333

MasterCard VISA

TOTAL 28 62

SALES SLIP

creasingly insular unity makes plain that the evolution of local societies followed no single course. Moreover, in many areas—particularly on the frontier—the trend moved in the opposite direction, toward the emergence of a series of small and highly autonomous communities. Over much of the region an intense localism continued to rule political and economic activity. This confusion of patterns was simply a mirror of the region itself—a profusion of societies, each attempting to define its separate future.

My objective in this study has been to describe the struggles of individuals and families to shape their own destinies in a period of rapid economic, political, and environmental change and to convey their experience in terms consistent with the circumstances in which they determined their actions. To people whose conceptions of the larger worlds beyond their home areas were fluid and situational, this analysis—based on the concepts of community and region—might well appear foreign or contrived. It clearly conflicts with the view that their descendants have largely adopted. But tribal or ethnic history puts stability in the place of movement and neat boundaries where complexity ruled. Describing the central Kenya past in regional terms opens up the flexible terrain on which nineteenth-century people saw themselves operating and shows quite explicitly the intricate layers and dynamism of nineteenth-century societies. The histories of communities in Mumoni, Migwani, Mbeere, and Embu reveal in plain terms how popular conceptions of identity evolved and shifted over time and according to circumstances. In contemporary Africa, ethnic boundaries are often the site of intensely bitter and violent conflict; and to many people—Africans and outsiders alike—tribalism represents an atavistic, seemingly insurmountable obstacle to progress.[25] Yet the history of central Kenya makes clear that in Kenya at least the roots of ethnicity are twisted and shallow. For those convinced of the inherency and intractability of ethnic animosity, the peoples of nineteenth-century central Kenya have a story to tell.

25. Elliot Skinner, "Group Dynamics in the Politics of Changing Societies: The Problem of 'Tribal' Politics in Africa," in *Essays on the Problem of Tribe*, ed. June Helm (Seattle, 1968), p. 171. Also Crawford Young, *The Politics of Cultural Pluralism* (Madison, 1976). Nowhere are such circumstances more evident than in present-day South Africa. D. W. Cohen discusses the pervasiveness of the tribal view in "History from Pim's Doorway."

People Interviewed

All interviews were conducted between January 1977 and April 1978 by the author or under his supervision. Most were recorded verbatim by hand from simultaneous translations. Interviews were conducted in Mumoni (northeast Kitui District), Migwani (north central Kitui District), in Kitui Town, in various sections of Mbeere (Embu District), in Kagaari and other areas of Embu (Embu District). Transcript copies have been deposited in the Kenya National Archives and with the History Department, University of Nairobi. The subjects are listed alphabetically for each area. A more precise area of residence is noted where relevant.

MIGWANI

Elizabeth Kitumba w/o Kisenga. Two interviews. Born in the late 1880s to 1890. Convert to Roman Catholicism.

Itali s/o Mwethya with Mumbi w/o Itali. Born, respectively, about 1900 and 1905.

Kaliungi s/o Ikenga. Born 1910s. Served in the army during World War II. Later became a headman.

Kasina s/o Ndoo. Two interviews. Born 1890s. Two of his father's brothers were, in succession, the first chiefs of Migwani under the British. Became a policeman and then himself became chief from 1927 to 1963. His reminiscences were published as a pamphlet. J. B. Carson, ed., *Life Story of a Kenya Chief* (London, 1958). Brother to Mbulwa s/o Ndoo.

Kikwae w/o Nthambu. Born late 1890s. Sister to Munyambu s/o Ngindo.

Kilungi s/o Kithita. Born late 1890s.

Kinyenye s/o Mbuvi. Born ca. 1910. Became a Christian in 1928. Has kept a written record of his life since 1929.

Wife of Kithusi. Born late 1890s.

Komba w/o Nzoka. Two interviews. Born early 1890s.

159

Matha w/o Ngumbi. Born about 1900.

Mavuli s/o Makola. Born about 1910.

Mbasia s/o Muliungi. Born about 1900.

Mbele w/o Nguli. Born mid-1890s.

Mbulwa s/o Ndoo. Born late 1890s. Brother to ex-senior chief Kasina s/o Ndoo.

Muito s/o Muthama. Born 1890s. Served in Carrier Corps, World War I.

Mukusu s/o Mututhu. Born 1890s. Served in Carrier Corps, World War I.

Mulango s/o Ngusia. Two interviews. Born about 1900.

Mulatya s/o Nguli. Born about 1900.

Muli s/o Ndulwa. Two interviews. Born 1890s. Served in Carrier Corps, World War I.

Munuve s/o Lingwa. Born early 1900s. Closely related to Ngavi s/o Mwanzi.

Munyambu s/o Ngindo. Born about 1900. Served as a headman for a period during the colonial years. Brother to Kikwae w/o Nthambu.

Munyasia s/o Kalwe. Was a minor local functionary in the colonial adminis- tration during the period around World War I. Born 1890s.

Musungu Kalola. Assisted by his wife. Born mid to late 1890s.

Mutia s/o Mboo. Two interviews. Born late 1890s.

Ndenge s/o Ngoma. Served in Carrier Corps, World War I.

Nelson Kangu s/o Imeli. Born about 1914. Inactive Christian convert.

Ngatu s/o Mauna. Three interviews. Born late 1880s or earlier. Employed by the British in the early days of colonial rule in a temporary force used to "punish" tax evaders.

Ngavi s/o Mwanzi. Born 1890s. Served in Carrier Corps, World War I.

Nguli s/o Kinuva. Born 1890s. Served in Carrier Corps, World War I. Later became a headman.

Nguli s/o Mbaluka. Born 1890s. Served in Carrier Corps, World War I.

Nguuti s/o Ndana. Three interviews. Born late 1880s to early 1890s. Served in the Carrier Corps, World War I.

Paul Ngutu s/o Ngutha. Three interviews. Born around 1900. Formerly an ac- tive Christian, was a member and president of the District Court in Kitui during the post–World War II period. Has been involved in official ef- forts to collect customary law.

Rose Makaa w/o Mutia. Born about 1895.

Sali w/o Mulewa.

Thitu s/o Nzili. Born 1890s. Was in the Carrier Corps, World War I.

Vungo s/o Ngonzi. Born about 1914. Grandson of Sila wa Ivuli and son of a court official. Served overseas in the armed forces during World War II.

Wamui w/o Munyasia. Born in the mid-1890s.

KITUI TOWN

Anonymous male elder. Born about 1900 in Kitui Town of a Kamba-speaking mother and an Arab or Afro-Arab father. Worked as a trader for various Indian shopkeepers in Kitui beginning in the 1910s. Participated in Na- tionalist Politics in the 1930s.

Hussein Juma. Born in Ulu (Machakos District) in the 1890s. Settled in Machakos Town and converted to Islam. Traded through Gikuyuland and Machakos and Kitui districts.

Meri daughter of Pereira. Born in Kitui early 1900s, daughter of a Goan who came to Kitui soon after 1900 in government service. He remained as a businessman, owning a plot of land and had an African wife. The informant is herself thoroughly incorporated into local Swahili society.

Mwalimu Charley. Born in eastern Kitui mid-1890s. Refugee to Embu during 1897–1901 famine. Went to work for colonial government in 1910s and attended school periodically. For many years a teacher in Kitui Town. Assisted Dr. Stanner in his research in Kitui in 1938–39.

Salim Ndongo. Born in the area north of Kitui Town early 1900s. Followed his father into the police and then joined the army, where he converted to Islam. Settled in Kitui Town.

Zura w/o Muhammad. Born in Ulu (Machakos District) 1890s. Came to Kitui Town because of famine. Married to a Swahili trader.

THARAKA

Maitha w/o Kang'uru. Interviewed near Tana River, Katse Location, Kitui District. Originally from Tharaka, west side of the Tana. Born around 1900.

Muthura s/o Nthiga. Interviewed near Tana River, Katse Location, Kitui District. Born 1890s. From Tharaka.

MUMONI

Ikiriki s/o Masila. Born soon after 1900. Katse Location.

Kalundu s/o Ndai. Interview by Charles Musyoka. Born about 1910. Katse Location.

Kaungo w/o Mutia. Born about 1900. Mivukoni Location.

Kauwima s/o Mutia. Born mid to late 1890s. Was a government-appointed elder and later subchief during the colonial period. Katse Location.

Kavindu s/o Ikunga. Two interviews. Born late 1880s to 1890 in eastern Mumoni. Was for many years, beginning in the 1930s, chief of Katse Location. Succeeded his brother in that post. Katse Location.

Kele s/o Kanandu. Born about 1905. Worked for many years in Mombasa.

Kiliungi s/o Muuru. Two interviews. Born mid to late 1890s. Originally from Tseikuru area. Katse Location.

Kimwele s/o Kyota. Born soon after 1900. Worked in the Nairobi area during the 1920s. Worked in the post office in Mombasa during the 1930s. Katse Location.

Kisalu s/o Kilatya. Born about 1905 in Ndatani in eastern Mumoni. Small-scale livestock trader between the World Wars. Tseikuru Location.

Kisilu s/o Katumo. Born 1890s. Served in Carrier Corps, World War I. Mivukoni Location.

Kiteng'o s/o Mutui. Born late 1890s. Worked in Mombasa early 1920s. Forced to work on railway construction 1920s. Tseikuru Location.

Kitevu s/o Ndaku. Born about 1905. Tseikuru Location.

Malila s/o Nzoka. Born about 1900. Worked in the Mombasa area for many years. Katse Location.

Manderi s/o Munzungi. Born early 1890s. Mivukoni Location.

Masila s/o Kivunza. Born late 1880s to early 1890s. Worked in Nairobi and

Thika prior to World War I. Served in Carrier Corps, World War I. Mivukoni Location.

Mathuva s/o Katui. Born late 1890s. Mivukoni Location.

Mati s/o Mwinzi. Born about 1900. Worked as an assistant to itinerant traders during the 1920s and 1930s. Katse Location.

Muasya s/o Munene. Born late 1890s. Tseikuru Location.

Mukungi s/o Masila. Born about 1905. Katse Location.

Mulanga s/o Ngile. Born 1890s. Served in Carrier Corps, World War I. Was a local elder in colonial administration and became a local policeman. Mivukoni Location.

Mulatya s/o Mutia. Two interviews. Born late 1880s. Served in World War I and was in the police in Nairobi before that time. Katse Location.

Muli s/o Kakuru. Three interviews. Born about 1905. Katse Location.

Muli s/o Sumbi. Interview conducted by Charles Musyoka. Born about 1900. During the 1920s worked on a settler farm and for the railway. Was a subchief in Katse for several years during the 1930s. Katse Location.

Munithya (or Kamau) s/o Mati. Born about 1900. Katse Location.

Munithya s/o Nganza. Born ca. 1905–10. His father's family originated in Tharaka. Katse Location.

Munyasia Mutilu. Interview by Charles Musyoka. Born 1890s to 1900. Possibly in Carrier Corps, World War I. Worked in Mombasa and Nairobi. Katse Location.

Munyoki s/o Mutui. Born mid-1890s. Served in Carrier Corps, World War I. Tseikuru Location.

Musyoka s/o Ndeto. Born ca. 1905–10. Forced into work during the 1920s. Katse Location.

Muthuku s/o Nzuvi. Born about 1905. Did forced railway labor, 1920s.

Muthungu s/o Musango. Born about 1900. Worked in Thika area during the 1920s. Mivukoni Location.

Muthuvi s/o Mui. Born about 1900. Mivukoni Location.

Mutisya s/o Muthaaka. Born about 1900. Originally from eastern Mumoni. Katse Location.

Muvali s/o Kilanga. Born in late 1880s to 1890. Circumcised in Embu, where he was a refugee from famine about 1898. Became a policeman in Embu. Later, returned to Katse. Katse Location.

Mwangangi s/o Mathenge. Two interviews. Born during the 1890s. Served in Carrier Corps, World War I. Katse Location.

Mwinzi s/o Kathinzi. Born late 1880s to 1890. Katse Location.

Nason Muindi s/o Ngumbau. Two interviews. Born about 1900. Worked in various areas during the 1920s and 1930s. Learned to read and write and converted to Christianity at this time. During the 1950s was a councillor and an elder of the District Court. Participated in the collection of data on customary law. Katse Location.

Ndithio s/o Mwangi. Born about 1900. Worked briefly as a policeman in Kitui during the 1930s. Katse Location.

Ngeri w/o Ngala. Born during the 1890s at Kyuso, northeastern Mumoni. Refugee in Chuka during the 1897–1901 famine. Her brother remained there. Katse Location.

Ngumu s/o Munithya. Born 1890s. Worked in Mombasa briefly between the World Wars. Mivukoni Location.

Ngungu s/o Mwaniki. Born about 1900. Mivukoni Location.

Nzila s/o Munyoki. Born shortly after 1900. Mivukoni Location.

Nzilu s/o Siongongo. Born about 1900. Worked for many years in Mombasa beginning about 1930. Katse Location.

Nzunya w/o Mbondo. Born 1880s. Lived in Chuka as a refugee during the famine of 1897–1901. Katse Location.

Paul Makuu s/o Kiwa. Born about 1920. Served overseas during World War II. Katse Location.

MBEERE

Abedinego Kagundu Njangaruko. Interview by Sam Nyagah. Born 1920s or 1930s. Keen interest in history and early convert to Christianity. Mavuria Location.

Anna Njira w/o Munyi. Born early to mid 1890s. Mavuria Location.

Benjamin Kau s/o Kimwele. Born in the mid-1930s in the Katse area of Mumoni, where his father (who came from Mbeere) had been raised after having been captured. Benjamin eventually went to Mbeere in the 1950s—first as a student and later to settle permanently. A devout Christian. Nthawa Location.

Cigana s/o Karere. Born 1890s. Served in Carrier Corps, World War I. Was an itinerant livestock trader. Ivurori area.

Gachone w/o Mburati. Born early 1900s. Mavuria Location.

Gachone w/o Rukeni. Born late 1890s. Mavuria Location.

Gatema Muyovi. Born 1890s. An interview with him appears in Mwaniki, *Embu Texts*, pp. 200–10. Kiambeere area.

Gicheche s/o Karuvia. Born early 1900s. Ivurori area.

Gitavi s/o Kunyira. Born late 1890s. Served in Carrier Corps, World War I. Mavuria Location.

Jimuko Ngonjo. Born early to mid 1890s. Kiambeere area.

Jonah Shirigu Muthinja. Two interviews. Born early 1890s [date substantiated by his 1934 marriage certificate]. Served in Carrier Corps and worked at the coast during the 1920s. Among the first in Nthawa to convert to Christianity. Received some education. Nthawa Location.

Kamdia Ndarabo. Born about 1890. Ivurori area.

Kanake s/o Gikathi. Born late 1890s to 1900. Worked as a local policeman about 1920. Nthawa Location.

Kanguru s/o Kirindi. Born 1890s. Worked at various times in the Nairobi and Thika areas. Mavuria Location.

Kigui s/o Kithaga. Interviewed with Nguru s/o Gatumbi. Ivurori area.

Kinyatta s/o Savana. Born late 1890s to 1900. Nthawa Location.

Konji s/o Ngai. Born early 1890s. Worked prior to World War I. Served in Carrier Corps, World War I. Nthawa Location.

Manunga s/o Nguci. Born early to mid 1890s. Worked at the coast and in Tanganyika. Chief of Nthawa Location from 1935 until the mid-1950s. Nthawa Location.

Maringa Maunge. Born late 1890s. Served in Carrier Corps, World War I. Mavuria Location.

Mbatia w/o Mukumi. Born 1890s in eastern Migwani, Kitui District. Refugee to Mbeere area during 1897–1901 famine. Married to local man. Mavuria Location.

Mbirano s/o Mwago. Born early 1900s. Mavuria Location.

Mbiringi Kathande. Born ca. 1900–05. Ivurori area.

Mbogo Ruturi. Born mid-1890s. Worked for considerable period in the Thika area. Mavuria Location.

Mucyoka s/o Kathata. Born early 1890s. Served in Carrier Corps, World War I. Mavuria Location.

Mutinda s/o Ruanyaki. Born about 1900. Ivurori area.

Muturi s/o Ruveni. Born late 1890s. Mavuria Location.

Mwageri Njuguara. With assistance from his wife. Probably born 1890s. Kiambeere area.

Mwige Kwigiriira. Born late 1890s. Mavuria Location.

Nderi Ndigica. Born 1890s. Forced to work on railway to Lake Magadi. Served in Carrier Corps, World War I. Worked also in Kibwezi. Ivurori area.

Ngai w/o Nthoroko. Born about 1900 in Embu, where her family were refugees. Nthawa Location.

Ngari s/o Matha. Two interviews. Born around 1900. Nthawa Location.

Ngira Katere. Born 1890s. Worked as local policeman at time of World War I forced recruitment. Mavuria Location.

Njiru s/o Mutemanderi. Born about 1905. Worked outside Mbeere. Nthawa Location.

Ngonju Ngunyaka. Born early 1890s. Mavuria Location.

Nguku s/o Kuliria. Born late 1890s. Served in World War I. Mavuria Location.

Nguru s/o Gatumbi. Interviewed with Kigui s/o Kithaga. Both are practicing *andu ago* (herbalists/specialists in supernatural). Ivurori area.

Njiru s/o Ngonjo. Born 1890s. Served in Carrier Corps, World War I. Worked in Kibwezi area. Mavuria Location.

Njuguna Kivuli. Born 1890s. Mavuria Location.

Njuthe s/o Rumbia. Rumbia (the informant's father) was chief of Nthawa Location from the arrival of the British until 1935. Nthawa Location.

Nthumbi s/o Gicere. Born ca. 1900–05. Went out to work a number of times for short periods. Nthawa Location.

Rudia Mairu w/o Mbiti. Born about 1905. Nthawa Location.

Ruguca Nthimbu. Two interviews. Born 1890s. Served in Carrier Corps, World War I. Nthawa Location.

Runji s/o Jigoya. Two interviews. Born 1890s. Mavuria Location.

Sarimu Njavari. Born early 1890s. Worked in Kibwezi area and in Mombasa. Served in Carrier Corps, World War I. Mavuria Location.

Syanderi w/o Muivia. Born 1890s. Kiambeere area.

Wagatu w/o Mucirwa. Born early 1900s in the Kiambeere area. Nthawa Location.

EMBU

Alan Kageta. Born ca. 1900–05. Kagaari Location.

Arthur Mairani. Two interviews. Born late 1890s. Forced to work on the Magadi railway. Became a policeman about the time of World War I. Attended school and became a Christian. Appointed chief of Gaturi in 1926, the first educated chief. Retired 1940s. An active Anglican and during the 1930s a fierce adversary of the Kikuyu Central Association.

Erasto s/o Runyenge. Born about 1905. His father, Runyenge, was appointed chief of Kagaari soon after the British arrived and remained in that office until 1939. Erasto was employed by the Agriculture Department. Runyenges area.

Gatere Kamunyori. Born about 1900. Interview by Gordon Njiru. Runyenges.

Gideon s/o Mwea wa Methumu. Born late 1890s. Kagaari Location.

Ginyane s/o Mkururu. Born 1890s. Kagaari Location.

Girishom Mukono. Two interviews. Born in the 1890s. A soldier or policeman during the time of World War I. Attended school and became a Christian. Prominent member of the Orthodox Church. Active in the Kikuyu Central Association. Detained during the Mau Mau Emergency. Kagaari Location.

Hezekiah Gataara. Born 1890s. Worked in Kibwezi and was impressed for labor on the Magadi railway. Served in World War I as a volunteer. Attended school occasionally and was among the first Christians in Kagaari. A leader of the Kikuyu Central Association.

Isaka Muragari s/o Njathumba. Born late 1890s. Worked in Nairobi area. Kagaari Location.

Jason Njigoru. Born about 1900. Became a Christian and received some education, 1920s. A close associate of Simeon Njage in trade and political activity. Runyenges.

Johana Kavuru s/o Muruanjuya. Born 1890s. Served in World War I. Kagaari Location.

Johana Mbarire. Two interviews. Born about 1905. A former headman. Kagaari Location.

Johana Ngondi. Early Christian (Roman Catholic) in Kyeni.

Kabogo s/o Gacigua. Two interviews. Born 1890s. An interview with him has been published in Mwaniki, *Embu Texts*, pp. 152–64. Kagaari Location.

Kamwochere s/o Nthiga. Three interviews. Born mid-1890s. Received some education and became a Christian in Nairobi, 1910s. Later an active trader in Embu and head of the local Kikuyu Central Asociation branch. An interview with him has been published in Mwaniki, *Embu Texts*, pp. 118–25. Ngandori Location.

Kanjama s/o Njanguthi. Two interviews. Born 1890s. Did forced labor on Magadi railway and served in Carrier Corps, World War I. Later convert to Christianity. Kagaari Location.

Lukah Nyaga s/o Kamuigu. Born 1890s. Kagaari Location.

Maritha w/o Nthereru. Born early 1890s. Kagaari Location.

Mbutei s/o Mwangai. Born 1890s. Served in Carrier Corps, World War I. Kagaari Location.
Mucuri Kanake. Born about 1910. Kagaari Location.
Munduwathara s/o Kunyaa. Born late 1890s. Worked outside Embu, 1920s. Kagaari Location.
Muruachuri Nyaga. Born about 1890. Served in army, 1914–24, and earlier in the police. Ngandori Location.
Muruakori s/o Gacewa. Two interviews. Born about 1890. Kagaari Location.
Muruamiti s/o Kathirikwa. Born about 1900. Kagaari Location.
Muruangerwe. Born probably 1890s. Kyeni Location.
Muruaringo s/o Muyakagio. Born late 1890s. Served in Carrier Corps, World War I. Kagaari Location.
Muruwanyamu Kathambara. Born about 1900. Kyeni Location.
Murwanthama s/o Gicandu. Born 1890s. Served in Carrier Corps, World War I. Kagaari Location.
Njorano Ndarwa. Born about 1900. Members of his family were pioneer settlers on the forest boundary in Kanja (upper Kagaari).
Paulo Gatema. Born mid-1890s. He was among the small group of boys who became Christians when the Anglican Mission was first established at Kigari, Embu in 1910. He has remained an active church member. Ngandori Location.
Paulo Njega. Born late 1890s. Worked in the Nairobi area where he received some education and became a Christian. Kagaari Location.
Rungai s/o Nthigai. Born mid-1890s. Kagaari Location.
Simeon Njage. Five interviews. Born about 1900. Worked for early Indian traders and was among the first Embu shopowners. Attended school and became a Christian, 1920s. Active in the Kikuyu Central Assocation. Close associate of Jason Njigoru. A prominent merchant in Runyenges.
Tirisa Kanyi w/o Mbarire. Born late 1890s. Assistance provided by her husband. In 1978 their son was an elected member of the national parliament. Kagaari Location.
Waicira s/o Ngura. Born in Kyeni. Worked at a Roman Catholic Mission near Nairobi and was in the army. When he returned to Embu he was one of the first local people to open a tea shop. Embu Town.
Waweru Kamwea. Born about 1905. Kagaari Location.
William Muriria. Born about 1900. Served in World War I. A former assistant chief. In 1978 his son was chief of Kyeni Location. An interview with him has been published in Mwaniki, *Embu Texts*, pp. 3–8. Kyeni Location.

Written Sources

ARCHIVES AND LIBRARIES

Public Record Office, London
    FO 2, Africa, Correspondence
    FO 107, Zanzibar, Correspondence
    CO 533, Kenya, Correspondence
Church Missionary Society, London (now Birmingham)
    J. L. Krapf Papers, Journals, CA5/16
Rhodes House Library, Oxford
    John Ainsworth, Diaries, 1895–1902, Mss. Afr. s. 377–378 (available on microfilm).
    Francis Hall Papers, Letters to Edward Hall, 1892–95 and 1895–1900; Diaries and other Papers including a draft paper on "The Kikuyu," 19 March 1894. Typescripts of originals (carbons at Syracuse University Library).
    C. W. Hobley, Original Safari Diaries, Mss. Afr. r. 143–148.
    H. J. Mackinder, Typescript Diaries prepared from the originals, Mss. Afr. r. 11–30.
    E. J. H. Russell, Diaries, 1895–1900, Mss. Afr. s. 118–122.
    J. A. Stuart Watt, "Recollections of Kenya, 1895–1963," Mss. Afr. s. 391.
Kenya National Archives, Nairobi (microfilms at Syracuse University Library).
    Annual Reports, Political Record Books, and correspondence files for Kenia, Ukamba, and Kikuyu Provinces and Embu, Kitui, and Machakos Districts.
    Kitui District, Local Native Council Minutes.
    W. E. H. Stanner, "The Kitui Kamba: A Study of British Administration in East Africa," 1939.
Embu County Council
    Embu District, Local Native Council Minutes.

Nairobi University Library
>   J. W. R. Pigott, "Diary of My Journey up the Tana River and Back Through Ukambani and along the Tabake River," 1889. Typescript of the original.
>   H. E. Lambert, "The Social and Political Institutions of the Tribes of the Kikuyu Land Unit of Kenya," 1945.

Roman Catholic Mission, Kabaa, Machakos District
>   Journal de la Mission de Notre Dame de la Rédemption à Kombe, 1912–20.

Syracuse University Library
>   Francis Hall Papers (see Rhodes House Library).
>   *Hearing and Doing* (continued by *Inland Africa*), the organ of the Africa Inland Mission, Philadelphia, Pa., 1896–1918. Published letters from missionaries in the field. Microfilm.
>   *The Taveta Chronicle*, the organ of the Church Missionary mission in Taita-Taveta, 1895–1901. Microfilm.

OFFICIAL PUBLICATIONS

Great Britain, Parliamentary Papers, "Report by Sir Arthur Hardinge on the British East African Protectorate for the Year 1897–1898 and including Mr. Charles Lane's Report on Kitui, Appendix A, 30 June 1898," London, 1899 (C. 9125).

Great Britain, Parliamentary Papers, "Reports Relating to the Administration of the East African Protectorate," October 1905, including a report on Ukamba Province by John Ainsworth, London, 1906 (Cd. 2740).

Great Britain, Kenya Land Commission, *Evidence and Memoranda*, 3 vols., Colonial no. 91, London, 1934.

British East African Protectorate, Native Labour Commission, 1912–1913, *Evidence and Report*, Nairobi, 1913.

BOOKS, ARTICLES, DISSERTATIONS, AND PAPERS
CITED IN MORE THAN ONE CHAPTER

Ambler, Charles H. "Central Kenya in the Late Nineteenth Century: Small Communities in a Regional System." Ph.D. Dissertation, Yale University, 1983.
———. "The Renovation of Custom in Colonial Kenya: The 1932 Generation Succession Ceremonies in Embu." Paper delivered at the African Studies Association, Annual Meeting, Madison, Wisc., November 1986.

Arkell-Hardwick, Alfred. *An Ivory Trader in North Kenia*. London, 1903.

Bernard, Frank E. *East of Mount Kenya: Meru Agriculture in Transition*. Munich, 1972.
———. "Meru District in the Kenyan Spatial Economy, 1890–1950." In *The Spatial Structure of Development: A Study of Kenya*, edited by R. A. Obudho and D. R. P. Taylor, pp. 264–90. Boulder, Col., 1979.

Berntsen, John L. "Pastoralism, Raiding and Prophets: Maasailand in the Nineteenth Century." Ph.D. dissertation, University of Wisconsin, 1979.

Boyes, John. *John Boyes, King of the Wa-Kikuyu*, edited by C. Bulpett. London, 1968 [1911].

Carson, J. B., editor. *Life Story of a Kenya Chief.* London, 1958.

Chanler, William Astor. *Through Jungle and Desert: Travels in Eastern Africa.* New York, 1896.

Clark, Carolyn. "Land and Food, Women and Power in Nineteenth Century Kikuyu," *Africa* 50 (1980): 357–70.

Clayton, A., and D. C. Savage. *Government and Labour in Kenya, 1895–1963.* London, 1974.

Cohen, David W. "Doing Social History from 'Pim's' Doorway." In *Reliving the Past: The Worlds of Social History*, edited by Olivier Zunz, pp. 191–235. Chapel Hill, N.C., 1985.

————. "Food Production and Food Exchange in the Precolonial Lakes Plateau Region." In *Imperialism, Colonialism, and Hunger: East and Central Africa*, edited by Robert Rotberg, pp. 1–18. Lexington, Mass., 1983.

Decle, Lionel. *Three Years in Savage Africa.* London, 1900.

Dundas, Charles. "History of Kitui." *Journal of the Royal Anthropological Institute* 43 (1913): 480–549.

————. "The Organization and Laws of Some Bantu Tribes in East Africa." *Journal of the Royal Anthropological Institute* 45 (1915): 234–306.

Fadiman, Jeffrey. "The Meru Peoples." In *Kenya Before 1900*, edited by B. A. Ogot, pp. 139–73. Nairobi, 1976.

————. *The Moment of Conquest: Meru, Kenya, 1907.* Athens, Ohio, 1979.

————. *Mountain Warriors: The Pre-Colonial Meru of Mt. Kenya.* Athens, Ohio, 1976.

Glazier, Jack. "Conflict and Conciliation among the Mbeere of Kenya." Ph.D. dissertation, University of California, 1972.

————. "Generation Classes among the Mbeere of Central Kenya," *Africa* 46 (1976): 313–26.

Gregory, J. W. *The Great Rift Valley.* London, 1968 [1896].

Guillain, M. *Documents sur L'Histoire, La Géographie, et le Commerce de L'Afrique Orientale*, vol. 2. Paris, 1856 [collected 1846–48].

Hildebrandt, J. M. "Travels in East Africa." *Proceedings of the Royal Geographical Society* 22 (1877–78): 446–52.

Hobley, C. W. *Ethnology of Akamba and other East African Tribes.* London, 1971 [1910].

————. "Nairobi to Fort Hall: A Survey of Ukamba Province." In *East Africa (British): Its History, People, Commerce, Industries, and Resources*, compiled by Somerset Playne, pp. 257–69. London, 1908–09.

Höhnel, Ludwig von. *Discovery of Lakes Rudolf and Stefanie: A Narrative of Count Samuel Teleki's Exploring and Hunting Expedition in Eastern Equatorial Africa in 1887 and 1888.* Translated by Nancy Bell. 2 vols. London, 1968 [1894].

Howard, Allen. "The Relevance of Spatial Analysis for African Economic History: The Sierra Leone-Guinea System." *Journal of African History* 17 (1976): 365–88.

Iliffe, John. *A Modern History of Tanganyika.* Cambridge, 1979.

Jackson, Frederick. *Early Days in East Africa.* London, 1969 [1930].

Jackson, Kennell A. "The Dimensions of the Kamba Pre-Colonial Past." In *Kenya Before 1900*, edited by B. A. Ogot, pp. 174–261. Nairobi, 1976.

Kenyatta, Jomo. *Facing Mount Kenya.* New York, Vintage edition, n.d. [1938].

Kershaw, Gretha. "The Land is the People: A Study of Kikuyu Social Organization in Historical Perspective." Ph.D. dissertation, University of Chicago, 1972.

Kjekshus, Helge. *Ecology Control and Economic Development in East African History: The Case of Tanganyika, 1850–1950.* Berkeley and Los Angeles, 1977.

Krapf, J. L. *Travels, Researches and Missionary Labours during an Eighteen Years Residence in Eastern Africa.* London, 1860.

Lambert, H. E. *Kikuyu Social and Political Institutions.* London, 1956.

———. "Land Tenure among the Akamba." *African Studies* 6 (1947): 131–47, 157–75.

Leakey, L. S. B. *The Southern Kikuyu before 1903.* 3 vols. London, 1977.

Lindblom, Gerhard. *The Akamba in British East Africa.* Uppsala, 1920.

———. *Kamba Folklore, vol. 3: Riddles, Proverbs and Songs.* Archives D'Etudes Orientales, vol. 20. Uppsala, 1934.

Lovejoy, Paul. *Transformations in Slavery: A History of Slavery in Africa.* Cambridge, 1983.

MacDonald, J. R. L. *Soldiering and Surveying in British East Africa, 1891–1894.* London, 1973 [1897].

Maher, Colin. *Soil Erosion and Land Utilization in the Embu Reserve.* Nairobi, Kenya Soil Conservation Service, 1938.

———. *Soil Erosion and Land Utilization in the Ukamba (Kitui) Reserve.* Nairobi, Kenya Soil Conservation Service, 1937.

Marris, Peter, and A. Somerset. *African Businessmen: A Study of Entrepreneurship and Development in Kenya.* London, 1971.

Mbithi, P., and P. Wisner. "Drought and Famine in Kenya." *Journal of Eastern Africa Research and Development* 3 (1973): 113–43.

Meinertzhagen, R. *Kenya Diary, 1902–1906.* London, 1957.

Miller, Joseph. "The Significance of Drought, Disease and Famine in the Agriculturally Marginal Zones of West-Central Africa." *Journal of African History* 23 (1982): 17–61.

Moris, Jon. "The Mwea Environment." In *Mwea: An Irrigated Rice Scheme in Kenya*, edited by R. Chambers and J. Moris, pp. 16–65. Munich, 1973.

Mungeam, G. H. *British Rule in Kenya, 1895–1912: The Establishment of Administration in the East African Protectorate.* Oxford, 1966.

Munro, J. Forbes. *Colonial Rule and the Kamba: Social Change in the Kenya Highlands, 1889–1939.* Oxford, 1975.

Muriuki, Godfrey. *A History of the Kikuyu, 1500–1900.* Nairobi, 1974.

Mutiso, G. C. M. "Kitui Ecosystem, Integration and Change." In *Ecology and History in East Africa*, Hadith 7, edited by B. A. Ogot, pp. 128–52. Nairobi, 1979.

Mwaniki, H. S. K. *The Living History of Embu and Mbeere*. Nairobi, 1973.

———. *Embu Historical Texts*. Nairobi, 1974.

———. "A Political History of the Embu, c. A.D. 1500–1906." M.A. thesis, University of Nairobi, 1973.

Neumann, A. H. *Elephant Hunting in East Equatorial Africa*. London, 1898.

Northrup, David. *Trade Without Rulers: Pre-Colonial Economic Development in Southern-Eastern Nigeria*. Oxford, 1978.

Orde-Browne, G. St. J. *The Vanishing Tribes of Kenya*. Westport, Conn., 1970 [1925].

Perham, Margery, ed. *The Diaries of Lord Lugard*, 4 vols. Evanston, Ill., 1959.

Peters, Carl. *New Light on Dark Africa*. Translated by H. W. Duicken. London, 1891.

Porter, Philip W. *Food and Development in the Semi-Arid Zone of East Africa*. Syracuse, 1979.

Rogers, Peter. "The British and the Kikuyu, 1890–1905: A Reassessment." *Journal of African History* 20 (1979): 255–69.

Routledge, W. Scoresby, and Katherine Routledge. *With a Prehistoric People: The Akikuyu of British East Africa*. London, 1910.

Saberwal, Satish. *The Traditional Political System of the Embu of Central Kenya*. Kampala, 1970.

Smith, Carol. "Introduction: The Regional Approach to Economic Systems." In *Regional Analysis*, edited by Carol Smith, vol. 1, pp. 3–63. New York, 1976.

Spear, Thomas. *Kenya's Past: An Introduction to Historical Method in Africa*. London, 1981.

———. *The Kaya Complex: A History of the Mijikenda Peoples of the Kenya Coast to 1900*. Nairobi, 1978.

Tate, H. R. "Notes on the Kikuyu Tribe of British East Africa." *Journal of the Anthropological Institute* 34 (1904): 130–48, 255–65.

Van Zwanenberg, R. M. A., with Anne King. *An Economic History of Kenya and Uganda*. Nairobi, 1975.

Waller, Richard. "Ecology, Migration, and Expansion in East Africa." *African Affairs* 23 (1985): 347–70.

———. "The Maasai and the British, 1895–1905: The Origins on an Alliance." *Journal of African History* 17 (1976): 529–53.

Watts, Michael. *Silent Violence*. Berkeley and Los Angeles, 1983.

Wolff, Richard D. *The Economics of Colonialism: Britain and Kenya, 1870–1930*. New Haven, 1974.

Index

Adoption, 12, 13, 25, 45

Africa: views of, 31, 112–13, 153–54; and ethnicity, 157

African history: precolonial, 4, 9; and colonialism, 8; and ethnicity, 4, 155–57

Afro-Arab traders: local contacts, 49, 73, 113; in long-distance trade, 68, 100–01, 102, 105–07; in regional trade, 101, 114, 133; competition with Europeans, 105–07; in towns, 111, 140

Age organization, 23–24; in Embu, 23; in trade, 75–76

Agriculture: expansion of, 9, 14, 116, 118–19; in Migwani, 15, 19; in Embu, 22; in Mumoni, 38, 40–41; practice of, 50–52, 120, 124–26; and drought, 52–54, 124, 147, 150–51; and trade, 58, 65, 115–21; in Mbeere, 65; and labor, 116. *See also* Crops; Farmers; Herders

Ainsworth, John (British official), 68, 108, 110; in Ulu, 107

Alliances, 108, 113, 114*n*, 152–53

Amulets, 49, 82, 94, 124, 142

Animal fat: traded, 57, 92

Apprenticeship, 61

Aro (people of Nigeria), 82*n*

Assimilation. *See* Incorporation

Atwa (people), 36

Authority: nature of, 25, 39–40, 41, 47–48; under British, 153. *See also* Power

Autonomy: local, 16, 35–36, 41, 42–43, 153; of region, 121, 152

axes, 91

Bananas: grown, 20, 22, 38; traded, 57, 58, 65

Bantu-speaking peoples of central Kenya: history, 9–10; collective identity of, 10, 35

Beads, 68

Beans: grown, 22, 58, 60; traded, 57, 58, 60, 65

Beer, 22, 26

Begging, 128

Blood (of cattle), 97, 126

Blood partnership: and trade, 66, 82–84, 102; and outsiders, 83, 84, 102; and migration, 134, 135, 147; repudiated, 147

Boundaries: of ethnic populations, 32, 34

Boyes, John (traveler), 113, 124

Bridewealth: and social relations, 18; and livestock, 66, 84, 97; and famine, 126. *See also* Marriage

British in central Kenya: local influence of, 8, 106, 110, 112, 114, 140, 152; resistance to, 46; attitudes toward, 95, 107, 140; expansion of, 105–08 passim, 112, 113, 152; policy of, 106–09 passim, 152–54; and trade, 107–08, 141; sources, 107*n*; and ethnicity, 112; and Great Famine, 122–23, 138–41, 149; administration, 140, 152–54. *See also* Colonialism in Kenya; European attitudes

British stations: local influence of, 25*n*, 106, 108, 139, 156; and slavery, 72; establishment of, 106, 111; and trade, 109–

British stations (*continued*)
  10, 140; and ethnicity, 112–13; and famine, 138, 141
Brokers, 47, 106, 114, 133; in Embu, 46–47; in local politics, 48, 104–05, 121; rise of, 73, 79, 102, 156; in Migwani, 102; and supply trade, 110, 115; and the British, 110, 152–53; and famine, 137–38, 148
Buganda, 106

Cannibalism, 95, 145*n*
Captives, 12, 133, 138
Caravans, 68; and supply trade, 101, 102, 106, 130
Cattle: and wealth, 26, 27, 39, 42, 54, 114; herds, 42, 54, 114; and nutrition, 97, 126; raiding, 99–100; trade, 103–04; disease, *see* Rinderpest. *See also* Livestock
Central Kenya region: population, 4–5, 5*n*; history, 4, 9, 114; geography, 4, 17; integration, 4, 50; identity, 35. *See also* Regional system
Central places, 104*n*
Charms, 49, 82, 94, 124, 142
Chiefs (colonial), 149, 152–53
Children: and violence, 82*n*, 100, 143, 147; health of, 97; exploitation of, 120–21; and famine, 143, 144, 146
Chuka (society), 21, 46, 142
Ciarume (from Mbeere), 25*n*
Circumcision, 45; and identity, 32–33, 44–45. *See also* Initiation
Clan membership, 33, 33*n*, 34, 35*n*
Clients, 12, 104. *See also* Patron-client relationships
Climate: zones, 51–52; and agriculture, 52, 117*n*; change, 56
Cloth: in trade, 47, 68; use, 94, 110–11, 121
Coastal traders. *See* Afro-Arab traders
Colonialism in Kenya: history, 3–4; precolonial impact on, 8, 122–23; intellectual basis of, 154. *See also* British in central Kenya
Commodities, 57, 60, 75, 91, 94; restricted, 58, 89; list of, 76; of Mount Kenya, 65, 72
Communities: defined, 4*n*, 7, 17, 18, 22, 31–36 passim, 44; identity of, 24, 28; and colonialism, 155
Conspicuous consumption, 67
Copper wire, 68

Cosmetics, 85
Councils of elders: in society, 24–25, 41; in Embu, 24–25, 45–46, 48
Crafts, 88–90, 104; production of, 89–90, 111
Crime. *See* Murder; Theft
Crops: 22, 38, 51–52, 57–60, 65, 85, 109, 116, 120, 151. *See also* Agriculture; Bananas; Beans; Maize; Tobacco
Cultivation: limits of, 21, 51, 52, 54; expansion of, 55, 116; density of, 118. *See also* Agriculture
Cultural traits: and identity, 32–33, 49. *See also* Subcultures
Currencies, 60, 89, 111
Customary law, 46; violation of, 82, 146–47

Dagoretti station, 116; and trade, 96, 108–11 passim; established, 105–07, 106*n*; and refugees, 100, 111–12; local impact of, 108, 110, 111–12. *See also* British stations
Dance organization, 24, 41–42, 67, 76
Death: in raiding, 100; and famine, 123–24, 128, 129, 132, 143–45, 150–51; views of, 127–28, 144–45, 151
Defense: and residence patterns, 28, 40. *See also* Military organization
Descent groups, 17, 18*n*
Dialects. *See* Language
Diet, 22, 60; and trade, 58, 60, 65; and livestock, 60, 97; and famine, 127
Disease (in humans): local views of, 81, 95; transmission of, 81, 141–42; and famine, 141. *See also* Smallpox
Disease (in livestock): and trade, 81; impact on Maasai, 98–99. *See also* Rinderpest; Tsetse fly
Diviners, 92
Divorce, 126
Donkeys, 90
Drought: occurrence of, 1, 22, 52–54, 95–96, 122, 147; and migration, 14–15, 52, 98; economic impact of, 52–54, 119–20; and livestock, 123
Dyes, 94

East Africa, 105–06, 114, 122
Eclipses, 95
Ecological zones, 51; and trade, 50, 55, 125
Ecological change, 55–57, 98
Elders: in society, 23, 25, 47–48

Elephants: hunting of, 47, 68, 69, 101; and pastures, 69

Elevation. *See* Topography

Embu, mentioned passim: ties to Mbeere, 5, 7, 63–67, 128–29; described, 7, 21–22; social organization, 18*n*, 20–23, 26, 30, 43–49; military organization in, 19, 47, 67, 148; economy of, 20, 22, 29, 43–44, 65–66, 118; view of outsiders in, 20, 44–45, 46–48, 82, 142, 142*n*, 148, 156–57; trade of, 22, 46–47, 65–66, 85, 88, 128–29, 154; population, 44, 44*n*; identity, 44–46; and the British, 46, 148, 152

Environment: in local history, 7–8, 55*n*; change in, 8, 55–56, 95, 98, 117–18, 151; of region, 51–52; views of, 55, 151

Erosion, 118–19

Ethnic conflict: and the Maasai, 111–12; and British policy, 112–13; and famine, 133–34, 142–43; in Africa, 154–55, 157

Ethnic identity: nature of, 5, 7, 32–35, 44–45, 154–56; and outside contact, 7, 83; and tradition, 9–10, 10*n*, 38, 156; and boundaries, 33–34, 35, 35*n*, 72, 155–56; and colonial rule, 34, 112, 154–55. *See also* Identity

Ethnic traditions: and history, 9–12, 9*n*, 10*n*; inconsistencies in, 33–34, 38; and identity, 33*n*, 156

European attitudes: toward local society, 34, 84, 108, 139; toward African society, 31, 95, 112–13, 153; toward slavery, 71–72, 71*n*. *See also* British in central Kenya

European imperialism: in scholarship, 3–4, 140; in East Africa, 8, 105–06; and slave trade, 71; local views of, 95

Europeans in central Kenya: local views of, 49, 105, 124, 137; actions of, 83, 105, 108–09, 111, 113. *See also* British in central Kenya

Exchange. *See* Regional system; Trade

Exploitation, 70; of women, 62, 133, 136

Exports: listed, 76

External contact: local views of, 17, 47–48, 140

Family unit, 32, 74–75; in famine, 135, 144, 150–51

Famine: causes, 1, 115; economic impact, 1, 62, 123, 125–27, 130, 132–33, 135; and migration, 14, 132, 136, 143–44; characteristics of, 52–54, 95, 96; and violence, 86; and disease, 122, 141. *See also* Famine of 1897–1901

Famine of 1897–1901 (the Great Famine), 1–4, 44, 122–49 passim; impact, 1–2, 26, 122–23, 143–52; and migration, 1–3, 48; in highlands, 2, 44, 48; and disease, 2, 141–44; causes of, 3, 95, 115–21; local views of, 3, 124, 137, 144–45; and trade, 5, 120; Europeans and, 8, 137–41, 152; names for, 122, 122*n*, 137; and death, 123–24, 132, 143–44; recovery from, 147–49. *See also* Smallpox

Famine relief, 139, 145, 149

Farmers: and hunters and herders, 12, 35, 36, 56; identity of, 35; and resources, 55, 119. *See also* Agriculture; Migration

Feasts, 26

Fiber string, 91

Food: 60, 108, 126, 127, 139; prices, 130–31

Food-livestock trade: patterns, 54, 57–58, 60, 65–67, 130; organization of, 60, 74–75, 130; and regional trade, 61, 65, 87, 88, 92, 94; local economies, 63, 65, 70; and migration, 63; and food shortages, 96, 129–30, 141; and external trade, 102, 119–20; in the 1970s, 154. *See also* Regional system

Forests, 55–56, 116, 119, 151

Frontier societies: diverse, 12, 14, 18, 36, 43, 157; settlement of, 12, 14, 36, 62, 98, 119; economies of, 15, 27, 98; and trade, 27, 62, 69, 98

Fuel, 57, 119

Genealogies, 38*n*

Generation organization, 23, 46

Giciaro, 82–84. *See also* Blood partnership

Gikuyuland, mentioned passim; settlement of, 10, 11, 56; frontiers of, 12, 43; and trade, 62, 75, 77–78, 85, 104, 117; economies of, 92, 96, 101; and Europeans, 108–11, 124; famine and, 128, 137, 142–45 passim, 151

Gikuyu-speaking people, 5, 23, 32, 33*n*

Goats: raised, 54, 98; traded, 61, 91, 103–04

Government. *See* Councils of elders

Guns, 113, 114

Supernatural powers (*continued*)
  in trade, 82, 92–94; explanation of
  events in, 95, 124, 137
Supply trade: scope of, 101–02, 109–10,
  115–16, 125, 126; and regional centers,
  102–11 passim; impact of, 113, 115–20
  passim, 125–26, 137
Surplus: production of, 52, 65, 67; disposition of, 67, 116, 130
Swahili society: in central Kenya, 111, 139
Syokimau (from Ulu), 92–93

Tana River, 30, 38–39; crossing of, 70, 79,
  80, 132; as boundary, 33–34; at famine,
  127, 132. *See also* Rivers
Technology, 55, 88, 113, 114, 116
Teeth carving, 32
Tharaka, 33, 37–38, 57, 92
Theft, 113, 136, 145–47, 149
Tigania (in Meru), 135
Tobacco: crop, 22, 92; traded, 22, 47, 91,
  92
Tools, 55, 85, 87, 88
Topography: and climate, 21, 38, 51, 53;
  and settlement, 21, 52; and trade, 57
Towns: established, 111, 139–40; inhabitants of, 111; and local society, 140
Trade (within central Kenya): basis of, 2,
  13, 22, 55, 66; organization of, 5, 22, 24,
  74–78, 84, 91–92, 101; with herders,
  13, 112; within communities, 22, 50; and
  migration, 28, 30–31, 62–63; and local
  societies, 28, 40–42, 50, 54, 66–67, 84;
  and leadership, 29, 77–78; patterns of,
  50, 57, 58, 62–63, 84, 87, 94, 151; evidence for, 58; historiography of, 59*n*;
  wholesale, 74, 91–92; routes, 80, 102,
  106–07, 130–31, 140; and supply trade,
  85, 102, 110, 113, 119; in iron, 87–89;
  in ornaments, 89–90; in natron, 90–92;
  in supernatural powers, 92–94; dangers
  in, 99; and famine, 125, 130, 136, 141,
  152. *See also* Commodities; Food-livestock trade; Ivory trade; Long-distance
  trade; Markets; Supply trade; Traders;
  Transportation
Traders: in food trade, 60; major, 68–69,
  70, 78; as disease carriers, 81, 143; and
  supernatural, 82; in towns, 111
Traditions. *See* Oral records
Transportation: difficulties of, 2, 78–82,
  132, 134; methods of, 80, 80*n*, 90, 132,

  134; in natron trade, 90–91; by rail,
  138–40, 146; in the 1970s, 154
Travel: attitudes toward, 49, 76, 134;
  means of, 75; and disease, 141, 143
Tribalism. *See* Ethnic conflict; Ethnic iden-
  tity
Tribute, 107–08
Tsetse fly: infestation, 54, 81, 98, 151

Uganda, 106, 107
Ulu: society, 20, 23–24, 33, 118; economy
  of, 62, 96, 101, 110–11, 118–19; migra-
  tion·in, 62, 134; views of, 93; and Europeans, 101, 108, 109, 110–11; impact of
  external trade on, 117, 120; and famine,
  125, 128, 129, 145–48
Uvariri (in Mbeere), 93–94

Vere wa Nzui (from Mumoni), 39–40
Victoria, Lake, 101, 106
Village concentration: and trade, 27–28,
  39*n*, 39–43, 63, 70; and famine, 151–
  52. *See also* *Mbenge* villages; Residence
  patterns
Violence: local, 24, 30, 41, 42; and trade,
  34, 82, 82*n*, 86; and ethnic conflict, 34,
  112–13; limits on, 44, 82*n*, 86, 99–100;
  causes of, 98–99, 113; and imperialism,
  107, 114, 152; and famine, 136–37,
  145–46, 149. *See also* Raiding

Wages, 61, 66
Wang'ombe (from Gikuyuland): power
  base of, 104–05, 113; actions of, 137–
  38, 156
Warfare. *See* Military organization; Raiding; Violence
Warlords: in central Kenya, 104, 113–14,
  137–38, 156; and the British, 152–53
Warrior class, 67, 147
Water supplies: and settlement, 41, 51–52,
  57; location of, 51–52, 81, 128
Wealth: accumulation of, 8, 15, 29, 40, 78,
  90, 114, 146–48, 151; and migration,
  14, 15, 137–38; and labor, 25–27; and
  leadership, 25, 114; views of locally, 26,
  48; and livestock, 27, 51, 66, 147–48;
  distribution of, 28, 42, 50, 67, 70, 121,
  148–49; equality of in Embu, 29, 48, 67;
  and trade, 68, 70, 105. *See also* Cattle;
  Labor; Leadership; Livestock; Trade